T5-CQA-394

Tools and Techniques to Inspire Classroom Learning

Also available from ASQ Quality Press

Orchestrating Learning with Quality
David P. Langford and Barbara A. Cleary, Ph.D.

Improving Student Learning: Applying Deming's Quality Principles in Classrooms
Lee Jenkins

The New Philosophy for K–12 Education: A Deming Framework for Transforming America's Schools
James F. Leonard

Kidgets: And Other Insightful Stories About Quality in Education
Maury Cotter and Daniel Seymour

Total Quality for Schools: A Guide for Implementation
Joseph C. Fields

The Quality Toolbox
Nancy R. Tague

Mapping Work Processes
Dianne Galloway

Team Fitness: A How-To Manual for Building a Winning Work Team
Meg Hartzler and Jane E. Henry, Ph.D.

The Change Agents' Handbook: A Survival Guide for Quality Improvement Champions
David W. Hutton

To request a complimentary catalog of publication, call 800-248-1946.

Tools and Techniques to Inspire Classroom Learning

Barbara A. Cleary, Ph.D.
Sally J. Duncan

ASQ Quality Press
Milwaukee, Wisconsin

Tools and Techniques to Inspire Classroom Learning
Barbara A. Cleary, Ph.D., and Sally J. Duncan

Library of Congress Cataloging-in-Publication Data
Cleary, Barbara A., date.
Tools and techniques to inspire classroom learning / Barbara A. Cleary, Sally J. Duncan.
p. cm.
Includes bibliographical references and index.
ISBN 0-87389-411-1 (alk. paper)
1. School improvement programs—United States—Case studies. 2. Learning—Case studies. 3. Elementary school teaching—United States—Case studies. 4. Classroom management—United States—Case studies. 5. Teaching—United States—Aids and devices. I. Duncan, Sally J., date. II. Title.
LB2822.82.C54 1997 96-44602
371.12—dc21 CIP

10 9 8 7 6 5 4

ISBN 0-87389-411-1

Acquisitions Editor: Kelley Cardinal
Project Editor: Kelley Cardinal

ASQC Mission: To facilitate continuous improvement and increase customer satisfaction by identifying, communicating, and promoting the use of quality principles, concepts, and technologies; and thereby be recognized throughout the world as the leading authority on, and champion for, quality.

Attention: Schools and Corporations
ASQC Quality Press books, audiotapes, videotapes, and software are available at quantity discounts with bulk purchases for business, educational, or instructional use. For information, please contact ASQC Quality Press at 800-248-1946, or write to ASQC Quality Press, P.O. Box 3005, Milwaukee, WI 53201-3005.

For a free copy of the ASQC Quality Press Publications Catalog, including ASQC membership information, call 800-248-1946.

Printed in the United States of America

Printed on acid-free paper

Quality Press
611 East Wisconsin Avenue
P.O. Box 3005
Milwaukee, Wisconsin 53201-3005

"To furnish the means of acquiring knowledge is . . . the greatest benefit that can be conferred upon mankind."

—John Quincy Adams
Report on the Establishment of the Smithsonian Institution

Contents

Figures

Preface

In the Babel of educational reform, teachers and administrators often find themselves listening to what seem to be multiple tongues. Not only are reformers speaking their own language, but they are talking so fast, they do not seem to have time to listen, to discern the patterns in others' language about schools, or to understand the connections between ideas and action. We have written this book because we know that teachers are going about the business of improving the learning process in their classrooms in spite of this often-emotional din that surrounds their profession.

Good teachers everywhere have common understandings and visions, whether they articulate them in the same words or not. Their common language is sometimes not words, but actions. After all, teachers tend to be doers. By piecing together what their actions *say*, patterns can be recognized. We wanted to find these patterns and help others benefit from them.

If someone were to suddenly blow the whistle on the interminable discussion of what is wrong with education and what schools should be doing, the ensuing silence might give us a chance to start from the beginning, to begin to identify a common language of improvement in schools, or at least to see common themes in the approaches to the complex problem of helping children to learn. We could even quietly tiptoe into classrooms and find out what teachers are really doing while the discussion rages.

This book is meant to tiptoe into the classroom and find teachers and their students doing what they do to advance their purpose. Such an intrusion may seem to lack context. It may seem disjointed from the larger purpose related to learning in the classroom, for it does not address the specific ways that the techniques described systematically relate to that purpose.

On the other hand, this work demonstrates through actual classroom examples the ways that good teachers are utilizing a variety of tools and techniques to advance learning. There is nothing new in that construct. What is new is the inspiration that always comes from visiting a classroom where learning is happening. It can take your breath away to hear children articulating ideas and to see their growth. This is the *doing* part of education—learning is, after all, active.

That is not to say that teachers only act, without the appropriate planning, study, analysis, and review that are fundamental to teaching and learning. Remember, we will be walking in on only one aspect of their learning cycle—the use of tools to bring about improvement in learning at all stages of the cycle.

An old Hebrew story tells of a man who was going crazy with all the noise in his house: His wife and children seemed to talk nonstop, and there was never any peace in his home. Looking for answers, he approached his rabbi. "My house is so noisy," he said. "I can't even hear myself think."

"Do you have any chickens?" the rabbi asked.

"Yes, of course."

"Put the chickens in the house with your family," was the rabbi's suggestion.

Since the man knew that one does not question the wisdom of a rabbi, he went home and did as he had been told. The din increased; however, now he heard not only the endless chatter of his wife and children, but also the pecking and chirping of the chickens he had brought into the house. He went back to the rabbi for further instruction.

"Do you have dogs?" the rabbi asked, when he heard the man's plea.

"Yes, I have five dogs," the man answered.

"Bring them into the house with the family and the chickens," the rabbi instructed.

Dubious, the man nonetheless followed the rabbi's instructions. What followed was the predictable cacophony of wife, children, chickens, and dogs—chattering, chirping, pecking, and barking.

On his third visit to the rabbi, the man received further advice. This time, he was instructed to bring his three cows into the house. Of course, the noise level increased with the addition of the cows' mooing and bellowing, and the man was more frustrated than ever. Returning to the wise rabbi, he said he did not think he could live in the house with all the noise, and felt he would have to leave in order to get some peace.

The rabbi, hearing the man's desperation, told him to take the chickens back to their coop, the dogs to their kennel, and the cows out to the barn. The farmer returned to his home and followed these instructions. Then he eagerly went back into the house.

Collapsing into his favorite chair, the man suddenly realized how quiet it had become. All he could hear now, he realized, were the voices of his wife and children, and he was grateful for the calm.

Perspective can alter things in unpredictable ways. We want this book to provide new perspective by focusing on what is happening in classrooms in all parts of the country. To do this, we need to eliminate the cacophony that surrounds these classrooms.

Using examples that show how specific problem-solving, planning, or improvement tools can help students learn, this is a handbook for that learning and for the improvement that can take place in the classroom.

In each chapter, a tool is briefly introduced. The heart of each chapter is the concrete examples of how students and teachers have used each tool to enhance their learning while improving processes. The cases cited demonstrate the creativity and flexibility that teachers and students can bring to bear in using the tools.

The examples are not business applications adapted to schools, nor do they relate to the administrative functions of school districts. Instead, they get into the classroom in fundamental ways: a lunchroom improvement project is undertaken not to improve the lunch process but to enhance students' engagement in learning in the time period after lunch. Students who struggle with alphabet recognition, teachers frustrated by their students' incessant questions about long division ("What do I do next?"), and professionals who want to bring about high-quality social studies learning are all subjects of this book.

We have drawn the examples from our experiences in our own classrooms and in those of others. Some have been used in specific quality improvement projects; others are applied to support the improvement process, but without using the terminology of quality improvement or total quality management (TQM). In every case, they are related to purpose—the advancement of the learning process—and are not taught as tools for their own sake.

The tools are arranged somewhat arbitrarily. We avoid classifying them as "statistical tools," "problem-solving tools," "tools for teamwork," and so on, because we have confidence that good teachers can figure out how each of the tools will work best in their own classrooms. We have grouped related tools, such as affinity and relations diagrams, since they are often used together. Some strategies, such as nominal group technique, are fundamental to the application of other tools in the collection.

Classroom benefits of using specific tools will provide a focus in each chapter. We do not want readers to forget the intimate connection between specific techniques and their purpose. Some of them support specific theories related to learning, such as Howard Gardner's research on multiple intelligences. Sources for further reading on various approaches are cited in the bibliography as well as the notes.

A feature that will enhance the applicability of the case studies is the occasional "Notable" observation, pointing out the rationale for a particular technique, giving a tip for applying it, or mentioning a caveat in using it. In this section, we will offer observations about possible next steps to get the most out of a particular tool and explanations about how the use of the tool has directly supported the learning process as it is currently understood. An "Application" section encourages readers to try out the tool on a process with which they are familiar.

In a way, this is a workbook. It is not meant to be read in a vacuum, however, or the applications simply filled in, so as to move on to the next tool. Instead, applications are meant to directly engage readers' classroom experiences. You may already have a situation or problem that is suitable for applying a given tool, or you may want to enlist the help of your students or colleagues in ferreting out a useful application.

In any case, we are eager for you to try these tools or to pick up on the tips offered by other educational professionals. And, we'd like to hear how you're doing.

Acknowledgments

We are grateful to those teachers and administrators who have given us the benefit of their experience. Our examples come from Ridgeview Elementary School, Ashtabula, Ohio; Norton Middle School, Grove City, Ohio; Marshall University Community and Technical College, West Virginia; Madison Street School, Ocala, Florida; Eighth Street School, Ocala, Florida; Silver Lane School, East Hartford, Connecticut; The Miami Valley School, Dayton, Ohio; Western Salisbury Elementary School, Allentown, Pennsylvania; and other schools in California, Ohio, Kansas, Kentucky, Tennessee, and Illinois that are not named because their stories are sometimes combined with other similar stories or are ones that we've heard from other teachers. By allowing us to use their stories, these teachers and students gave us permission to tiptoe into their classrooms and see what they are doing to enhance learning and to build knowledge. We are grateful to others who have contributed their ideas or reviewed the manuscript: Mike Cleary, John Duncan, Steve Kreitzer, our own students, and those at PQ Systems (including Linda O'Malley) who have supported our efforts to put this book together.

With them, we invite you to step into those same classrooms with us and see what's really going on.

Introduction

If learning lies at the heart of a school's purpose for being, any improvement that is to be substantive must address learning itself. As we are precipitously close to another century, we are fortunate to know so much more about how the brain functions in the process of learning than anyone could have imagined at the threshold of the last century—or even three decades ago. Once real-time magnetic resonance imaging (MRI) became possible, only three or four years ago, scientists could begin to actually watch the brain as it carries out various processes, including thinking. Neuroscientists, psychologists, and educators are all contributing to what has become known as the *cognitive revolution*.

Regardless of how much we know about the brain and its functioning, however, or what we can see as the brain goes about its business, this knowledge will have relevance to classrooms only when we have figured out what it means to the learning process. A scientist can identify the ways in which a dyslexic child is able to process sounds or symbols, for example, as Robert Sylwester (1995) has pointed out. What remains is to identify the strategies that will put this knowledge to use—currently uncharted territory in many respects.

Progress has been made in understanding how learning happens, and we will need to take this advancement into consideration as we envision classrooms of the future and in the present. Both the important theories that lie behind classroom learning and the tested processes that translate those theories into learning are critical to improving the learning process and its environment. We leave those discussions to others who have already approached them thoughtfully and to those who will continue to examine the important foundations on which learning is built and the context within which it happens.

It is up to classroom teachers to develop approaches to learning. As we have noted, teachers are already pursuing creative and interesting strategies to support learning in their classrooms. A variety of other strategies and tools exist as well, not only in the classrooms of other teachers, but also in the world of human resources and organizational development, including the world of total quality. Cumulatively, many of these strategies have advanced and supported learning for adults as well as children. Understanding their connection to learning—for many, an intuitive connection—will be enhanced as our understanding of the brain and its function expands. It is critical for educators to stay tuned to the research related to learning, so that their classrooms make sense with respect to the purpose of learning.

Problem-solving and analytical tools that have come to be associated with quality improvement have given demonstrated support to the learning process. Sometimes, however, these tools seem to classroom teachers to have little relevance. These teachers may feel that since their schools or districts are not really involved in total quality or continuous improvement, changing the system on their own is a far too daunting task. In the meantime, however, they are actually using these or other tools to advance their own purposes in the classroom.

These tools and strategies can indeed have a profound meaning to the teachers who are engaged in the everyday learning activities of schools, because the tools can be used to directly support the learning process in which teachers are so passionately immersed. Improving learning is something that teachers know about, regardless of their understanding of TQM or CQI and its implications. In fact, without ever calling

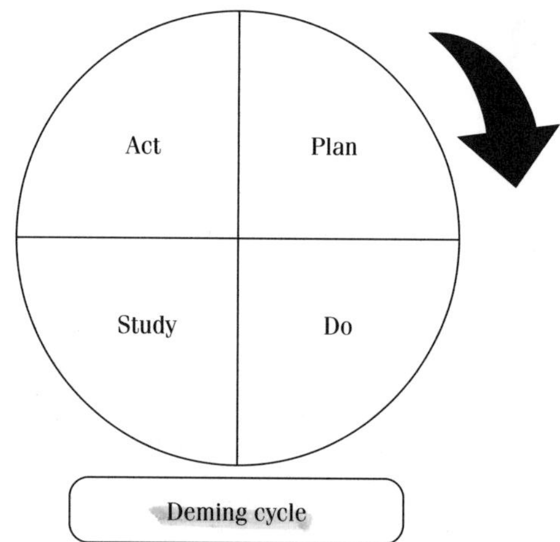

Figure I.1: PDSA cycle.

it process improvement, teachers are doing process improvement every day of their lives. TQM represents only one part of the system of learning. Although its theory, process, and tools can provide fundamental support to that system, it is nonetheless only a part of the process.

Common language of the classroom might begin with the idea of *purpose*. Teachers know why they are doing what they do. It is, after all, learning that lies at the heart of the classroom experience. The tools and strategies that are presented here—for that matter, all tools and strategies of the classroom—must advance that purpose. Otherwise, they can be seen only as busywork for educators and students alike.

Of course, neither the discussion of purpose or the use of tools and strategies alone offers a step-by-step process for carrying out the classroom purpose. One way to approach that process lies in understanding, as much as possible, about the learning process: how the brain functions in enlarging knowledge and making the vital connections among data, information, understanding, and wisdom that builds a system of knowledge.

Another process that is vital to improvement of classrooms and of learning is that of the plan-do-study-act (PDSA) cycle (Figure I.1) of W. Edwards Deming (1986). While discussion of this process lies outside the purview of this book, the PDSA cycle warrants close examination by those interested in systemic change and improvement in schools. An example of work undertaken by a school team within the context of the improvement cycle appears in the final chapter of this book. At that point, readers will have learned about the same tools and techniques used in the PDSA cycle.

It is not tools alone, but tools within the context of process, and above all of purpose, that will bring about lasting improvement in schools. The contribution of tools and strategies is that of supporting purpose and processes that advance the improvement of learning.

References

Deming, W. Edwards. 1986. *Out of the crisis*. Cambridge, Mass. MIT Center for Advanced Engineering Study.

Sylwester, Robert. 1995. *A celebration of neurons: An educator's guide to the human brain*. Alexandria, Va.: Association for Supervision and Curriculum Development.

Chapter 1

Going with the Flow

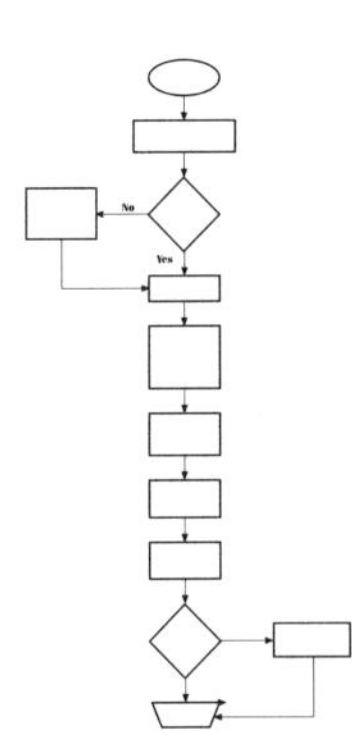

Introducing flowcharts

Walking into any elementary classroom, one is always struck by the colorful work of children posted on bulletin boards and walls. In some schools, though, this work is not just the usual set of drawings for Mother's Day or seasonal collages of bunnies and leaves. These are supplemented by equally colorful papers—flowcharts are everywhere. Some of these are accompanied by drawings or photographs of children. Children at the drinking fountain. Children lining up for music. Children putting away library books. The flowcharts and accompanying pictures are reminders that these young students have documented the everyday processes of their classroom experience, and these are the maps to those processes.

Children at the youngest levels of school can use flowcharts as they address the challenges and processes of their classroom experience. Even those who have not yet learned to read or write can create flowcharts by using photographs or drawings of the steps in a process. Older students can create flowcharts of increasingly complex problems and processes.

Flowcharts illustrate all the steps in a process. When more than one person is involved in a process, the appropriate tool is a *deployment flowchart*. When only one person is engaged in a process, a simple *process flowchart* can be used. Some standard symbols used in flowcharting are shown in Figure 1.1. While some of these symbols are usually associated with deployment flowcharts and others with process flowcharts, they are often used interchangeably.

Knowing when to use flowcharts becomes increasingly easy with experience. Flowcharts are used to help define a system and understand how a particular process works. They can also be used to review processes after they have been changed, as a way to document a standard procedure and record the improvement. For example, getting ready to leave a classroom for music class is a process that can be documented with a flowchart. If a step in that process is changed—lining up differently or leaving at a different time—a new flowchart documents that change.

Flowcharts can be used in classrooms at all levels, lunchrooms, administrative offices, homes, and teachers' workrooms. Flowcharts are useful wherever processes take place. Flowcharts are used because they provide valuable information about the way in which a process happens. All the steps in that process, the order in which they are undertaken, and the decisions that are involved as the process proceeds can all be seen on a flowchart.

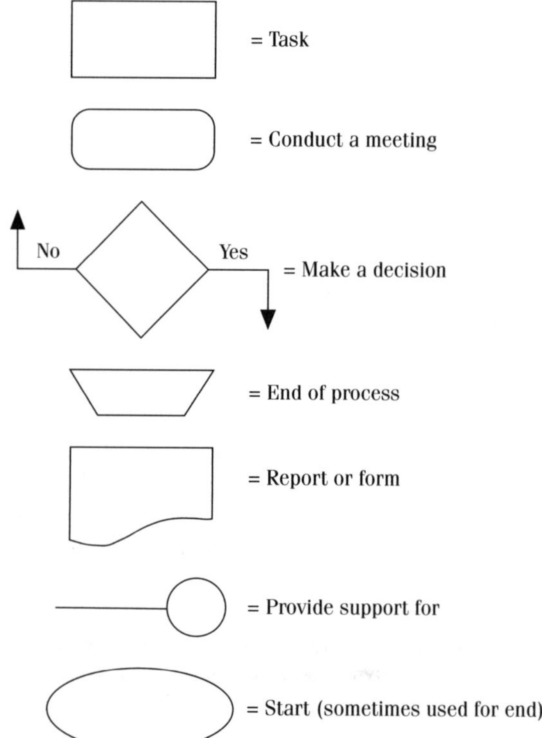

Figure 1.1: Flowchart symbols.

Classroom benefits

When students create flowcharts of familiar processes, they begin to take responsibility for those processes. Dependence on a teacher or other adult diminishes as young people see processes as their own. A flowchart for a particular process provides a record of the standard way to approach that process. This record may help to diminish the inconsistencies that are frequently found in math processes, for example. (When you borrow from the tens column in order to subtract the ones column, where do you write the borrowed number?)

By enhancing students' responsibility for their own learning, this tool can support and promote active learning, rather than the transfer of information that sometimes characterizes classroom learning.

Example: Organizing dismissal time

A classroom of fourth graders in an Allentown, Pennsylvania, school wanted to provide more time during the school day to complete homework, so that they would not have to take so much work home. Since the number of hours they spent in school was fixed and was not likely to change, the students realized that they would have to eliminate some of the time that was wasted during the school day and use that time for homework. These nine-year-olds decided by using brainstorming and nominal group technique (chapter 14) that the end of the school day bore the greatest promise for increasing efficiency and adding productive minutes to their school day.

The fourth graders studied the dismissal system over a period of several days, recording the steps in the process and deciding on the appropriate problem-solving tools to help them describe the way the dismissal system was working at the outset. They determined that a flowchart would be the most useful tool for the process.

Information about the dismissal time was gathered within the classroom. Students determined when the process actually began (with a signal from the teacher), watched each other get ready to go home, and tracked the process on a flowchart. Figure 1.2 reflects the dismissal practice.

A follow-up exercise to determine how much effect the improved efficiency actually had on homework completion involved collecting data with two different tools. The first of these related to the amount of time students spent during the day completing homework assignments. A run chart (chapter 9) was used here. For the second approach to monitoring the improvement, the teacher kept a check sheet (chapter 2) to reflect the number of homework assignments submitted. Later, a scatter diagram (chapter 6) demonstrated the relationship between these two events.

A by-product of creating the flowchart was enhanced efficiency in the dismissal process. Students became more aware of their preparations for dismissal and kept better track of their book bags and homework notebooks in order to increase their own efficiency.

Examples: Managing long division and subtraction

A fifth-grade teacher in Ocala, Florida, presented the fundamentals of long division to her students. By introducing the vocabulary of *quotient*, *dividend*, and *divisor*, and repeating the cycle of dividing, multiplying, and subtracting that make up long division problems, she gave students time to practice on their own and to ask questions until the process had been well-defined and the class seemed to grasp the fundamentals.

For further practice, she asked students to do several problems on their own, using two-digit dividends and one-digit divisors. She was dismayed by the number of times students raised their hands with the comment, "I don't remember what to do next," since she had felt that every student had understood the sequence of steps in the division process.

"Let's walk through a problem once more," she said to the students, and after they had listed all the steps, they constructed a flowchart to show the relationship of the individual steps to the whole. After "testing" the flowchart by trying out problems and applying it, the students and teacher agreed on the process and made their own individual copies of the flowchart for reference as they went through their own sets of problems.

The teacher noticed that the questions stopped almost entirely. But more important, students referred to their flowcharts less. No longer was the teacher responsible for answering questions or repeating instructions; each student was responsible for his or her own learning. And the mastery of long division was proportionately accelerated.

As in other classroom applications of quality tools, this example clearly demonstrates how these tools can subtly change the way students learn by shifting responsibility for the process from the teacher to the learner. Figure 1.3 shows the students' flowchart for long division.

After hearing about the long division flowchart, a second-grade teacher in the same school decided to use the tool for subtraction. Her students went through the steps of the

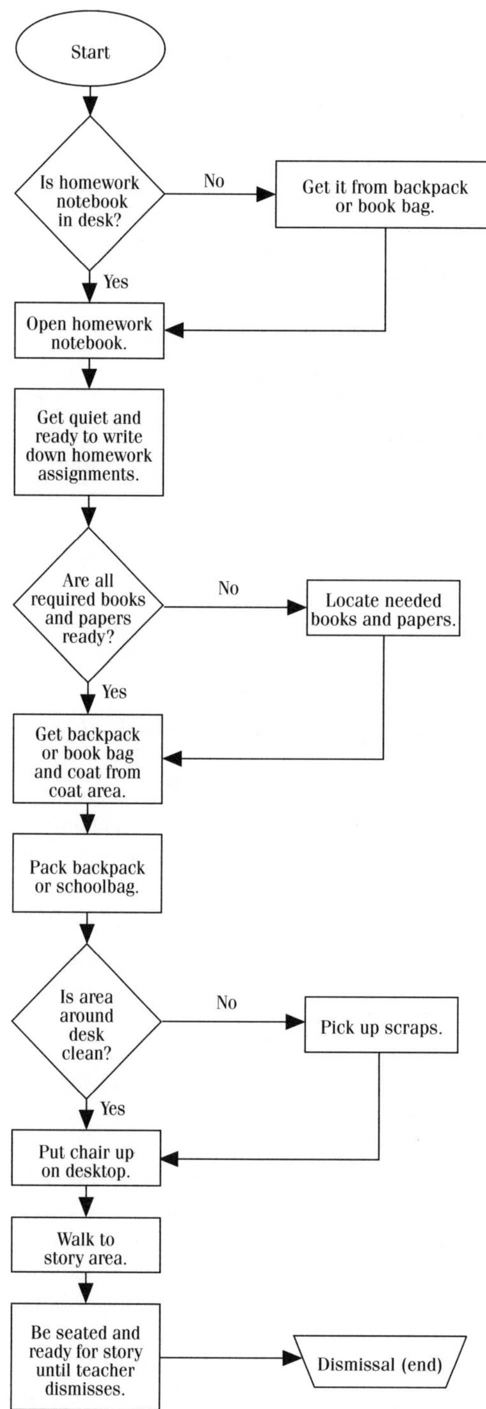

Figure 1.2: End-of-day dismissal process flowchart.

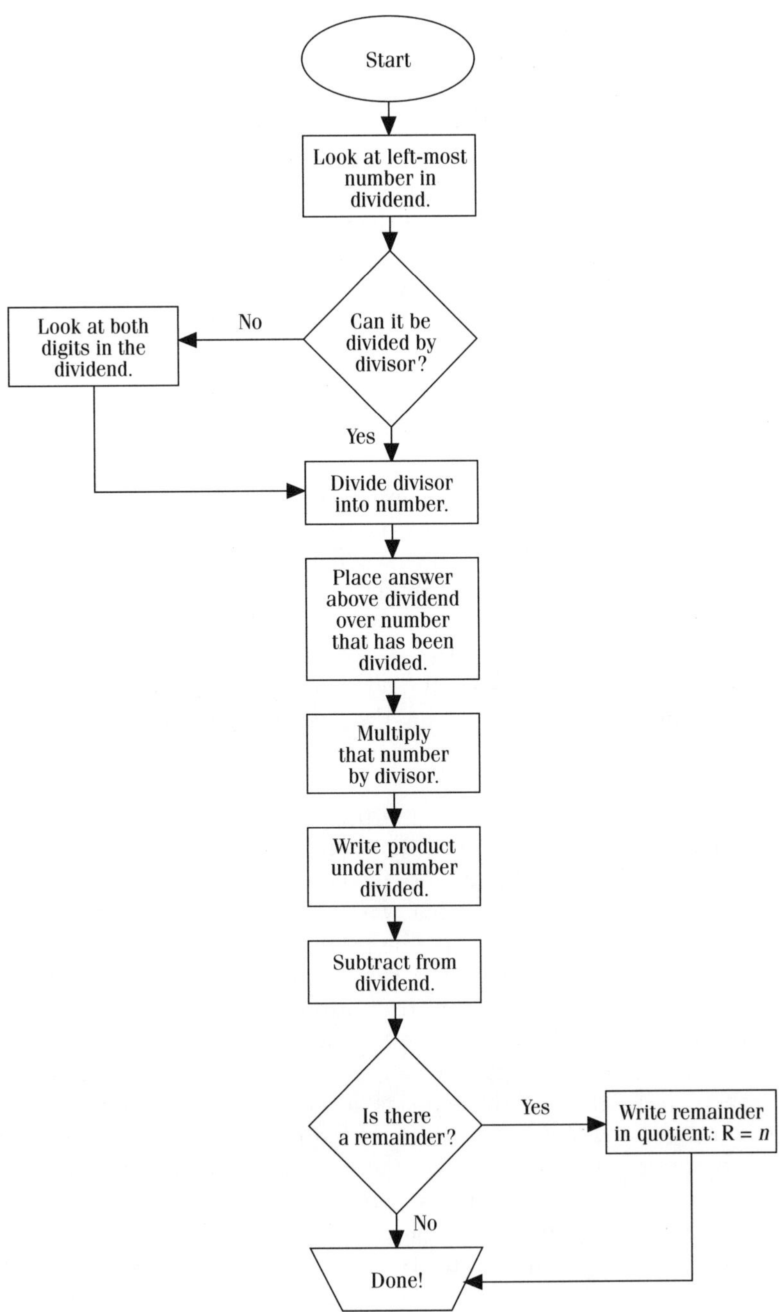

Figure 1.3: Long division flowchart.

subtraction process and created a flowchart for themselves in the same way that their older counterparts had illustrated long division.

Since the skills had been learned some weeks prior to the exercise, the teacher observed that the flowchart not only helped the second graders to standardize the way in which they subtracted, but it also caused them to reflect on the process in a new way. Between the time they had been introduced to subtraction and the time that they created their flowchart, the students had done countless subtraction problems. Some of them had become careless in their application of the learning, and others had still not mastered the sequence of steps. In this case, the flowchart helped them to further cement the learning they had already experienced and the practice they had already had. The second graders' flowchart is illustrated in Figure 1.4.

Example: Communicating with parents

Increasingly, schools are recognizing the important role that parents play in their children's education. Many schools, however, wrestle with handling this role in the most appropriate way. While a parent may know a great deal about his or her child's learning and can contribute that knowledge to the classroom teacher's ability to help that child learn, it is professional educators who know most about educational development and curriculum. Potentially, parents can resent teachers' unwillingness to share more with them about their child's learning; and teachers can become frustrated by parents' perceived meddling in classroom processes. Improving the communication between parents and the school can greatly enhance a child's learning experience, but this communication can be a thorny issue.

In an independent school in Ohio, administrators and teachers became increasingly aware of inconsistencies in the ways in which parents were involved in the communication process relating to their children's school experience. In some cases, parents were first contacting the headmaster to discuss what was happening in their children's classrooms, rather than contacting the teachers first. The problem was one of encouraging communication, but ensuring that such communication was clear and appropriate, and that it would support the learning process rather than interrupt it.

Administrators began with a flowchart for each level of the school—lower, middle, and upper. They indicated the appropriate steps to be taken in communicating with appropriate school personnel. With feedback loops to ensure that parents are satisfied with strategies and that the door remains open for further discussion about a situation, the chart also clearly communicates that all contact with the school is characterized by appropriate steps. If a parent has a question about a tuition statement, for example, it is clear that the business manager's office is the place to begin communication. If, on the other hand, a parent's question or comment deals with the classroom teacher, the communication must begin there.

The flowchart is distributed to parents new to the school as well as to those who initiate any contact with the school and are unfamiliar with the process. What has ensued is a diminished sense of uncertainty ("Whom do I call?") and a greater level of communication. If, for example, a situation is resolved in a way that is satisfactory to the parent, the teacher is informed of this even when this has happened at the administrative level. It is the parent's responsibility to let the teacher know that he or she is satisfied.

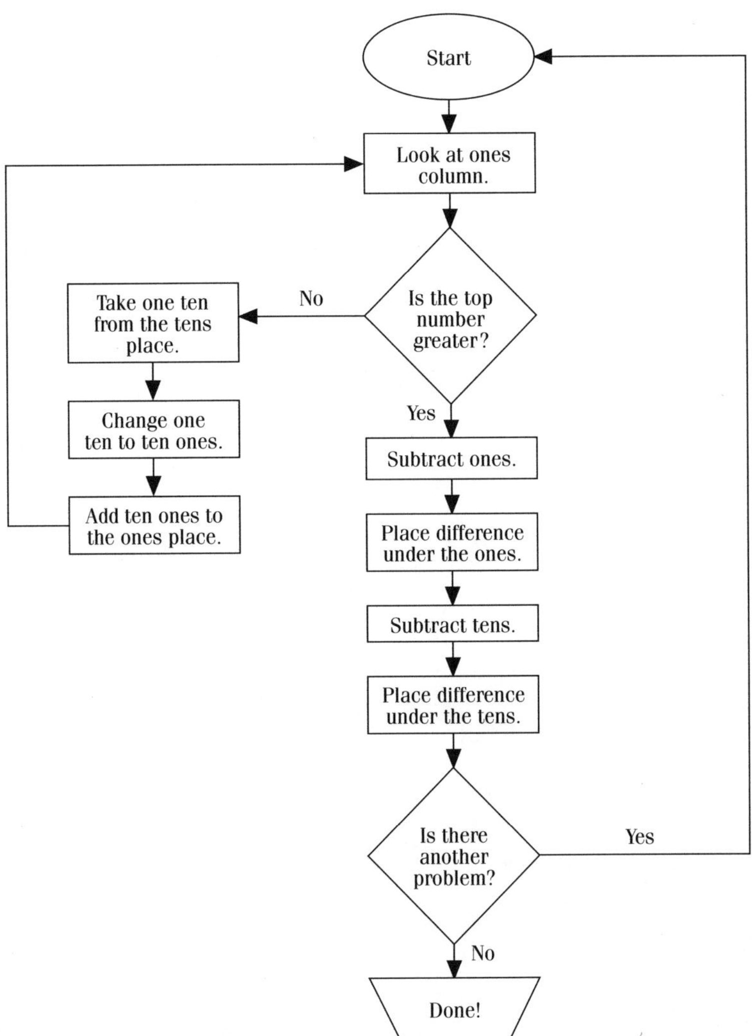

Figure 1.4: Subtraction flowchart.

The flowchart that is used for contacts for lower school and middle school students is seen in Figure 1.5. Figure 1.6 reflects the upper school process.

Example: Deployment flowchart for social studies

A process can be illustrated with a deployment flowchart as well as with a process flowchart. Both charts list the steps in order. In addition, the deployment flowchart provides information about the person or position responsible for each step. When more than one person is involved in the process, it may be useful to have this information. A deployment

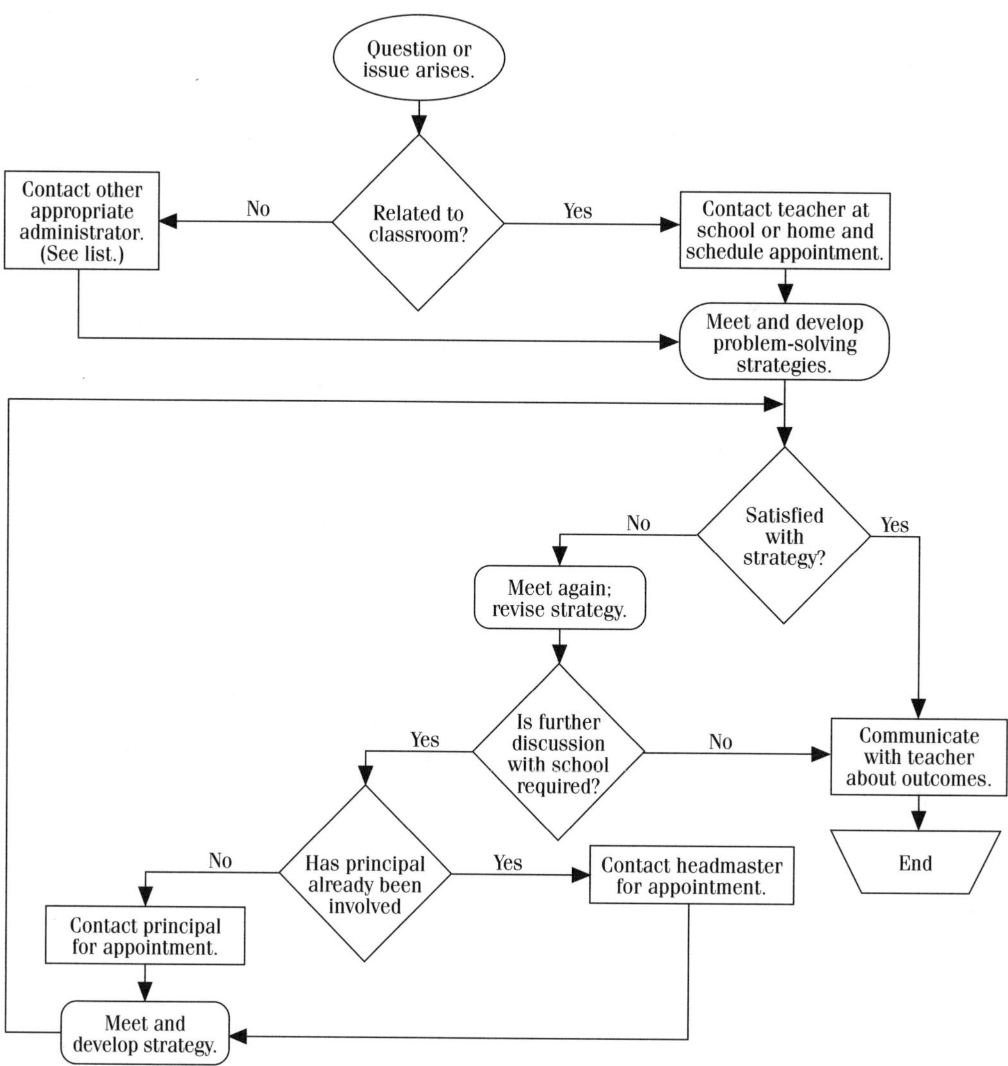

Figure 1.5: Lower school problem-solving process flowchart.

flowchart created by a group of teachers at Ridgeview Elementary School, Ohio, demonstrated the give-and-take responsibilities of student and teacher in a history-geography unit in social studies (see Figure 1.7).

In this example, the two people involved in the process—student and teacher—have different responsibilities, but work together to develop the student's knowledge of history and geography. The flowchart begins with the student's need: "knowledge of history and geography." It seems to suggest that the process will never end, since each mastery of a concept leads to the introduction of a new concept. Of course, this is the way that the process of accruing knowledge really works. But to indicate that there is a way to break out of this loop, this may be done with the use of a drop shadow behind the "introduce new concepts" task box. A drop shadow in any flowchart indicates that another flowchart

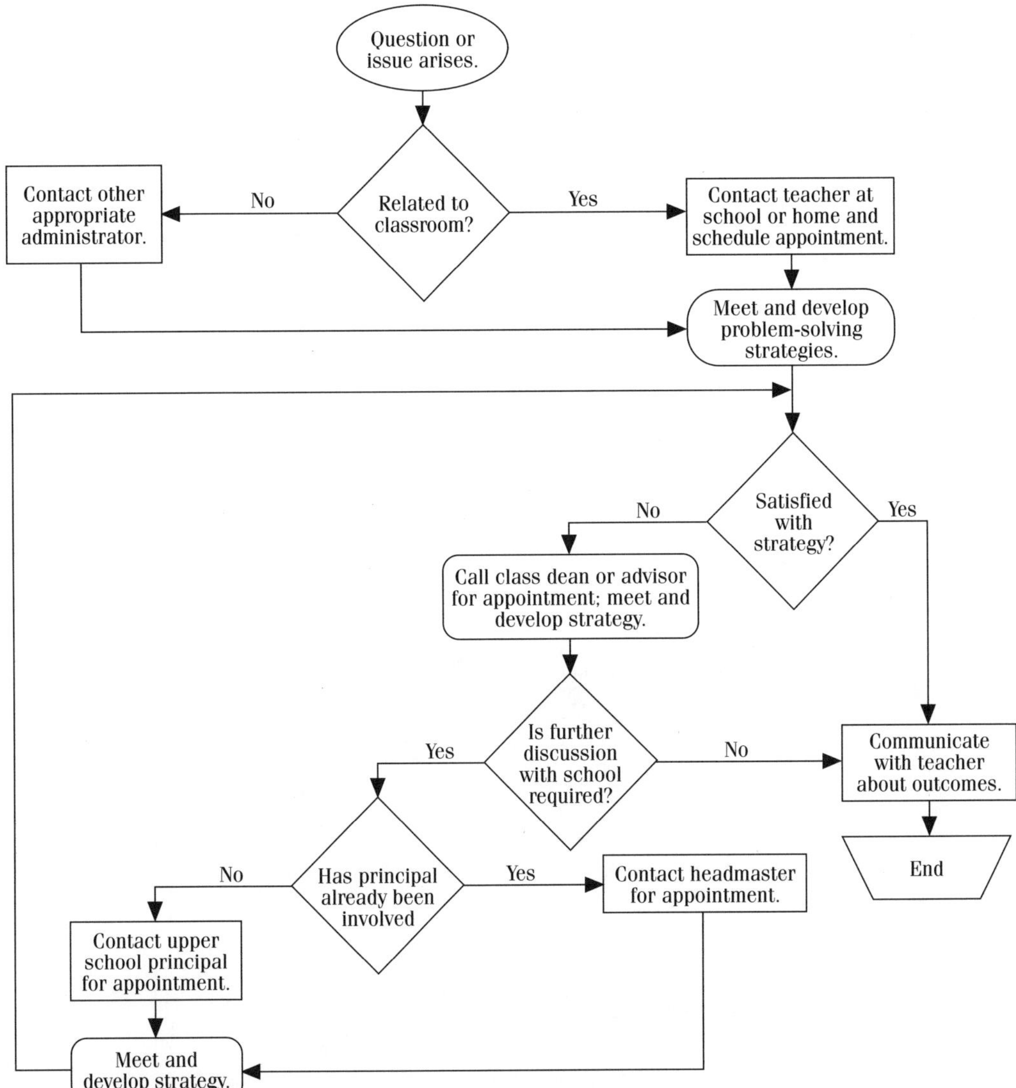

Figure 1.6: Upper school problem-solving process flowchart.

exists to further pursue this task. In this case, the second flowchart might indicate what the arbitrary end point might be—the conclusion of the school year, for example—and delineate the concluding tasks of the study.

Example: Math class

A class was offered to new students at Marshall University Community and Technical College in West Virginia. Students had to demonstrate their need for special help with math skills prior to beginning the mathematics curriculum at the college. Their college

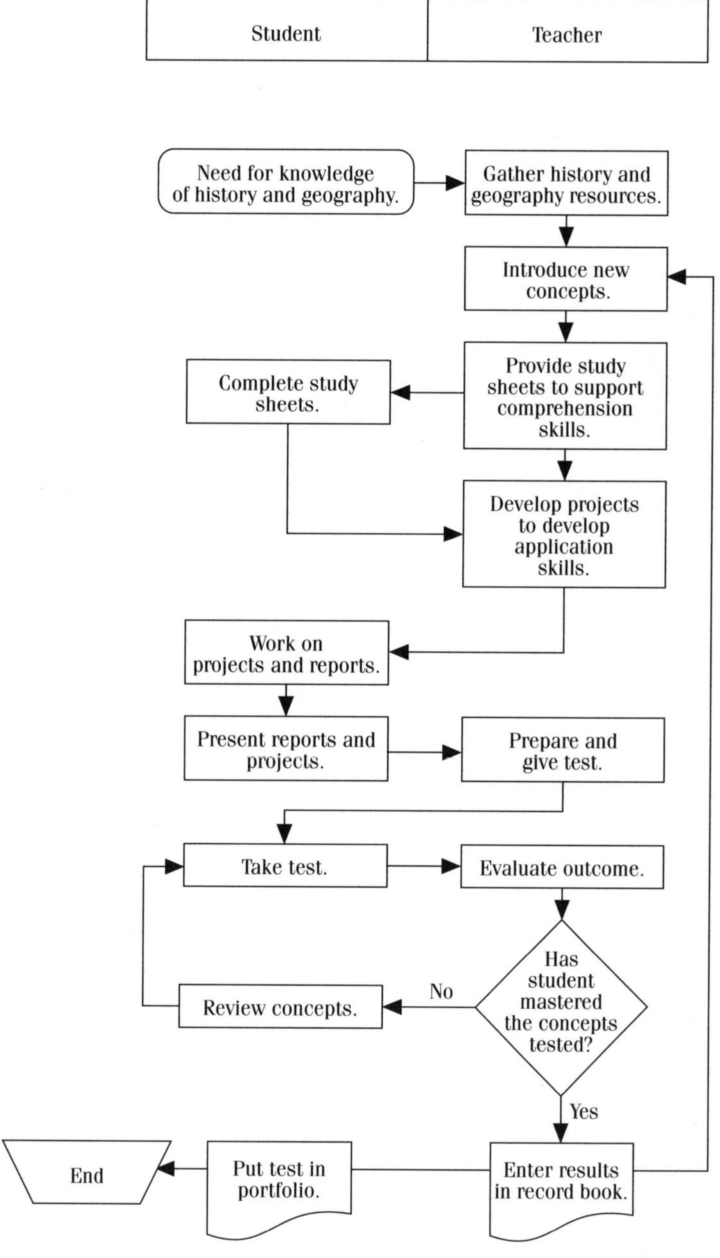

Figure 1.7: History-geography process deployment flowchart.

admission tests indicated gaps in concepts, and the course was designed to address these one at a time.

The professor used a variety of tools to support and expand student learning, but flowcharts provided a particular appeal to the students. After learning a particular application, the class would work together to create a flowchart for that concept, reinforcing each

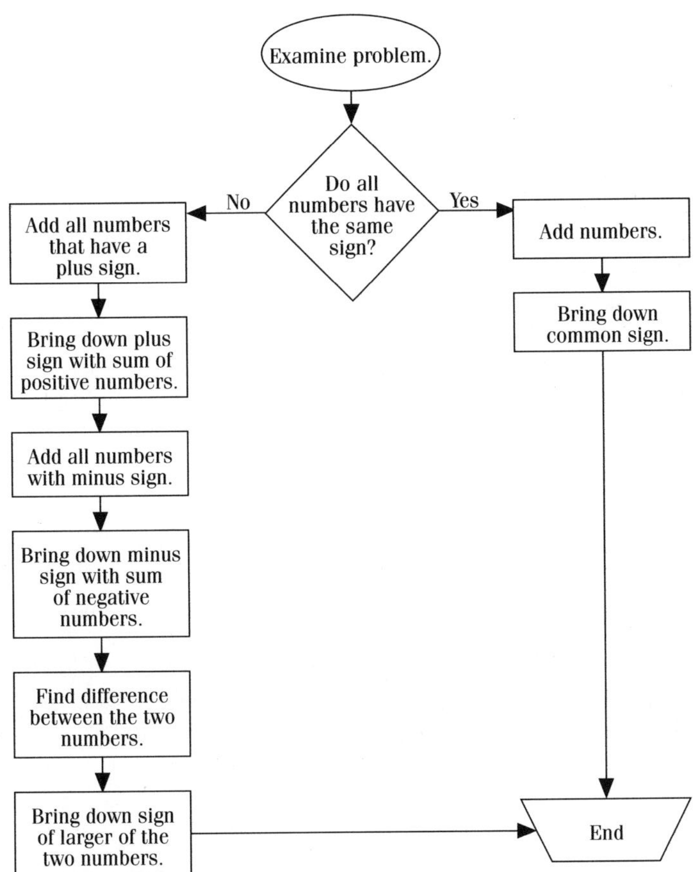

Figure 1.8: Adding signed numbers flowchart.

other's learning in the process of discussion and applying the flowchart to future applications. Just as in the case of the long division flowchart, these college students found that once they had created and used the flowchart, the application became easier and the tool was no longer necessary as they approached individual problems. Figure 1.8 illustrates one of their flowcharts, relating to adding a series of signed numbers.

Just for fun

A class of sixth graders at Norton Middle School in Grove City, Ohio, decided to use the flowchart to illustrate the steps of the human digestive system. While they had fun speculating about the progress of chewed food through the body and recording that progress on a flowchart, there could be little doubt that after they had created the flowchart, they better understood the digestive process.

Notable

As noted, dependence on a teacher or other adult diminishes as young people see processes as their own. Flowcharts, like other tools, will reflect increasing sophistication as students grow in their knowledge and skill.

Likewise, when flowcharts are applied to interfaces between teachers and other parts of the system—internal or external—what ensues is not only an improved process, but also an enhanced opportunity to improve the learning in the classroom. To be sure, there are times when creativity is to be emphasized, rather than agreeing on a standard approach to a process. Frequently, however, steps in learning must be standardized in order to avoid confusion or even danger. One would not want to be in the position of deciding on the escape route during a fire drill by brainstorming and thinking of all possible creative approaches.

Application

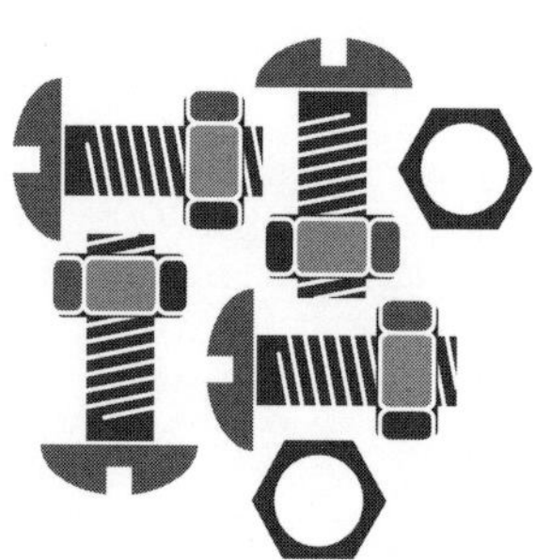

Using the flowchart symbols shown in Figure 1.1, draw your own flowchart for a process with which you are especially familiar. It may be something from your daily life (sorting the mail or assembling a new toy, for example) or from your own classroom experience. (How about that fire drill example?) After you have created the flowchart, try walking through the actual process, using the chart as your guide.

Chapter 2

Checking the Facts

Introducing check sheets

Every teacher in the world uses check sheets: a list of student names checked for homework; an attendance report; a milk money list; and a field trip supply check. Many other day-to-day activities require the use of check sheets. A check sheet provides a simple way to gather simple data, usually of the yes-no variety. Check sheets help to keep track of when things have happened or have not happened.

When used to their full potential, check sheets can become blueprints for further analysis or action. They provide a way to record more than one kind of information at a time. In fact, they are most useful when they do this. Because it is not known how data will later emerge into patterns, it is generally a good idea to collect more information than seems to be needed, so that it can be stratified or broken down for analysis later. After all, one never knows when "a fact may flower into a truth" (Thoreau 1845).

If teachers are annoyed by interruptions to their classrooms, it might seem to be sufficient to simply record the number of interruptions. Tick marks could represent the number of incidents. In order to do anything about the interruptions or to recommend changes, however, it will be far more useful to know *when* each interruption occurred (day of the week, time of day), *why* it took place (message from office, speech therapist sends note to student, and so on), and perhaps other supporting information. These data also will be useful during a later analysis.

Students can also use check sheets. In fact, some of the data that teachers record could just as easily be kept by students, enlisting their participation in the record keeping as well as in any planned change that may be pursued. If a student knows exactly when he or she has failed to hand in homework, and the check sheet reveals that these failures have often occurred on Mondays, that student may want to review the activities or distractions that have contributed to the lapses. When a child regularly forgets milk money, it is more important to understand exactly when this has happened than to know only how many times that child has forgotten. Then, this information can guide future actions for the child by developing the why of the incident.

A check sheet can take on a variety of forms. It may be a grid or matrix, where information is entered to reflect more than one factor (time, date, yes/no) at the same time. Figure 2.1 is a check sheet of children turning in milk money. This chart provides only minimal information. For example, the number of observations is insufficient to perceive any real patterns. If check sheets had been kept for several weeks instead of only one, then it might be seen that Lisa forgets her milk money every Monday. Erica, who appears on this list never to have her milk money, was absent the week this check sheet was maintained and, in fact, usually brings her money promptly. On the other hand, Paul seems to have had a perfect week for this particular chart, but has not had such a week for the

Name	Mon.	Tues.	Wed.	Thurs.	Fri.
Paul	✔	✔	✔	✔	✔
Lisa		✔		✔	✔
Alycia	✔	✔			
Matt			✔	✔	
Carl		✔	✔	✔	✔
Kascha	✔	✔			
Liz	✔	✔	✔	✔	
Erica					

Figure 2.1: Milk money turned in check sheet.

entire year until now. Data can mislead if it is insufficient or if it has been gathered without enough supporting information.

Classroom benefits

As teachers attempt to reach students by understanding their particular gifts or "intelligences" (Gardner 1983), they find that different approaches to learning support different intelligences. For example, using check sheets supports both visual and kinesthetic intelligences when children maintain their own charts. When a student makes a mark that records an aspect of his or her work, that act reinforces the student's learning. The responsibility for learning is subtly shifted from the teacher, with his or her grade book filled with every record, to the student, who is now responsible for some of his or her own record keeping. While this shift may seem to be a small one, it is fundamental to developing and enhancing the student's ability to take responsibility for learning.

Maintaining portfolios and other records of student learning is enhanced with the use of check sheets. Nothing could be more dramatic in a conference with a parent who insists that a child is doing every homework assignment than for the child to voluntarily show the parent a documented check sheet in the child's own handwriting showing the contrary.

Example: Fourth-grade writing

A fourth-grade class at the Eighth Street School in Ocala, Florida, developed rubrics to assess good writing practices. As part of that assessment, students used check sheets. While it is clear that this tool cannot provide the complete picture of what constitutes good writing, the teacher helped students to develop definitions of several components, so they could review their own work and determine which of these components were present and which were missing.

In addition to the simple list that would help students focus on particular components, the young writers provided additional analysis of their skills by evaluating each component on a scale of 1 to 6 (low to high) (see Figure 2.2). The list included the following components of writing.

Student: Karla Assignment: Character analysis, *To Kill a Mockingbird*		Date: October 17
Characteristic	Comments	Evaluation (1–6 low to high)
Main idea	Atticus is courageous.	5
Focus	Described incidents that show courage.	5
Grammar	Some comma errors; good use of capitalization.	4
Spelling	Seven errors; "Atticus" misspelled throughout.	2
Structure	No topic sentence used in third paragraph.	2
Use of supporting details	Good use of examples to support main idea.	5

Figure 2.2: Writing evaluation check sheet.

- Unity: Having a main idea
- Clear focus
- Grammar
- Spelling
- Structure
- Use of supporting ideas

The tool helped students to analyze their own writing problems, as they carefully reviewed each of their papers to assess these components. In addition, the teacher developed a system in which individuals' check sheets were overlaid to give a class profile. In this way, the students and their teacher were able to identify their greatest strengths and challenges. When they saw, for example, that grammar represented the weakest area on a given paper, they collectively knew that they needed to work on this skill.

Example: Class participation by gender

After attending a workshop relating to gender-appropriate education, a middle school teacher became more aware of the relative attention he was giving to boys and girls in his English classroom. The workshop leader had shared data that suggested that boys often demand and receive more attention in discussions than do their female counterparts. The English teacher wanted to evaluate his own behavior in order to assess whether he was reinforcing "typical" male-female classroom roles.

The teacher constructed a check sheet to gather data about the number of times that students spoke in class for any reason—to answer questions, to respond to behavior reminders, and to ask for something. He found that it was difficult to keep track of these contacts himself, since he was involved in other tasks relating to classroom management and facilitation, and he would often forget to tally every student contact. To improve his data-gathering system, he asked an interested colleague to tally the data, with the promise

Class discussions: Gender analysis		Class: Period II, English 7-A
	Boys	Girls
Mon. 10/8	卌 卌 III	卌
Tues. 10/9	卌 卌 II	IIII II
Wed. 10/10	卌 IIII	IIII
Thurs. 10/11	卌 II	卌 卌
Fri. 10/12	Test: No discussion	
Mon. 10/15	卌 IIII	卌

Figure 2.3: Discussion analysis by gender check sheet.

that he would do the same for her. The colleague agreed to participate in the data gathering every day for a week. The check sheet that the colleague put together appears in Figure 2.3.

The record was interesting, because it seemed to indicate that boys were receiving slightly more attention through teacher contact than were girls. The English teacher noted that on the day prior to a test, girls were more actively involved in discussions and participated in the class more frequently than the boys. Following the test, however, this pattern seemed to change. The teacher realized that the data deserved more analysis. For example, it would be important to know more about the kind of contact that each student had received. It may be that the boys were given more negative attention than girls or that the quality of the contacts might be different for the genders. Were girls receiving more intellectual support, for example, while boys were primarily admonished for their behavior?

Now that he had become more aware of his contacts with students, the English teacher found that he was able to collect his own data. He kept the check sheet clipped to his literature book, and as he walked around the classroom and interacted with students, he noted the interactions on his data sheet. This time, however, he stratified the data by noting the kind of interaction. He also noted the number of students present in the class each day, so that he would be able to determine not only how many students had interactions with him, but the proportion of the total class that this number represented. The second check sheet, Figure 2.4, shows this information.

After the English teacher had gathered the data and analyzed it, he discussed it with his students. Their insights were helpful to him as he worked toward eliminating gender bias in his classroom. The discussion also helped the students understand and monitor their own behavior with respect to their contact with the teacher. The exercise, which had begun as a professional development issue, became a source of mutual interest for the teacher and his students. Follow-up data were recorded by a selected student using a check sheet.

Example: Feeding the goldfish

Among the classroom assignments for kindergartners in a Connecticut classroom are changing the calendar, collecting the scissors, feeding the goldfish, selecting a story to be

Class discussions: Gender analysis 2		Class: Period II, English 7-A								
Number present	Mon. 23		Tues. 20		Wed. 19		Thurs. 22		Fri. 19	
	Boys	Girls	Boys	Girls	Boys	Girls	Boys	Girls	Boys	Girls
Responding to question	卌	II	III	卌	III		卌	卌	卌	卌 I
Asking for something	卌 III	IIII	卌	III	卌	IIII	卌		IIII	II
Volunteering in discussion	卌	III		卌	IIII		卌		卌	
Inattentive comment	IIII	II	III		卌		卌 IIII	卌	卌 III	
Talking to neighbor	卌	II	II	卌	卌	II	IIII		卌	卌
Follow-up comment	卌	II	III	II		卌	卌	IIII	III	IIII

Figure 2.4: Gender analysis: Class participation check sheet.

read aloud, erasing the chalkboard, and turning off lights as the class goes out to recess. The teacher helped students manage these tasks by using a check sheet. Each time a child completed an assigned task, he or she would check it off on a large chart that was posted in the classroom (see Figure 2.5). A separate list identified the initials of the child who was responsible for a task each day.

Although it represented a simple record of the tasks, in this case, the value of the check sheet was to reinforce the sense of responsibility that each child felt for a given task. It gave a sense of completion to the contributions that the children made to the smooth management of their classroom and provided a picture of tasks that were often overlooked. For example, it seemed hard for the children to remember to turn off the lights when they found themselves last in line. The teacher was able to discuss the issue with the children, who came up with a new approach to the problem. A second child was assigned to close the classroom door, and together the last two children would remind and help each other with their respective tasks. By recording the children's initials in a separate place, the chart avoided placing blame on individual children who had forgotten to do their tasks.

Example: Math skills

A fifth-grade classroom utilized the check sheet as a way for students to chart their own progress in gaining competency with particular math skills. They had already used cause-and-effect diagrams (chapter 3) to determine the greatest contributor to wrong answers on math problems. Both Sara and Karl found that their greatest number of errors in problems—in decimal problems, fractions, or story problems—was related to simple arithmetic errors. They realized that this pattern had an impact on a wide variety of math problems, whether they were multiplication, division, subtraction, or addition problems. They

Classroom duties																				
	M	T	W	T	F	M	T	W	T	F	M	T	W	T	F	M	T	W	T	F
Calendar	X	X	X	X	X	X	X	X	X		X	X			X					
Scissors	X	X	X		X	X	X	X	X	X	X	X	X	X	X					
Fish	X	X	X	X	X		X	X	X		X		X	X	X					
Story	X	X	X	X	X	X		X		X	X	X	X		X					
Chalkboard	X	X	X		X	X	X	X	X		X	X		X	X					
Lights		X	X	X	X	X	X		X		X			X	X					

Figure 2.5: Classroom duties check sheet.

wanted to keep records that would indicate the times that the errors were most likely to occur. Although check sheets can be used by individuals for their own use, it is often helpful to have more than one student pursuing the data gathering and analysis, for they will find support in each other's progress as well as their own. They will also be able to brainstorm about the kinds of data that they want to collect.

Figure 2.6 reflects Sara's record of her own arithmetic errors. She was able to clarify the areas where she needed additional practice. In this case, multiplication appeared to be one of these. She was able to see that her difficulties were not in doing a particular kind of problem (story problem, fractions), but were related to specific operations.

Errors in arithmetic: Sara																
	Problem set #1				Problem set #2				Problem set #3				Problem set #4			
	+	−	×	÷	+	−	×	÷	+	−	×	÷	+	−	×	÷
Decimals	IIII	II	IIII	III		𝍸			𝍸		𝍸			𝍸		
Fractions	𝍸 I		𝍸 𝍸	𝍸			𝍸		IIII	II	IIII		III		𝍸 𝍸	III
Story problems			IIII	II	IIII	III				𝍸	𝍸 III		III			
Whole numbers	IIII	II	IIII	𝍸			𝍸 I		III				𝍸			III

Figure 2.6: Sara's math check sheet.

Notable

If students are to evaluate their own work, it is important for them to know that data entered on a check sheet are *not* to be used for their grades. In fact, it is usually best for them to tally their own check sheets and share them with their teacher only in individual conferences that are not related to grading. One way to de-emphasize the grading process is to gather group check sheets. By compiling the students' check sheets—overlaying them, so to speak, for a cumulative profile—the teacher's emphasis becomes one of promoting improvement for the entire class without focusing on individual performance.

Application

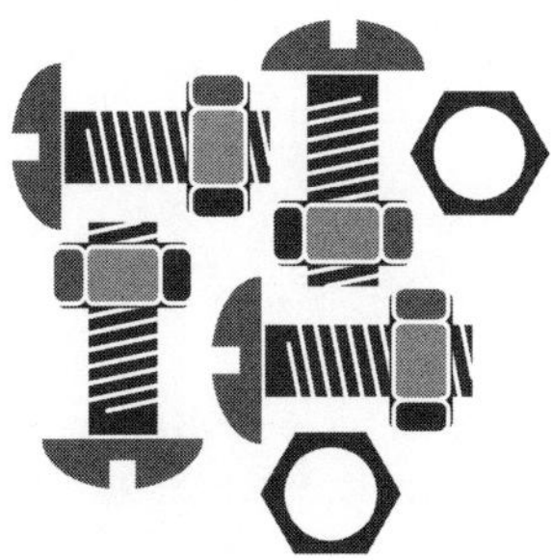

Notice how much more observant you become when you have decided to collect data by means of a check sheet. For example, if you record the number of times children begin a task without a reminder, you will undoubtedly become more aware of how often this happens. Collecting data and sharing it provides a way to reinforce positive behavior in the classroom.

References

Shanley, J. Lyndon, ed. 1974. *Henry David Thoreau: Walden* (1845). Princeton, N.J.: Princeton University Press.

Gardner, Howard. 1983. *Frames of mind: The theory of multiple intelligences*. New York: Basic Books.

Chapter 3

Getting to "Why?" with Fishbones

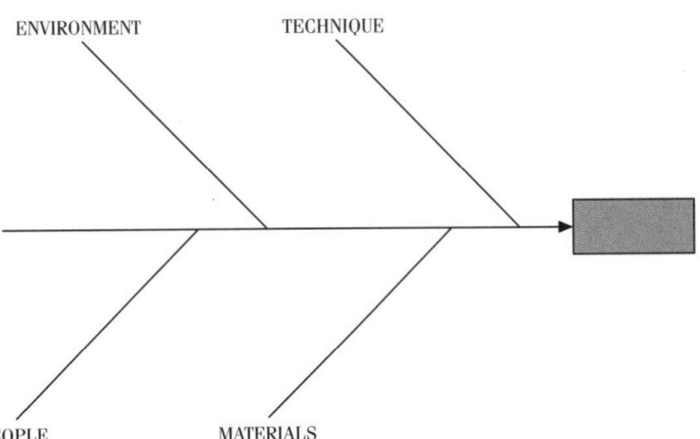

Introducing cause-and-effect diagrams

From the time a child can talk, his or her overriding question is "Why?" Cause-and-effect diagrams help children continue to ask that question throughout their lives.

Cause-and-effect, or Ishikawa diagrams, build on brainstorming; that is, speculation about various factors that help to bring about a particular effect. They are sometimes referred to as *fishbone diagrams* because they look like an x-ray of a fish. Children can create cause-and-effect diagrams in the classroom; and teachers can find them useful in assessing the reasons for problems in a child's learning. Once people learn to use these diagrams, they will begin thinking about ways to apply them to a variety of problems, events, or circumstances.

Usually organized around central categories, the fishbone chart begins with a central spine that points to the effect that is under scrutiny. Other "bones"—traditionally organized as causes that relate to people, methods, materials, environment, and machines (or technology)—can be labeled in ways that are appropriate to the effect being studied. For example, "students" or "skills," can be used instead of "people" or "methods."

Start with a common example. As a parent, how many times have you sopped up spilled milk at the dinner table after a child has inadvertently knocked over a glass? Does this also happen in the lunchroom at school?

In a brainstorming session, family members have identified these causes for the milk spills.

1. Glass is too full.
2. Youngest child Charlie's chair is too low to reach the glass safely.
3. Glasses have stems that are unstable.
4. Charlie isn't paying attention.
5. Charlie's brother is distracting him.
6. The glass is on the wrong side of the plate. (Charlie is left-handed.)
7. Charlie doesn't like milk.
8. Everyone is yelling at the dinner table.

In this case, where the temptation is generally to reprimand the child for carelessness, the focus can be taken away from blaming little Charlie and setting about to analyze the situation further. Instead, family members can observe how many times the milk spills,

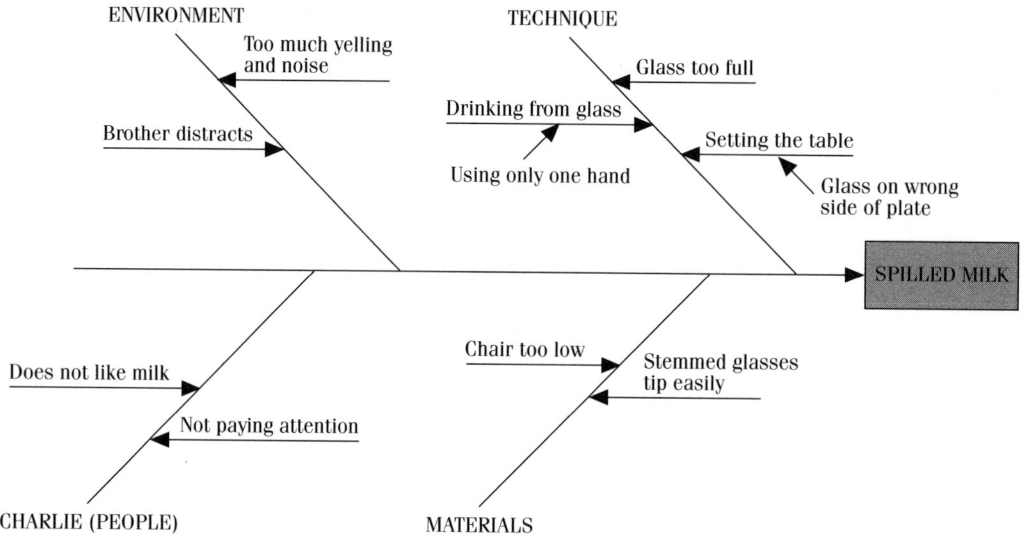

Figure 3.1: Spilled milk cause-and-effect diagram.

and then begin to use a cause-and-effect diagram to organize their observations about the reasons for these spills. Categories that are generally assigned to the bones of the cause-and-effect diagram include people, techniques or methods, environment, and materials. In this case, technology probably does not apply, and there's no use stretching or artificially adding reasons just to make the example fit (see Figure 3.1). The people category focuses on Charlie, so his name appears as the category.

Analyzing the chart

Once the cause-and-effect diagram has been constructed, everyone involved has an opportunity to identify the causes and their graphic connection to the outcome—the spilled milk. It is clear that the situation will not change in a permanent way, however, until the family determines that it will work on a single cause. If all the causes are seen as equally destructive, and every classification is changed immediately, family members will never understand what represented the most important cause for the spilled milk. Without this focus, the issue will become unnecessarily complex, and probably no permanent change will take place. The family may pursue the improvement process by identifying what it feels is a root cause—let's say number 6: The glass is on the wrong side of the plate. The next step is to test the theory by changing the setup. Charlie can reach his glass when it is on the left side of his plate; so when the table is set, it is arranged this way. Further observation might reveal fewer incidents of spilled milk, and the change can become a permanent part of the family's meal pattern.

Classroom benefits

Although the immediate temptation is to use cause-and-effect charts only to rout out the reasons for problems or failures, they can be equally useful in analyzing events or reproducing positive results. A child who has produced an outstanding report on eagles and other birds of prey, for example, can be encouraged to review the reasons that the report was so successful. The technique shores up the learning process by emphasizing skills of analysis and critical review of processes. The diagram is so easy to use that small groups of children, or even individual students, can apply it on their own once they have learned how to manage it. While it is intimately connected with other techniques—brainstorming and data gathering, for example—a cause-and-effect diagram can represent a visual event that will continue to remind students of the ways they have approached problems in the culture of their classroom. And the diagram will help students probe more deeply into the reasons that events or problems have occurred. It advances learning by organizing thinking around causal or contributing relationship factors.

Example: Learning intervention

A team composed of teachers, a lunchroom aide, a speech therapist, a psychologist, a learning disabilities teacher, a nurse, a supervisor, a parent, and the principal at Ridgeview Elementary School in Ashtabula, Ohio, used a cause-and-effect diagram as a part of its efforts to improve students' reading and writing fluency. The team narrowly focused on students with special problems in word and letter recognition skills, asking, "Why do students have poor reading and writing skills?" The Ridgeview team's cause-and-effect diagram is shown in Figure 3.2.

This case, as with many others, demonstrates why the Ishikawa diagram cannot stand alone. It is not an end in itself, but only suggests ways to proceed with improvement. The team developed an improvement theory that focused on specific causes it identified as most critical, all relating to the students. These are circled on Figure 3.2. In addition to honing in on these causes, the diagram was useful in supporting and understanding the larger processes of reading and writing.

The adults addressing the children's problems in reading and writing proceeded to test their theory: If a particular approach, what was termed the "fold-in method," were used, if parents were solicited to give extra help with spelling, and if students had more practice with dictated sentences, then students would see more success. The adults tested their theory by continuing to collect data, monitor progress, and observe outcomes.

Example: World War II

Here, a group of middle school students in Ohio used the cause-and-effect diagram to organize their thinking about a historical event. They were cautioned about oversimplifying such a complex event, but they wanted to think about some of the causes of the war itself, in the context of understanding how World War II happened to break out when it did. The students focused on general conditions that contributed to the eruption, rather than specific invasions or battles that created actual events.

- People
  —Racial hatred
  —Ethnic fighting
  —Desire for revenge
  —Jealousy of others
  —Greed

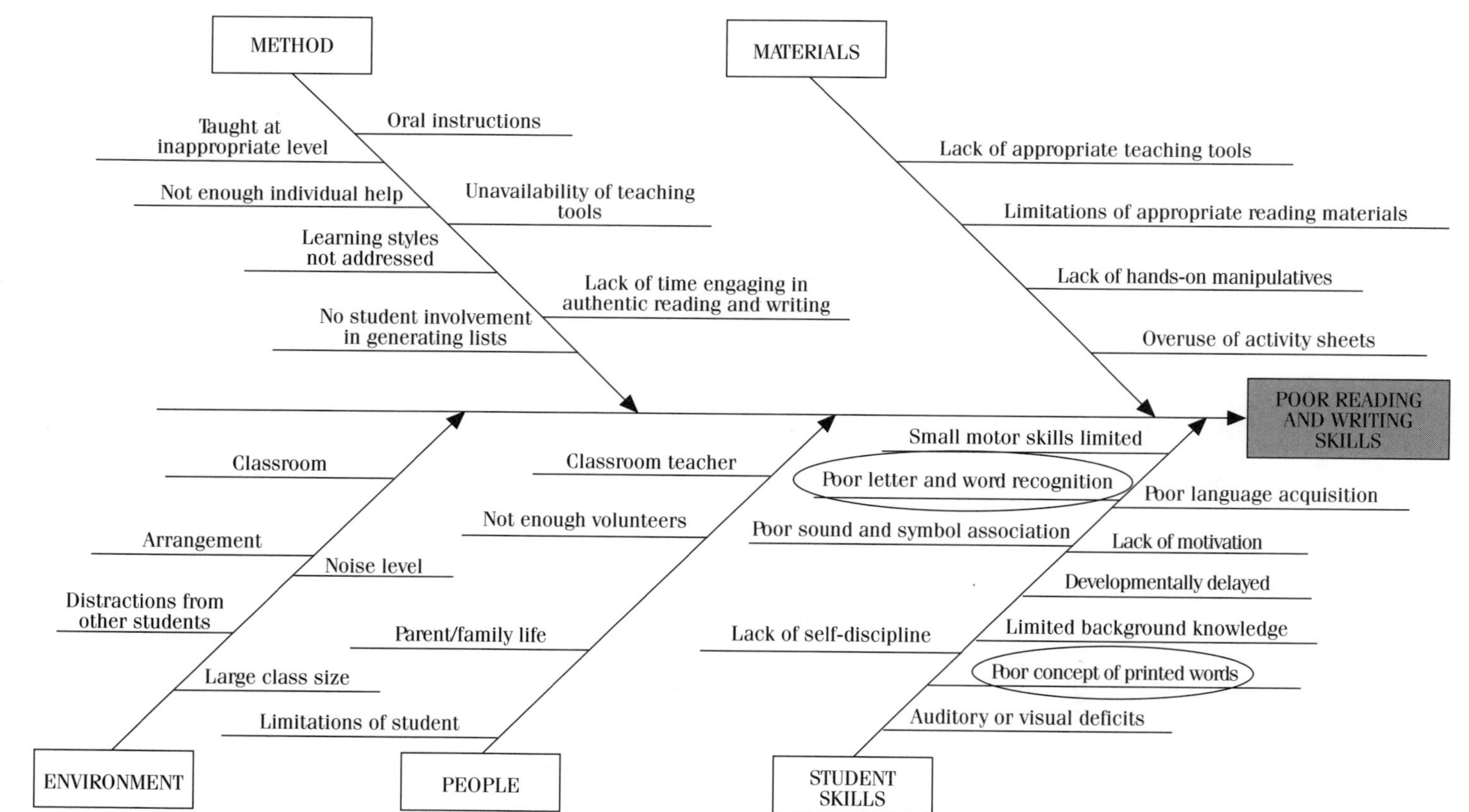

Figure 3.2: Reading and writing skills cause-and-effect diagram.

—Economic threats
—Need for more power
—Nationalism
—Charismatic, evil leader
- Materials
—Weakening economy
—Shortages of goods
—Unfair distribution
- Methods
—Lying about motivations
—Manipulative leadership
—Flawed agreements
- Environment
—Suspicion of neighbors
—High unemployment
—Inflation
—Injustices
—Shortages of goods
—Witch-hunting atmosphere

With each of the causes listed, the analysis could go deeper by making that cause the effect; that is, moving it to the "head" of the fish. What, for example, were the factors that contributed to the high unemployment (one of the causes of the war, in the earlier analysis)? One of the powerful features of cause-and-effect analysis is that it can be pursued at deeper, increasingly focused levels.

An interesting discussion might ensue if students were to create a cause-and-effect analysis about the factors that keep wars from happening. This represents a variation on the tool, where a hypothetical, opposite situation is the focus for the analysis. So-called "negative cause-and-effect" exercises are useful in developing different perspectives.

Example: Vocabulary

A group of reading students found that they could never transfer their acquisition of vocabulary words that they had looked up in the dictionary to actually understand the words in their reading. They felt that the vocabulary tests did not help them learn and that their vocabulary skills were fairly weak. Figure 3.3 shows the students' cause-and-effect diagram.

As they analyzed their chart, the students realized that their preparation for vocabulary tests was just that—preparation only for the test, rather than a commitment to learning new words that would help them in their reading. They began to discuss how their mastery of words could be demonstrated in ways that had more meaning to them. Eventually, the students worked with their teacher to develop a reading-based series of vocabulary exercises that developed their confidence in reading unfamiliar words and adding them to their vocabularies.

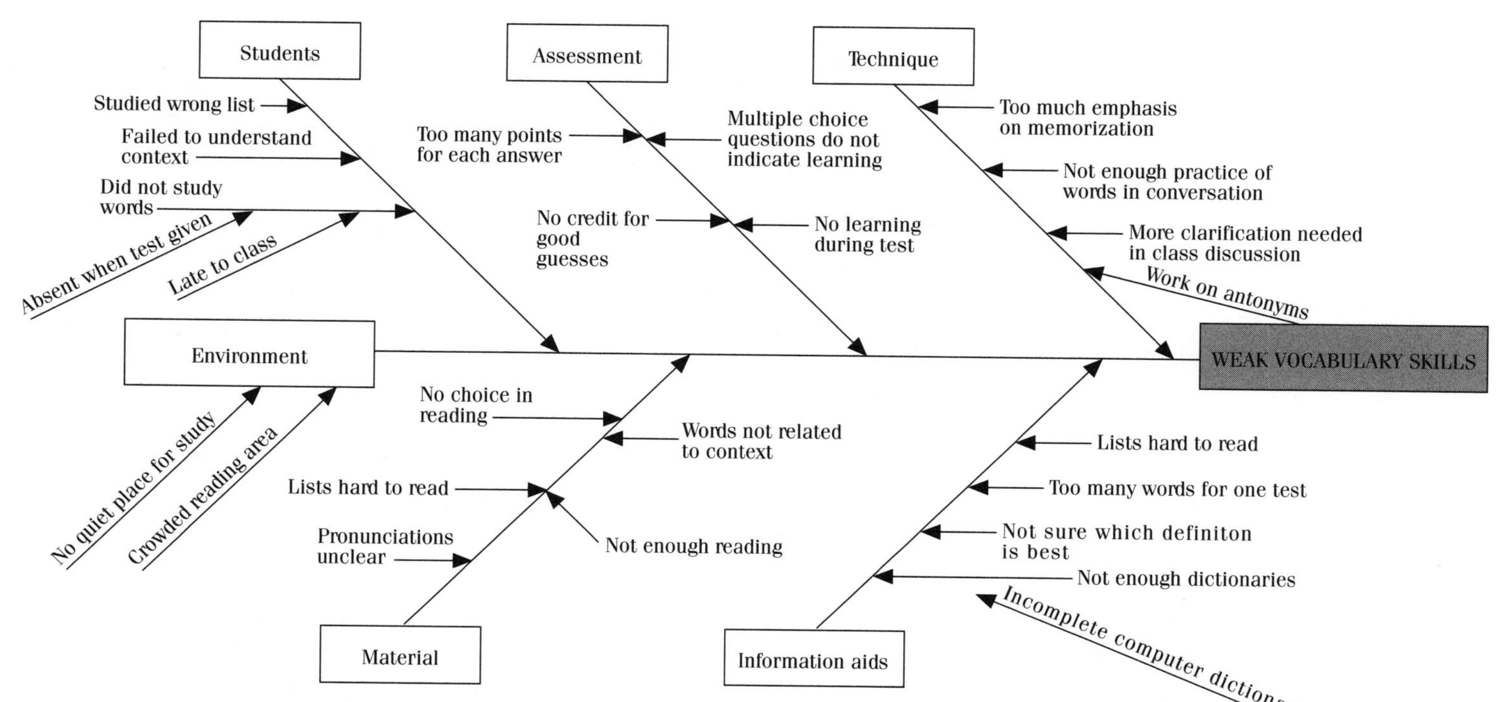

Figure 3.3: Vocabulary cause-and-effect diagram.

Example: Second-grade writing

Why is it that students can earn As on every single spelling test and yet seem unable to spell at all in the context of their written expression? Every teacher has faced this conundrum. Math teachers, too, know students who ace the multiplication tables and yet make multiplication errors time after time. A team in Ocala, Florida, addressed this kind of discrepancy.

Cause-and-effect analysis can be pursued by teachers, students, administrators, or teams that represent all of these groups. One such mixed team in an ASQC Koalaty Kid school was comprised of the principal, a learning specialist, several teachers, a teacher's assistant, students, a parent, and business sponsor representatives. (The Koalaty Kid Initiative represents the effort of ASQC to support training in quality theory, process, and tools for educators and students.) The team addressed the issue of improving student writing and, as part of its analysis, created a cause-and-effect diagram to reflect the causes for weak spelling on classroom assignments.

This diagram represented part of an ongoing project to improve the second graders' writing, and the team applied a variety of tools to that improvement effort. An example of a control chart as well as a Pareto diagram that was used in the same improvement project are examined later in this book. The cause-and-effect diagram (Figure 3.4) focuses on the spelling skills reflected in student papers.

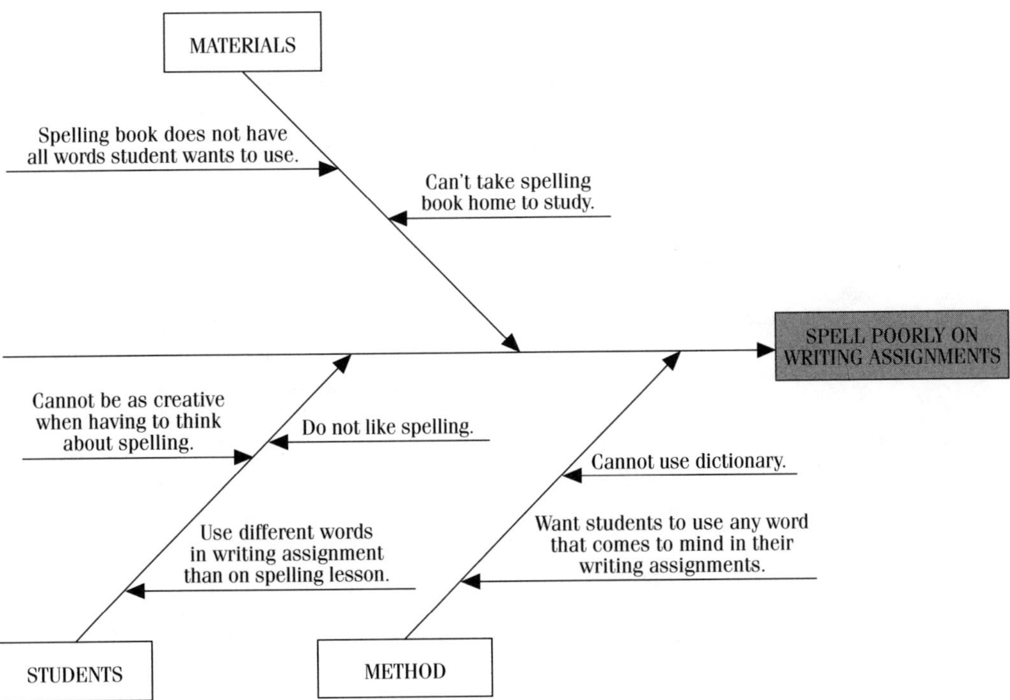

Figure 3.4: Second-grade spelling and writing cause-and-effect diagram.

Notable

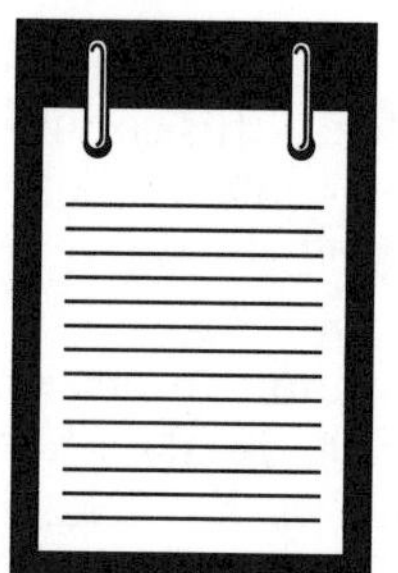

While cause-and-effect diagrams are useful for organizing thinking about factors that contribute to a particular outcome, they are flexible enough to apply to the learning process in a variety of ways. Once students have created a cause-and-effect diagram, they can begin to discuss the most important, or root causes. Then, the students can develop a second cause-and-effect diagram with that cause becoming the effect. This process generates deeper analysis as students delve beneath the surface of events or outcomes.

If, for example, students determine that the most important cause for the development of slavery in this country was the need for cheap labor, the next phase might pose the factors that contributed to this need. For deeper analysis, the cause-and-effect diagram helps students productively focus their thinking in a way that continues to ask the important question, Why?

When students begin cause-and-effect analysis, their responses may at first seem to be superficial or obvious. Using this second- and third-layer approach will help them go beyond their initial observations and begin to uncover deeper causes. At the same time, their own thinking will become deeper, and they will find that they are expanding their ability to go beyond the superficial.

One caution is in order with respect to cause-and-effect analysis. The temptation is often to go immediately to this tool, often before other information has been considered and analyzed. One team created a fishbone diagram to examine the reasons for poor performance in math—a highly general effect of a variety of causes. If the team had first considered check sheets and Pareto analysis related to the kinds of math errors, it would have noted that most of the difficulty was associated with multiplication skills. Whenever students were called upon to multiply, whether in story problems, long division, or algebraic equations, they were more likely to make errors. The cause-and-effect analysis could have been more useful if "multiplication errors" had been at the head of the fishbone, rather than simply "poor performance in math."

Application

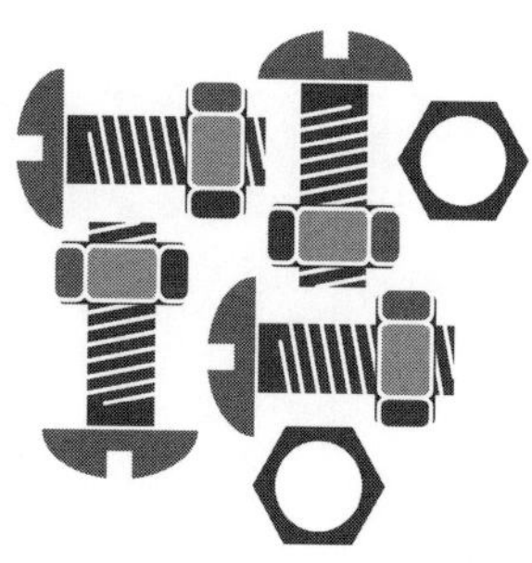

Consider creating a cause-and-effect diagram that relates to your classroom situation. You can do this alone, developing causes with which you may already be familiar, or with others who share the same situation. Begin by thinking of a question; for example, why is it so difficult for the third grade to settle down after lunch? You might consider doing this with individual students, where they may analyze the reasons for their own tardiness or for a specific academic problem they may be having. If possible, consult other related data that you may already have.

Chapter 4

An Affinity for Organized Thinking

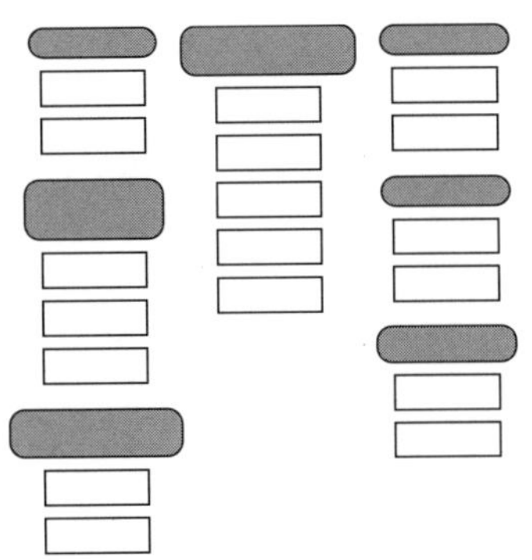

Introducing affinity diagrams

Grouping ideas offers another approach to developing analytical thinking skills. Affinity diagrams help to make connections among ideas, sometimes organizing chaotic thinking into manageable groups for further analysis.

Teachers have used affinity diagrams as a way to organize thinking or approach problems, often without calling the technique by name. Affinity diagrams are among the most useful classroom tools, since they are so versatile and can be used to great advantage for both children and adults. Affinity diagrams provide ways to spread the thinking around, to acknowledge everyone's ideas, and to enhance creativity in the thinking process. Affinity exercises are nonthreatening and can be produced almost anonymously. They can be adapted spontaneously to nearly any process, at any stage of problem solving.

Like other learning tools, the affinity exercise begins with a kind of brainstorming. In this case, each participant records ideas one at a time on separate pieces of paper. Ever since Post-it™ notes were invented at the 3M Corporation, this type of sticky note has become an integral part of the affinity exercise, but it can be equally effective using scraps of recycled paper, 3″ × 5″ cards, or memo pads. The value lies in the thinking process rather than in the finished product. In fact, the affinity diagram can often be discarded after the exercise has been completed.

After an issue or question has been identified for further exploration, the first step in creating an affinity exercise is recording ideas in no particular order, one at a time, on separate pieces of paper. After all students have had an opportunity to record ideas, the entire group works together—without talking—to collect the ideas around recognizable themes or ideas. Depending on the size of the group, these can be arranged on a table for everyone to see or can be taped or stuck to a wall or chalkboard as they are grouped. The key to this stage of the process is that the ideas can be moved around and regrouped, as particular themes or connections emerge. Figure 4.1 reflects the groupings that emerged from food lists.

Knowing when to use an affinity diagram is less important than knowing how to use it, since it can be safely developed whenever a class is at its wit's end in solving a problem; when a small group of students is dominating a discussion; when there are a myriad of possibilities to answer the question why; or when a teacher senses a need for a change of pace in a discussion or problem-solving exercise. In other words, most days of the week call for an affinity exercise. Of course, if this is the only tool in the teacher's bag of learning devices, students will quickly become tired of using it, and its effectiveness will be diminished.

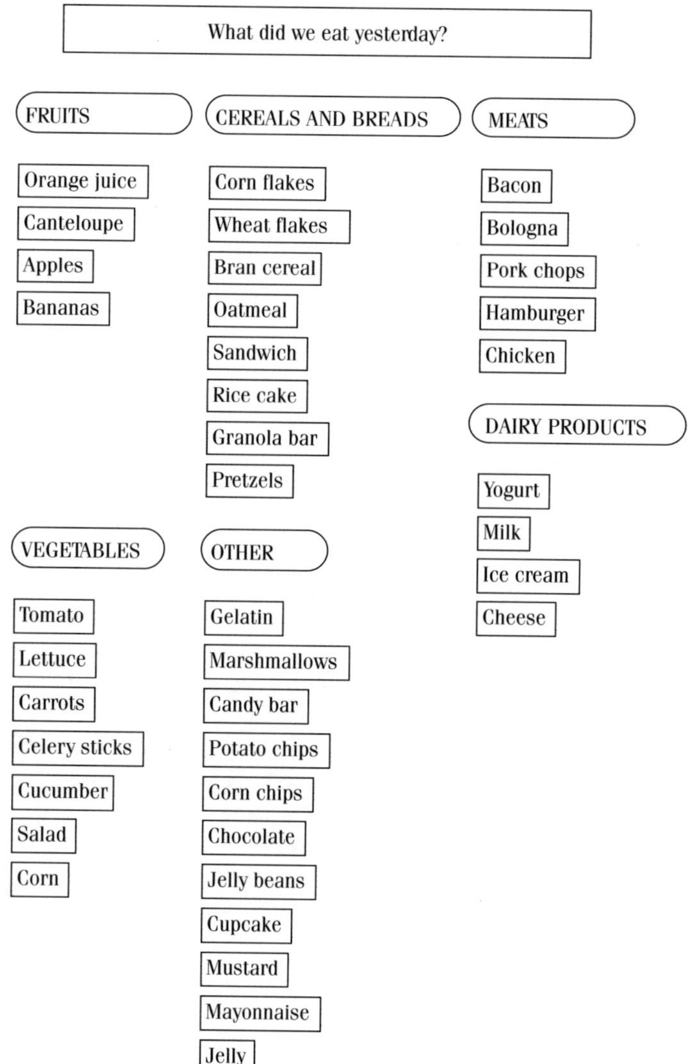

Figure 4.1: Foods affinity diagram.

It may be important to prioritize the items generated in an affinity diagram. If so, a second tool, nominal group technique (chapter 14), can be applied to identify a most important theme among those that emerge or to help make a decision about the items should that become necessary.

Classroom benefits

This tool accommodates a wide variety of learning styles and thinking patterns. A learning style that Donna Markova (1992) calls "consciously visual" is a good example. This child learns best by seeing; however, the kinesthetic learner also benefits, by actually writing an idea down, then attaching the note to a wall or walking around a table looking at others' ideas. The *Myers-Briggs Personality Inventory* identifies the person who needs to think a moment before speaking, as opposed to those who learn by actually saying something aloud. The affinity diagram helps this personality type by giving time to think and then record ideas.

Because everyone participates in this exercise in an equal way, those who are quick to wave their hands with "answers" do not have a chance to overshadow those who are more thoughtful in their responses. This builds a sense of confidence for all members of the class, since all ideas are given a sense of validity without criticism or judgment.

Example: Social sciences

A class of fourth-grade social studies students in Buckeye local schools (Ohio) approached their required Ohio history and geography unit in the same way that students often respond to mandated curriculum. After introducing this unit to students over a period of years, the teacher anticipated their boredom, inevitable questions about why they had to study their own state history, and their dread of long reading assignments and required reports. The teacher used the affinity exercise to break down some of this anticipated resistance and found that this year, the students' study was far more productive, because they felt they had a say in what they were learning and how they would learn it.

The teacher asked students what they thought they needed to know about their own state. On sticky notes, they generated their ideas and framed them as questions (for example, "What crops are grown in Ohio?"). They grouped their questions into categories as a class, and the questions fell into a number of topic areas: Ohio's native populations, products, history, geography, government, industries, and so on. All categories were parts of the original curriculum unit that the teacher had planned, but since the students had developed the questions themselves, they were far more eager to pursue the study. When the teacher asked, "How can you find the answers to your questions?" students offered suggestions about on-line and library sources, field trips, and interviews that would generate the information they needed.

In this case, the teacher took advantage of the affinity process to help students plan their work. Because she was also interested in the process of framing appropriate questions, she was able to utilize the exercise to develop this skill at the same time. The entries on the affinity diagram, shown in Figure 4.2, are, for the most part, framed as questions. Some of the questions are closed, seeking only specific information; but as chapter 15 suggests, the exercise also stimulates students to ask open questions that will help them develop deeper understandings of causal and other relationships related to information.

Example: California history

In a similar example, another group of intermediate-level students organized their own study with an affinity diagram. The study of California history has been part of that state's curriculum for generations. When a curriculum is not only required but also repeated year after year, it is sometimes difficult for both teachers and students to feel that there is anything new to learn about a particular subject.

What do you want to learn about Ohio?

OHIO IN PREHISTORIC TIMES

Were there any dinosaurs?

PEOPLE AND AREAS

Who are the famous people in Ohio?

What famous monuments or buildings are in Ohio?

What customs are unique to Ohio?

Are there any ghosts in Ohio?

How did the Civil War affect Ohio?

What part did Ohio play in the Underground Railroad?

What presidents came from Ohio?

MANUFACTURING

How does manufacturing contribute to Ohio's wealth?

What are Ohio's natural resources?

How are they used in manufacturing?

What fuels are used?

Where are factories located?

What products are manufactured in Ohio?

What inventions contributed to manufacturing?

CLIMATE

Are there any tornadoes in Ohio?

Are there any earthquakes in Ohio?

GOVERNMENT AND SYMBOLS

What and how did Ohio become a state?

What is the state tree?

Who designed the Ohio state flag and when?

What are the surrounding states and how are they similar to and different from Ohio?

What is the origin of the name "Ohio"?

How does early government compare and contrast with today's government?

LAND FORMS

Where are Ohio's forests?

What animals are native to Ohio?

What plants are native to Ohio?

EARLY OHIOANS

Were there any mound builders in Ohio?

Who and when were the first settlers?

Why did the settlers come to Ohio?

What Native American tribes were here?

What did the settlers bring with them?

Did any of my ancestors come to Ohio?

Where did early settlers practice religion?

CITIES AND TRANSPORTATION

What is Ohio's population now? 100 years ago?

What is the major transportation form? Now? During early settlers' time?

What are major highway systems in Ohio?

What is the crime rate in Ohio and why?

Where are Ohio's greatest cities?

LAKES AND RIVERS

What rivers and lakes are in Ohio?

Is there any major flooding in Ohio?

What dams exist in Ohio?

How was the shape of Ohio formed?

What is Ohio's highest point?

What are Ohio's famous bridges?

How do the Great Lakes affect Ohio?

How can we use maps to locate rivers and lakes in Ohio?

AGRICULTURE

What type of farming is done in Ohio?

What is the impact of dairy farming in Ohio?

Figure 4.2: Ohio social studies affinity diagram.

An affinity diagram, however, can enlist the minds of fifth graders not only in structuring the study but also in thinking of ways to approach that study. One group brainstormed about the somewhat daunting task that lay ahead. What did students need to learn, and how would they learn it? They arranged their responses to the first question in the following list prior to creating the affinity diagram.

In our study of California, we need to learn about the following:

- Who was here first?
  —Earthquakes
  —Coastal fog
  —Terrain
  —Weather
  —Government
  —Politics
- Gold Rush
  —Harbors
  —Islands
  —Our ancestors
  —Population
- Spanish influence
  —Jobs
- How the border was determined
  —Flag
  —Rivers
  —Schools
  —Statehood
- Hollywood
  —Famous people
  —Constitution
  —Governor
- Spanish missions
  —Famous bridges
  —Universities
  —Cities
  —Farming
  —Animals
  —Industries
  —Crops
  —Leaders
  —Ethnic makeup
  —Architecture
  —Water supply
  —Transportation
  —History

Students grouped these topics, which fell into larger categories such as history, transportation, geography, economics, population, and politics. It is not hard to imagine these categories; they probably closely reflect the required sections of the mandated curriculum.

Nonetheless, the fifth graders who compiled this list considered it their own and proceeded accordingly. Once the items were grouped into the affinity diagram in Figure 4.3, the students talked about the "how" of their learning. What, for example, would be the best way to learn about California's rich historical fabric? They decided that a second affinity diagram would help them to further break down aspects of the state's history. Then they saw a variety of approaches to learning.

As they created the affinity diagram, students began to see that history could not be studied in isolation from other aspects of the state and its development. Politics and geography, for example, helped to determine leadership trends. Events were to be considered in a broader context than chronology alone. Their next step was to create projects that would support not only their learning about specific aspects of the state's development, but also help them to understand the culture reflected in this development.

They designed interviews, written reports, conversations in Spanish, field trips, and mapmaking projects. One student, determined to make a model of the Franciscan mission at San Luis Obispo, found that the model involved understanding the purpose of the mission as well as the available materials and labor sources. What had begun as a simple list of what had to be done resulted in a comprehension of the complexity of the topic itself and of the interconnections of learning.

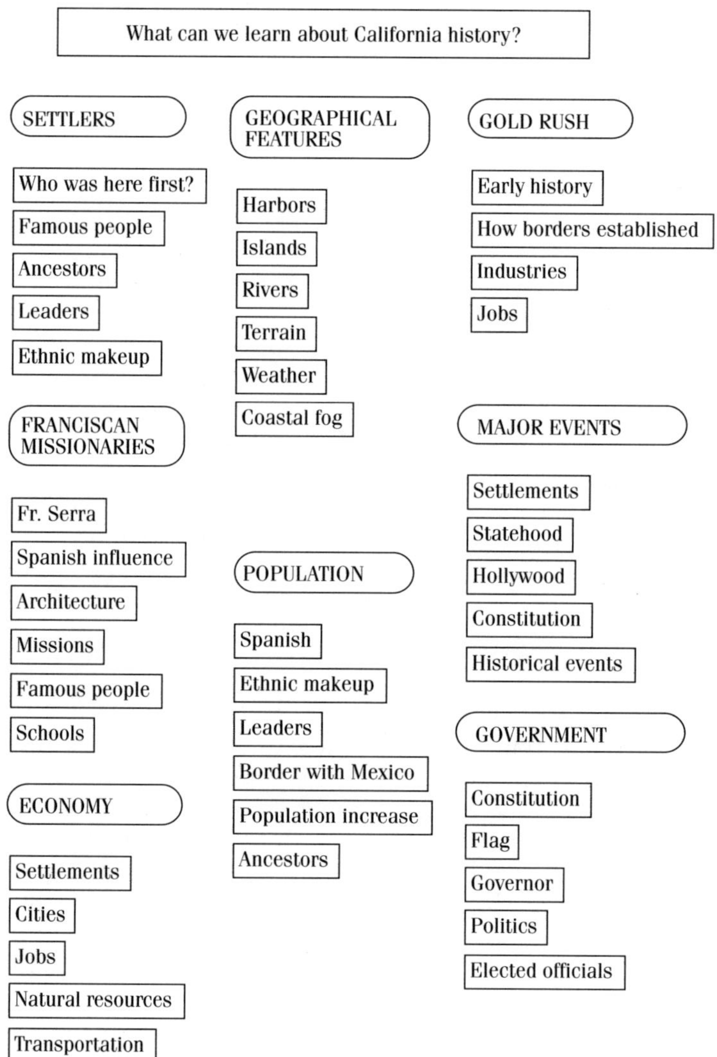

Figure 4.3: California history affinity diagram.

Example: The Scarlet Letter

High school juniors studying Hawthorne's *The Scarlet Letter* used affinity diagrams to initiate discussions about a character in the novel. The enigmatic little child, Pearl, had a bundle of qualities, some of which seemed to be quite natural and childlike, others that could be interpreted as preternatural or at least precocious for a child of her age. Before the class began to debate which character traits fell into each of these groupings or to explain the behaviors in terms of personality, the teacher urged the students to record everything they observed about the child and to include a brief example of each trait. For example, one of the sticky notes looked like this.

Comfortable in the woods: Animals came up to let her pet them

Because they were writing their ideas, rather than simply calling them out, students came up with many more examples than they might have in a discussion alone. Another example of "at ease in natural setting" was "the brook seemed to be talking to her." After students had recorded their initial ideas, they posted them on the chalkboard. Figure 4.4 reflects this list, simplified, without the examples.

- Bright: learned crafts easily
- Intuitive: could sense her mother's pain
- Mischievous: made an A from green burrs
- Curious: asked questions about Rev. Dimmesdale
- Aggressive: threw stones at taunting children
- Sensitive: responded to Dimmesdale's attention
- Spoiled: had tantrums when she did not get her way
- Self-aware: knew of her own beauty
- Independent: would not come to the governor in the garden
- Loving: responsive to mother's care
- Bold: asked Mistress Hibbins if she were a witch
- Imaginative: created her own games and fantasies
- Lonely: had no friends her age
- Comfortable in the woods: animals came up to let her pet them

At this point, the affinity diagram has served the purpose of generating ideas. The teacher may decide that it has already been useful and leave the posted ideas for students to refer to during discussion. A second step, however, is to ask students to organize the notes, grouping like ideas together. They will see that although classmates may have provided different examples, many of the traits will overlap. The next step might be to group them according to whether they represent natural childish behaviors or something that can be interpreted as preternatural, as Pearl's contemporaries were wont to do. The students chose to simply classify the character traits they had listed, with respect to various

What character traits can we identify in Pearl?		
Bright	Bold	Bratty
Learns easily	Imaginative	Aggressive
Sensitive	Lonely	Spoiled
Intuitive	Isolated	Self-aware
Mischievous	Honest	Independent
Curious	Smart	Loving
	Frank	

Figure 4.4: Character traits affinity diagram.

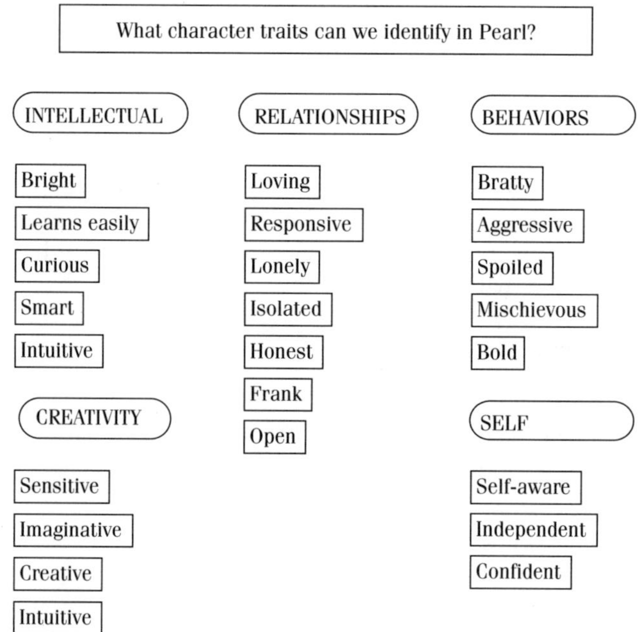

Figure 4.5: Pearl's character.

aspects of personality or makeup, and then later returned to their examples to discuss the ambiguity of each characteristic (see Figure 4.5).

In this case, the discussion of Pearl's character is an outgrowth of the thinking that students have already done, both alone and together. It represents a natural expression of that thinking, rather than just a way for the teacher to check whether or not the students have done the reading. Frequently, teachers note that with this kind of investment in "prework," students' participation in discussions is not only more thoughtful, but also more active. Even their body language will be positive. Remember that the point is not to elicit the right answer but to generate many ideas that will build skills of analysis and deep thinking. Then, the affinity diagram has served its purpose.

What if students post a number of answers that show lack of understanding or misinterpretation of the reading they have done? Teachers find that students will take care of these matters themselves when they are given a chance to do so. Usually, they will gently point out their classmates' errors or give additional information that will clarify what someone else has said. This, too, is a powerful by-product of using tools such as affinity diagrams in the classroom.

Just for fun

A group of very young children (prekindergarten) brainstormed about all the parts to a horse. They came up with an extensive list representing their pooled knowledge about hooves, tails, manes, stomachs, and other features of the animal, drawing pictures for each part so everyone in the group could "read" the list. Their teacher asked them to group the various parts according to what worked together.

They were able to organize their long list according to various needs and functions of the horse—eating, walking, digesting food, neighing, staying warm, and so on. What had begun as a simple vocabulary lesson relating to "horse words" ended in enhanced understanding of how the parts (or processes) of the horse worked together to create an interdependent system.

Notable

This chapter has shown how affinity diagrams help to organize ideas (character analysis of Pearl), as well as curriculum units (Ohio and California history units). Affinity diagrams are among the most useful classroom tools because they are so versatile. For example, they can help organize events, supporting students' planning and making life easier for educators. Affinity diagrams can organize brainstorming about topics for papers that students are writing. They can help students prepare for something that will require various supplies ("What will we need for our overnight astronomy trip?" can help them not only to anticipate their need for flashlights, but also to actually remember to bring their flashlights—since, after all, this was their own idea.)

A fund-raising activity for the student newspaper can be organized by means of affinity diagrams, as can building or understanding a physical object. By naming parts and grouping them, students expand their analytical abilities and enhance their creativity.

Application

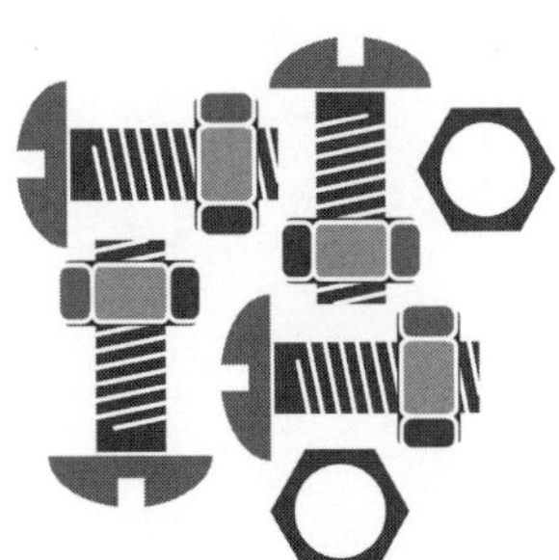

Try using an affinity exercise to help students focus on an upcoming activity or study. For example, what are their expectations about a field trip to the planetarium? You may be surprised to find what they anticipate, and the exercise may help you to clarify any expectations that are unrealistic.

With your students' parents at an open house, try using an affinity diagram to share what they've heard about school this year. This will lighten your session, and you may learn something you had not anticipated!

References

Markova, Donna. 1992. *How your child is smart: A life-changing approach to learning*. Berkeley, Calif.: Conari Press.

Myers, Isabel Briggs. 1980. *Gifts differing*. Palo Alto, Calif.: Consulting Psychologists Press.

Chapter 5

Understanding Relationships and Their Complexities

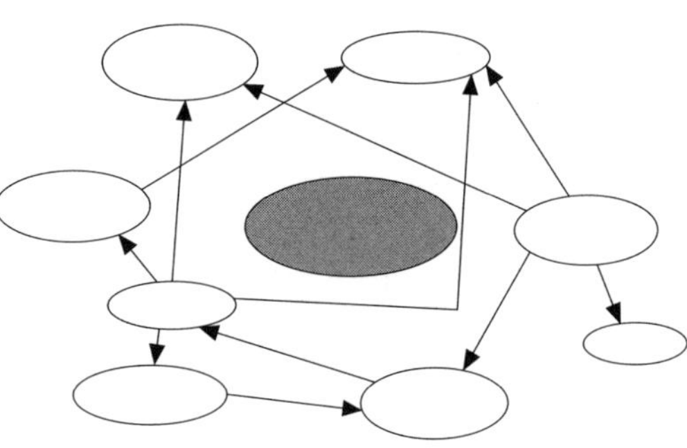

Introducing the relations diagram

"Let us settle ourselves, and work and wedge our feet downward through the mud and slush of opinion and prejudice and tradition and delusion . . . till we come to a hard bottom and rocks in place which we can call reality" (Thoreau 1845, 99).

Thoreau could have used a relations diagram, if he really wanted to get to the bottom of things.

The relations diagram can be a useful approach to taking cause-and-effect or affinity analysis a step further, since it presents a visual connection among causes and effects or primary drivers and their outcomes. Generally, if the issue in the center relates to a problem, *root causes* must be sought, while if it is another kind of issue, it is *primary drivers* that are revealed. For example, if a teacher is seeking to get to the bottom of her discovery of paint spattered in the art room, she wants causes. On the other hand, if a class is looking for factors that led to Goodyear's invention of vulcanized rubber, students might look for primary drivers.

It is possible for an effect to be a cause of something else, creating a tangled web of relationships. The relations diagram helps to sort this out and to analyze the relationships among a variety of issues or questions. Ultimately, it helps to identify the primary cause or driver; that "hard bottom" of which Thoreau speaks.

Beginning with an issue framed in the form of a question or issue will help to identify and clarify contributing factors. The relations diagram, with its central issue in the center, reflects a number of related issues surrounding this question. An empty relations diagram template appears in Figure 5.1.

After the related factors have been identified, arrows are drawn to show what causes what. That is, if one factor seems to lead to another or is involved in that second factor, an arrow will indicate this relationship (see Figure 5.2).

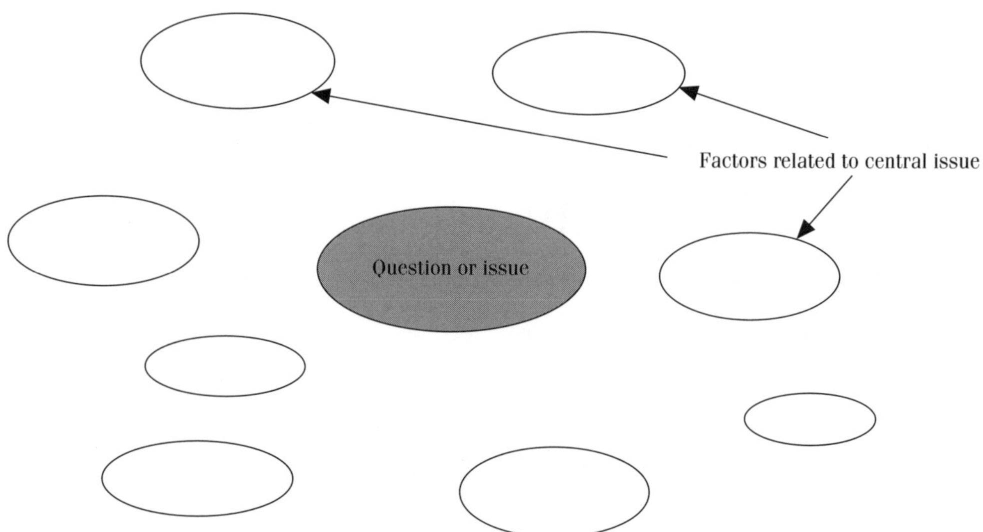

Figure 5.1: Sample relations diagram template.

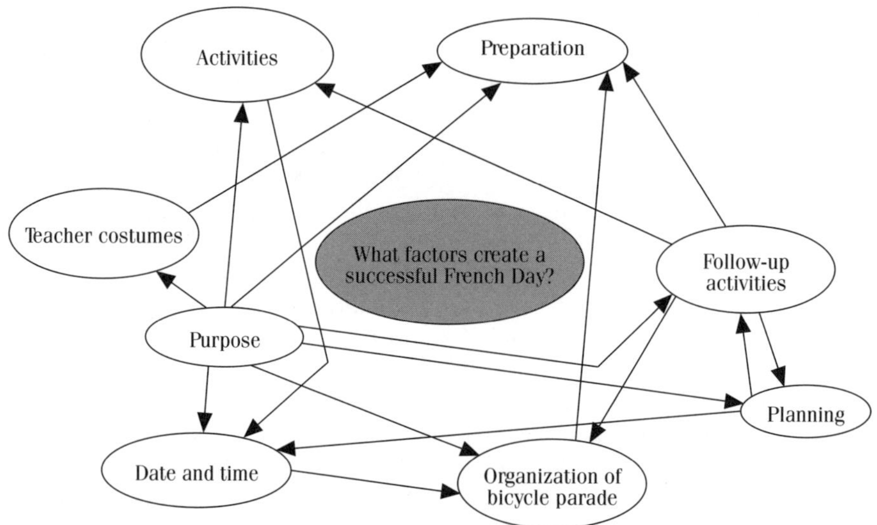

Figure 5.2: Factors related to French Day relations diagram.

Analyzing the chart

Primary analysis takes place in the construction of the chart itself. That is, each individual factor is considered with respect to its relationship with every other factor. Ensuing discussion will help to clarify the relationship, and the arrow will document this relationship.

A relations diagram that focuses on the planning for an annual French Day experience appears in Figure 5.2. It demonstrates factors that relate to the success of the event.

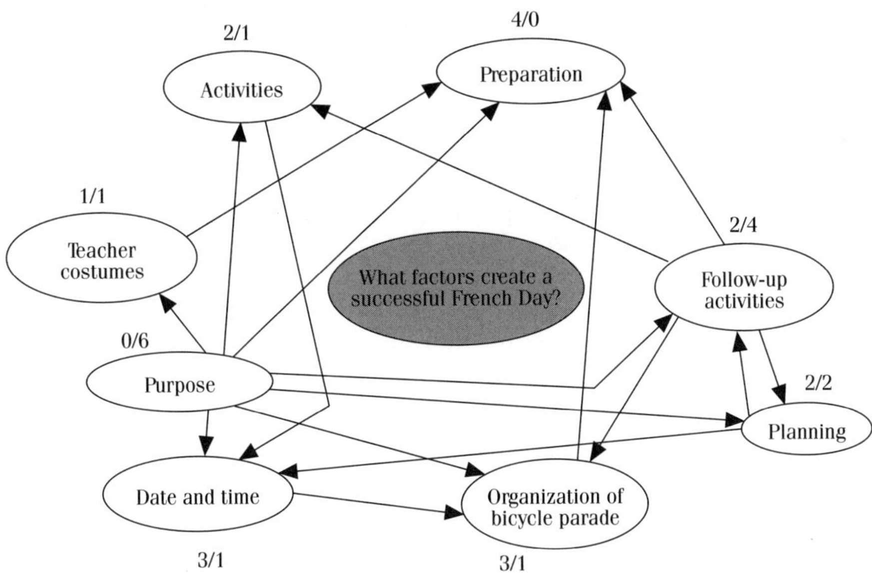

Figure 5.3: French Day diagram with numbers.

In this case, drivers rather than causes account for the success of the day, but the thinking process is the same.

The final step in creating a relations diagram is to count the number of arrows that point toward each factor and those that point away. This count is recorded next to each factor in Figure 5.3, showing a completed relations diagram for the French Day discussion.

The relations diagram in this example provided a way to focus on the important issues and to establish the most important issues—clearly, the purpose of the field trip and the follow-up activities. This can be determined by the relative numbers of arrows in and out. Root causes or primary drivers are the categories with the greatest number of arrows going out. Root effects or outcomes are those with the greatest number of arrows going in. As they engaged in the discussion of these issues, the students identified the importance of the purpose. At this point, they might draw a double box around the primary driver, or purpose, to emphasize its importance. As the figure shows, follow-up activities are critical outcomes or effects of successful planning for French Day.

Classroom benefits

Thinking skills that contribute to the analytical exercise of creating a relations diagram are critical to students' growth and learning. Discerning what is important, establishing priorities among issues, considering others' ideas, and anticipating experiences will all help to enhance the experience not only of the field trip under scrutiny, but of learning itself. By helping to sort out complexities without oversimplifying them, the exercise helps students deal with complexity itself and with the ambiguities that often surround issues.

Relations diagrams can be used in practical matters (such as planning field trips) and in academic ones. The diagrams help to clarify issues related to the discussion of literature or history, for example, and to plan the processes that contribute to student learning in every subject and class.

English teachers often lament about their students' inability to understand subordinate clause constructions. Often, this difficulty reflects limited thinking about the relationships among ideas, rather than a purely grammatical limitation. If, for example, one understands the relationship between one idea—it is raining—and another—I need my umbrella—then the expression of those ideas and their relationship becomes easy. "Because it is raining, I need my umbrella." Relations diagrams encourage the kind of thinking that helps students identify relationships, especially causal ones, among factors or ideas.

Example: Analyzing A Christmas Carol

In a discussion of Charles Dickens' *A Christmas Carol,* middle school students used a relations diagram to wrap up their discussion of Scrooge and his character. In this case, an affinity diagram could have generated discussion of character traits, as in the example related to *The Scarlet Letter* in chapter 4. The relations diagram provides further insight, however, into the causal relationships among various contributors to Scrooge's situation (see Figure 5.4).

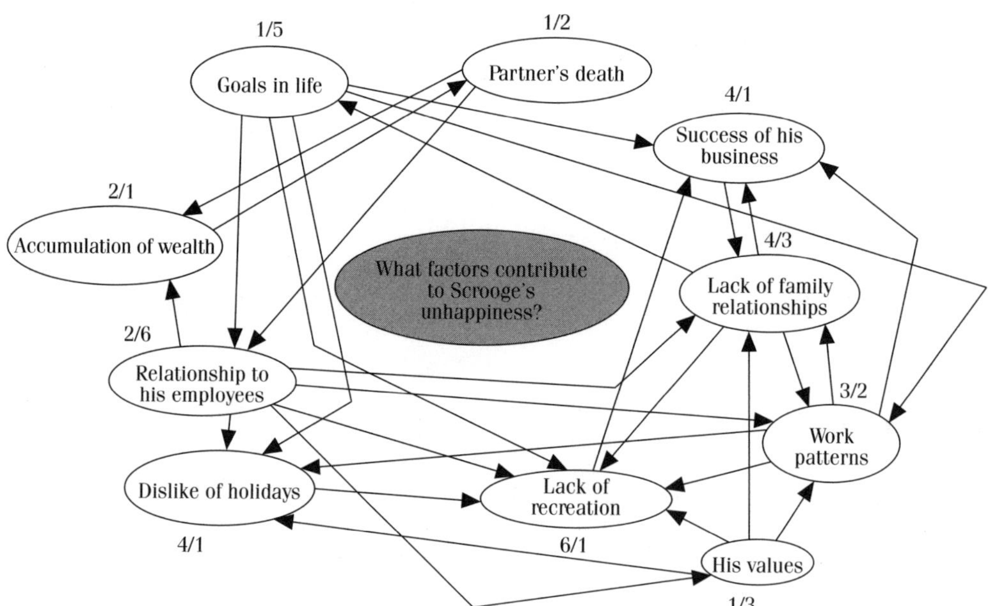

Figure 5.4: Factors related to Scrooge's unhappiness relations diagram.

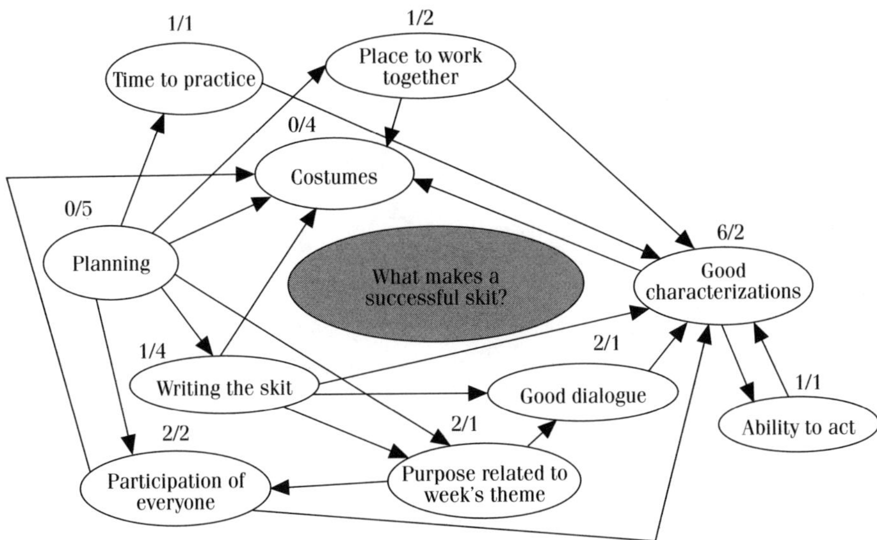

Figure 5.5: Creating a skit relations diagram.

Example: Planning a skit

Understanding relationships among apparently disparate factors is critical to event planning. Once a group of students understood the factors that were most critical to the success of their spirit week skit, they were able to focus on those factors to create the success they wanted (see Figure 5.5). In this case, the students realized the importance of having a purpose that would be related to the theme of the week and then fitting the other characteristics of a good skit to that purpose. They found themselves focusing not only on the final product, but also on the values that were important to them in the process; for example, having a high level of participation from their class.

Example: Writing a news story

Sometimes students want to charge off to do an assignment, without realizing the various factors that will make the assignment easier or better. In this journalism class, a relations diagram helped students to see the connections among skills of interviewing, preparing, and writing a news story.

Figure 5.6 demonstrates some of these relationships and highlights the most critical factors to the success of the finished product. In this case, the preliminary exercise of creating a relations diagram will help students evaluate their work as they create it and after it has been finished. As we know, grades provide very little information to students about ways in which the work can be improved. Knowing at the outset, however, that the success of a news story will depend in part on the quality of the interview will help students *prevent* the kinds of mistakes that they might otherwise make.

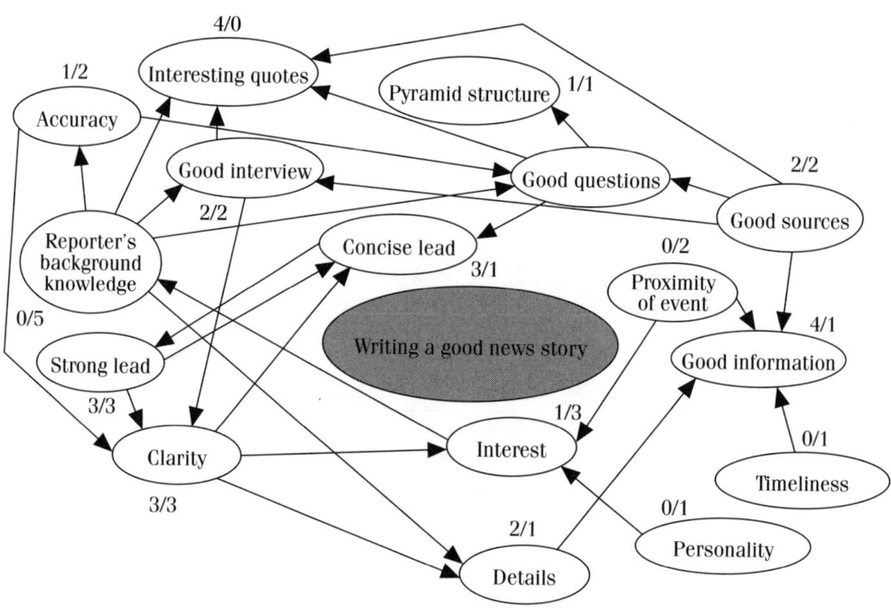

Figure 5.6: News story relations diagram.

Notable

Do not use a relations diagram to document a process or to create a classroom visual that will improve a bulletin board display. The value of a relations diagram does not lie in the finished product, but in the process of creating it. It is a messy process—one that generates discussion and sometimes disagreement about what causes what, and whether something is really a cause or an effect.

Relations diagrams can be generated by groups; for example, by small teams of students and teachers or an entire class. Relations diagrams may also be useful to an individual who is considering various aspects of an issue. It may, for some, provide a way to organize thinking to prepare for a writing exercise or a test, or to pursue causal relationships that are important preparation to leading a discussion.

Unlike other tools, the relations diagram will probably not be especially useful in communicating to someone who has not been a part of creating it. The analysis can be transferred to another format to make it more user-friendly, but the power of the relations diagram lies primarily in its contribution to the thinking process.

Application

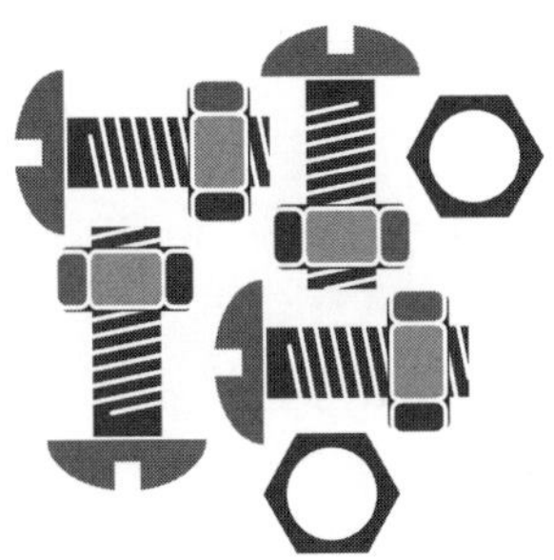

As you begin to construct a test or writing assignment for your students, try using a relations diagram to clarify your own understanding about various aspects of the subject. Or, using the cause-and-effect diagram that you created in chapter 2, pursue further analysis of the causal relationships that you identified there.

Reference

Shanley, J. Lyndon, ed. 1974. *Henry David Thoreau: Walden* (1845). Princeton, N.J.: Princeton University Press.

Chapter 6

Scattering the Connection

Introducing scatter diagrams

The unique vocabulary of parenthood is replete with advice about the connections between two factors. "If you don't get enough sleep, you'll be sick for your final exams." "I told you that if you didn't keep the gas tank at least a quarter full, you'd run out of gas some day." "If you don't lock your locker, someone will steal your lunch money." "Unless you review every day, you'll do poorly on the test."

Professional experience gives both teachers and parents license to make these connections based on long observation and hunch, and frequently these intuitive gleanings are right on target. The scatter diagram provides a way to validate gut feelings about the connections between two factors, to objectively communicate about these connections, or to revise conclusions about them.

Teachers are generally convinced that students who frequently miss class can never learn anything about the subject. Yet many have had the experience that one American literature teacher had with a student who repeatedly missed class because of what was eventually diagnosed as school phobia (although his teachers did not know that at the time and were resentful of his "attitude" toward their classes).

The English teacher, determined to "show" this student that he had to attend class to learn about American literature, gave him a challenging test about *The Scarlet Letter*. Many of his classmates who had attended class regularly actually failed the test, and the teacher was convinced that this student, too, would do poorly. Imagine her amazement when he got an A on the test. He had loved the novel, had read and studied on his own, and had mastered the central themes and concepts of the book. In his case, there was apparently no relationship between class attendance and learning—shocking as that may seem to those who spend their lives in classrooms. This case is a single example that may not be true for an entire class, but it demonstrates the complexity of issues that may be involved, beyond creating a simple hypothesis.

A scatter diagram is a simple graphical tool that helps to illustrate a theory about relationships between factors and to reflect possible correlations between two factors. One factor, the dependent variable, is believed to be affected by another, the independent variable, and data are gathered to verify or discount that effect.

A scatter diagram is based on data collected with some other tool, such as a check sheet or grade book grid. Data representing the two factors may have been collected with two different tools, and are brought together in the scatter diagram. There must be sufficient data collected to provide statistical integrity in the analysis. Patterns, after all, must represent enough data to really become patterns. While the number of data points may vary among different topics that are charted, conclusions that are based on more data will be more reliable than those based on less data.

Collecting data to examine the relationship between average weekly homework scores and test grades yields the following list. Note, for scatter diagrams, it is not necessary to have time-ordered data.

Percentage of homework completed		Average test grade
Week 1	37	79
Week 2	24	30
Week 3	59	55
Week 4	75	70
Week 5	57	63
Week 6	82	75
Week 7	33	40
Week 8	90	82
Week 9	72	80
Week 10	81	80
Week 11	86	83
Week 12	94	82
Week 13	50	48
Week 14	93	86
Week 15	85	79
Week 16	70	68

The numbers are entered on a scatter diagram that has been labeled to indicate the two factors. Any other information that will be useful, such as class name, dates, and so on, should be entered on a header for the chart. The scatter diagram reflecting the listed data appears in Figure 6.1.

Analyzing the chart

Interpreting scatter diagrams means identifying patterns. A positive correlation between two pairs of data (homework averages, test grade averages) suggests a conclusion that if one of the pairs increases, the other is likely to increase as well. That is, if homework averages go up, so will test grades. Positive correlations are reflected in patterns that seem to go somewhat steadily from the lower left to the upper right of a scatter diagram.

Negative correlations, meaning that when one factor increases the other will diminish, are suggested in patterns that seem to descend in a path from the upper left to the lower right of the diagram. If such a pattern appeared on the chart in Figure 6.1,

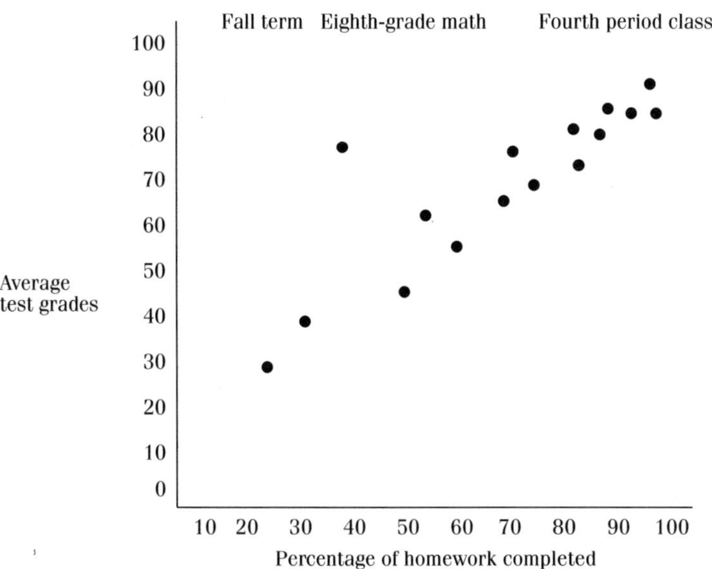

Figure 6.1: Homework and grades scatter diagram.

it might be concluded that higher homework averages are related to lower test grades. That is not the case here. Although the pattern does not go neatly from left to right, this can be attributed to the fact that the class rarely had test scores or homework averages below 50.

Sometimes no conclusion can be reached between two sets of data. That is, there may be absolutely no correlation between two factors. "The more vegetables you eat, the better you'll do in school" might produce a scattered or circular pattern (Figure 6.2) rather than a linear one.

If the points on the chart seem to go one direction and then drop or rise, there may be a point of diminishing returns. An example might be "The more time students spend studying the Constitution, the better they will do on the civics test." It may be that test scores will be higher over time when students invest more time in preparation. After a certain point, however, more time alone will not bring about continued improvement in test scores. There is, after all, a point of diminishing returns, beyond which the benefit of additional investment of time and energy will not pay off in better performance (see Figure 6.3).

Classroom benefits

Scatter diagrams can be maintained by individual students who want to try out various behaviors or approaches. When they are created in a class, to reflect the behavior or approach used to an entire group, the conclusions can be useful in discussing that approach and taking steps to improve one factor or the other.

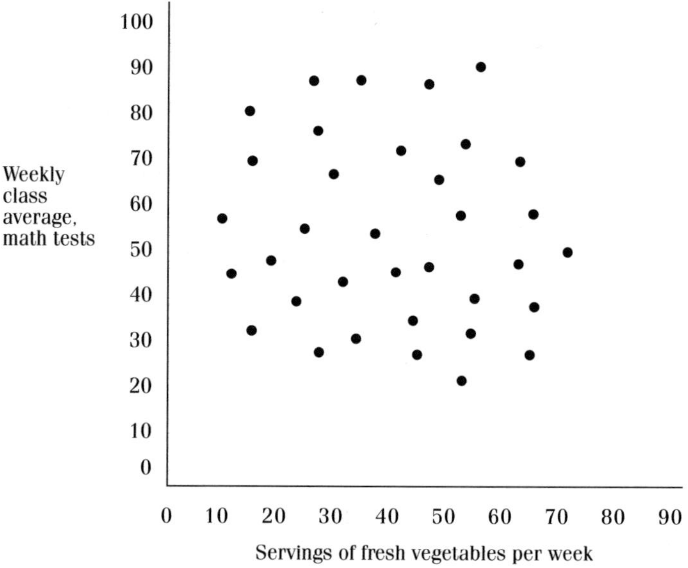

Figure 6.2: Good grades and vegetables scatter diagram.

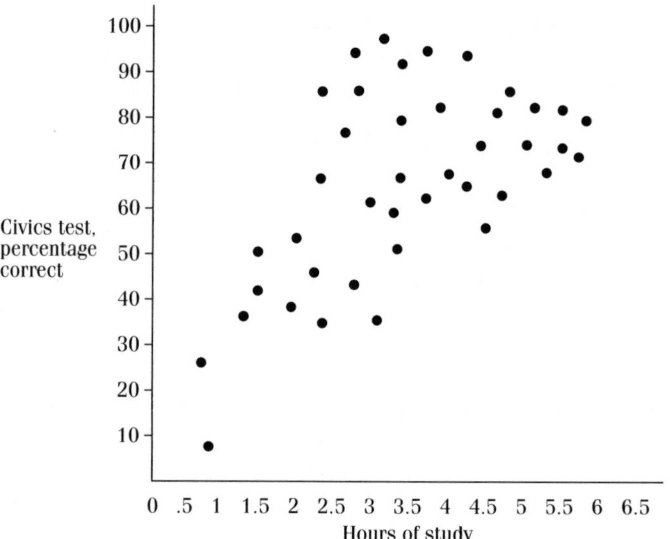

Figure 6.3: Studying and civics test scatter diagram.

Teachers can productively use scatter diagrams in their professional behaviors as well. One group of teachers successfully argued that when they had time to work together in planning, their students performed better in class, basing their conclusion on data that had been collected over time.

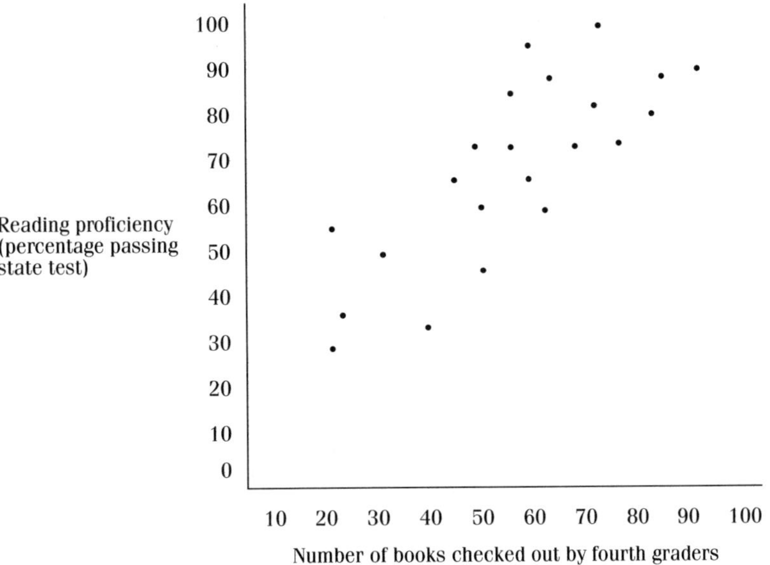

Figure 6.4: Library use and reading scatter diagram.

Example: Library use

Standardized tests that are administered to measure the performance of students throughout a district, school, or state often seem to have little to do with patterns of genuine learning or improvement. This is often a source of frustration to educators.

In one large school district, however, teachers were determined to make the mandated testing as useful as possible in advancing their own goals for their students. Therefore, they kept records not only of performance on proficiency tests that measured reading skills, but also of the number of books checked out of the school library. Their hypothesis was that if children were checking out books (presumably in order to read them), their reading skills were likely to increase.

The scatter diagram that was used for a group of fourth graders who took their state test for the first time indicated a slightly positive correlation between the percentage of students who passed the test on the first try and the number of library books checked out. See Figure 6.4 for the data.

Example: Class size and disciplinary actions

Class size remains a somewhat controversial issue, with various studies cited to show that students do much better in smaller classes, or conversely that class size has no impact on learning. See *What Research Says about Class Size* (1986).

When class size increases, most educators and many parents intuitively feel that the quality of the learning process may decrease. A scatter diagram based on disciplinary

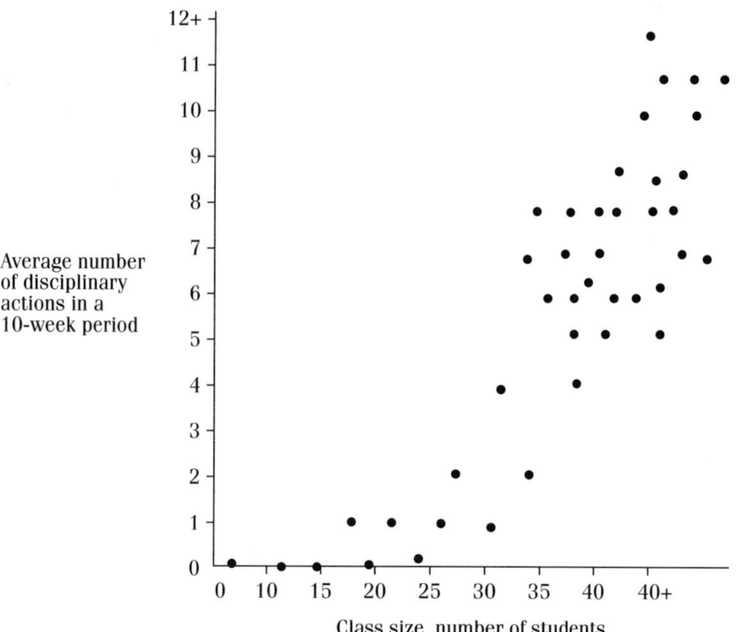

Figure 6.5: Class size and disciplinary actions scatter diagram.

actions as they relate to class size produces one way to interpret the issue of class size, although many other variables may exist and must also be considered before drawing conclusions.

The scatter diagram represented by Figure 6.5 seems to identify a positive correlation between the number of disciplinary actions taken in a school district and the class size (ratio of students to teachers). Caution must be exercised, however, for these actions included everything from disciplining students who had worn hats in school to dealing with a case of assault. Furthermore, it is clear that with more students, more *opportunities* for disciplinary actions will exist. Nonetheless, the data seem to suggest that there are far fewer incidents in very small classes than in very large groups.

Educators and parents would be hard pressed to show that having large classes actually caused any of the disciplinary actions, since so many other factors might be involved. Scatter diagrams do not prove causal connections; they can only suggest whether or not a relationship between two factors exists. It is nonetheless interesting to examine the data in Figure 6.5.

Example: Grades and service

Sometimes a scatter diagram will undermine rather than reinforce a hypothesis. This was the case in a study of middle school students. Their teachers had speculated that those with higher grades were probably more likely to be involved in service activities outside of school, including those rendered through scouting, church affiliation, or community groups. It always seemed that the highest achievers were those who were most busy with

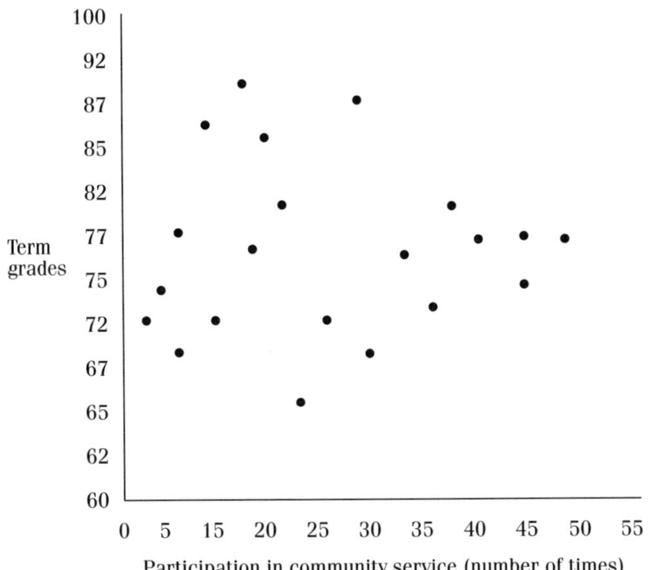

Figure 6.6: Grades and community service scatter diagram.

a variety of other activities, and the teachers tested their theory by collecting data over a period of several years and preparing the scatter diagram reflected in Figure 6.6.

The scatter diagram suggests almost no correlation in the groups studied. Some of the high-achieving students in the middle school population were indeed involved in a variety of community service activities. But so, too, were students who experienced less classroom success. Caution must be exercised as well when there may be two separate subgroups in the population. After analyzing the scatter diagram, the teachers pursued their examination of the data further with the help of cause-and-effect diagrams (chapter 2) and other tools.

Example: Reading speed and comprehension

Another example of the principle of diminishing returns might be illustrated in an analysis of reading speed. In increasing the pace at which children read, the objective is to enhance efficiency while maintaining high levels of comprehension. (Eyes can move down a page at lightning speed, but if they do not understanding what they have seen, what's the point?)

To monitor this process, an Ohio reading teacher collected data based on three minutes of reading for speed for each student and measured comprehension with a short test. The teacher plotted the results on individual scatter diagrams and then compiled these to show the trend for a group of 10 students.

The results are shown in Figure 6.7. The scatter diagram indicates that when speed goes up, comprehension likewise increases—to a point. Ultimately, the speed of reading and comprehension of what is read will no longer reflect a positive correlation.

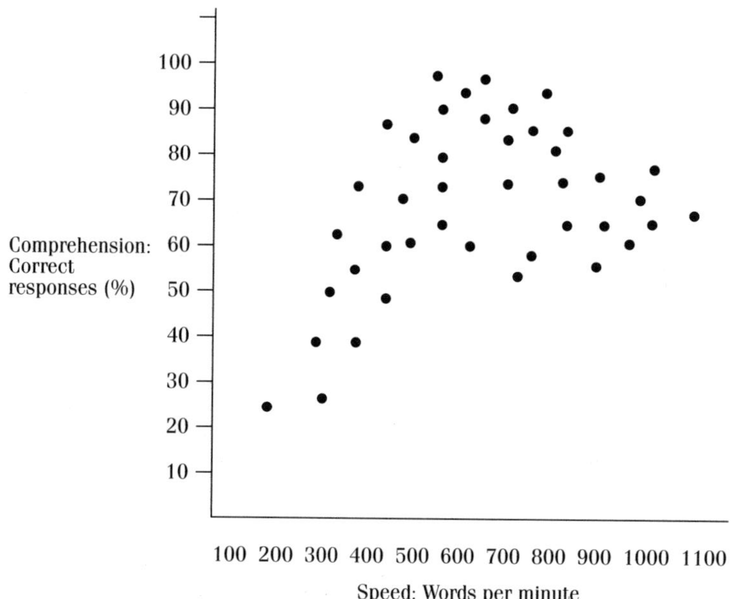

Figure 6.7: Reading speed and comprehension scatter diagram.

Notable

In developing a scatter diagram, it is sometimes, but not always, useful to compose a hypothesis in the form of an "if. . . then" statement. For example, "If I study more frequently, I will learn more French verbs," is a hypothesis that can be tested by a student who collects data on his or her individual performance. The amount of study in minutes can be seen to correlate with the number of verbs that are mastered.

If a positive correlation seems to exist, action that is taken can be based on that correlation, or further analysis might be appropriate. In the case of the just-cited hypothesis, the student has little to lose by taking the action of increasing the frequency of study. In a more complex hypothesis, where a proposed action may be time-consuming or expensive, one would certainly want to study the theory further. "If more natural light is available, children will read more" may be supported with a positive correlation on a scatter diagram. But since it will be very costly to install additional windows or skylights in the classroom, additional persuasive data will undoubtedly be demanded.

The definition of terms must be clear in beginning a scatter diagram analysis. A clear operational definition for each part of the hypothesis is important. In the earlier example, the student must understand what "study more frequently" means and be consistent in its application. If he or she studies one verb every five minutes and counts each of these sessions as separate from the others, "more frequently" may actually involve less cumulative time and effort than twice-a-day sessions of 20 minutes each.

Application

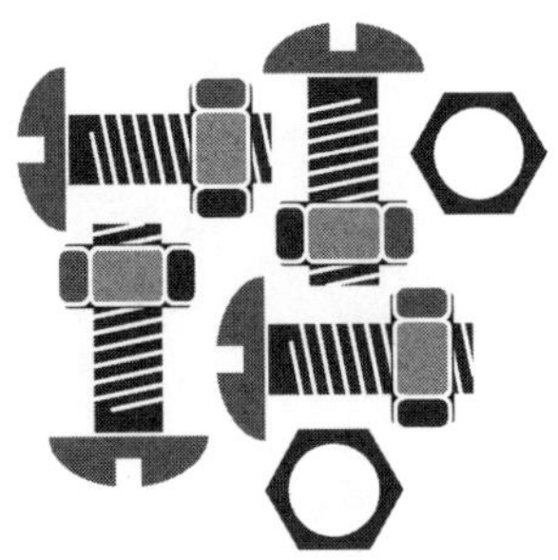

Think about a relationship between two apparently separate factors in your classroom. This may involve connections between ambient temperature in the room and test scores, seat position and participation in discussions, parent attendance at conferences and student participation in class activities, or other factors. Collect data for the two separate factors and then create a scatter diagram to reflect the correlation, if any, between them.

Reference

What research says about class size. 1986. Washington, D.C.: Professional and Organizational Development Research Division. Also see, Porwoll, Paul. 1978. *Class size: A summary of research*. Arlington, Va.: Educational Research Service.

Chapter 7

Separating the Few from the Many

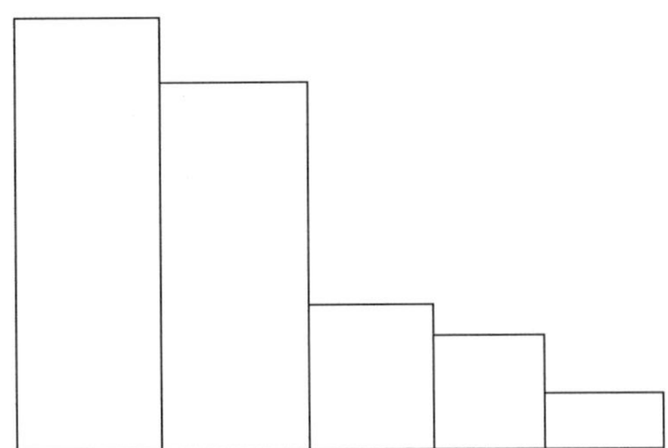

Introducing Pareto diagrams

Separating the few events that seize attention from the many that escape notice helps to create better understanding of situations and events. Pareto analysis, named for the Italian sociologist and economist Vilfredo Pareto, is a bar chart that represents data ranked by category. Pareto noticed an uneven distribution of economic resources. He saw that a great deal of wealth was concentrated in the hands of a few, while most of the population was poor. His analysis graphically demonstrated this distribution of wealth.

The purpose of a Pareto chart is to separate the significant aspects of a problem from the trivial ones (Ball et al. 1991). If, for example, disciplinary actions are broken down by category, it might be found that students' most frequent violations relate to tardiness to class or disrupting class. Other infractions such as fighting or vandalism may be more serious but occur with far less frequency.

Pareto analysis is useful to prevent overreacting, among other things. Classroom rules are sometimes made on the basis of a few incidents that do not really reflect the general pattern of behavior. A teacher uncovered an elaborate cheating scheme where students were taping sheets with vocabulary words to the underside of tables and then using small mirrors to read them. A new rule went into place: No mirrors were to be used in class. The teacher was reacting to a single use of mirrors, when, in fact, most of the time students—if they had mirrors at all—were using them for benign purposes.

The Pareto diagram also helps to keep perspective on things. In another behavior-related situation, a team of teachers and the school principal found themselves deliberating for hours about how to discipline two eighth-grade girls who had gone off campus and picked flowers from a neighbor's yard to comfort another student whose dog had been killed. Engaged in serious discussion about violations of rules and the ensuing risk, the committee suddenly realized how much time they had spent on this incident that was probably harmless and certainly not one that was likely to recur, rather than focusing on problems that might affect more students or occur with more regularity.

Making a Pareto diagram begins with collecting data. This can be done with the use of a check sheet (chapter 2) or a frequency table that records not only each incident, but also its cumulative frequency. Before data are entered, a Pareto diagram looks like Figure 7.1.

What makes a Pareto chart different from other bar charts is that the data are arranged in descending order with respect to its frequency of occurrence. The incident or event that happens most often is on the left, descending to that which occurs least frequently.

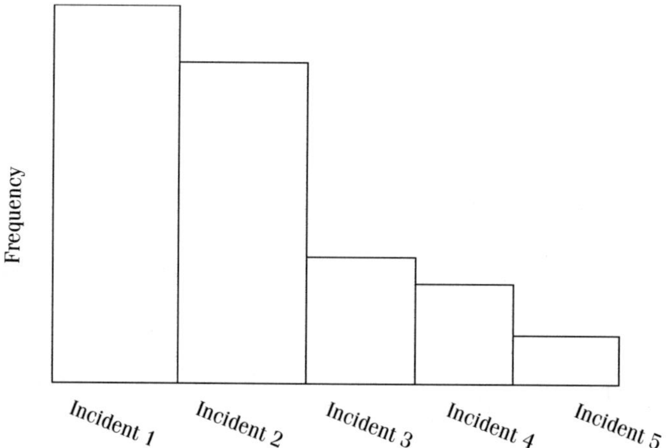

Figure 7.1: Pareto diagram.

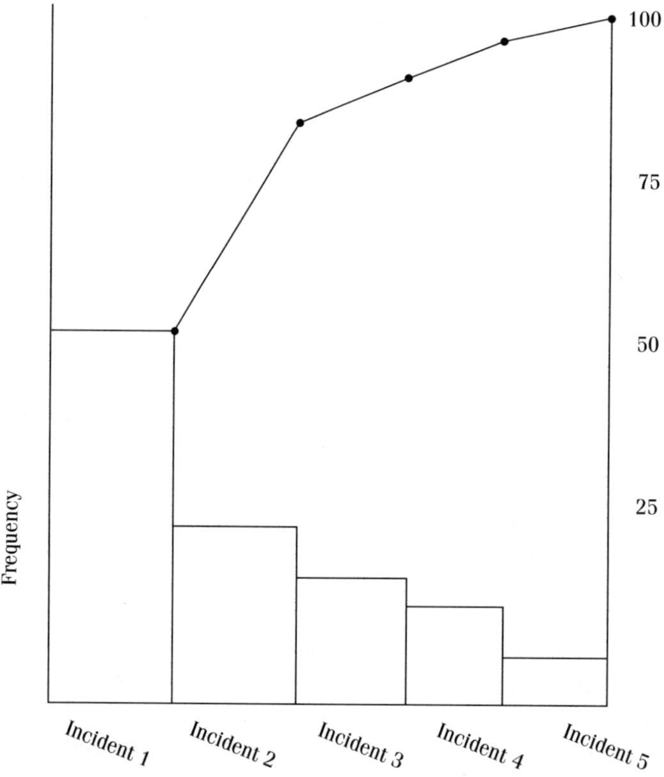

Figure 7.2: Pareto diagram with cumulative percentages.

Sometimes, a cumulative percentage line is used to indicate how the categories add up proportionately. If this is done, percentages are entered along the right side of the chart (see Figure 7.2).

Analyzing the chart

After the data have been entered on the Pareto diagram, the single bar that seems to stand out from the others should be examined first. If there is no such thing—if all the bars are about equal, for example—the Pareto diagram's usefulness in separating the trivial few from the significant many is limited. In this case the diagram reflects the fact that there are no significant many categories. At this point, it may be helpful to break down the categories further. In the case of disciplinary cases, for example, if there is very little difference among the categories, further information can be gleaned by selecting one of the categories for further analysis. If tardiness is one of the categories, data can reflect tardiness in various classes or homerooms, or at different times of the year or month. In this way, the question "Where (or when) is the greatest incidence of student tardiness?" is further pursued.

If, however, one or even two bars seem to stand head and shoulders above the others, it will become clear that in order to have the greatest effect on the problem with a single change, that change must address these areas. The analysis has been helpful in determining where to invest energy in bringing about improvement.

Remember that Pareto analysis helps to identify the events that happen most frequently. It does not identify those that may be the most serious or may, in fact, demand priority attention. Discipline problems, for example, may be primarily related to tardiness; but if even a small number involve assault or physical harm, then these must be addressed first.

Classroom benefits

Building on other tools of analysis, the Pareto diagram helps to establish perspective. The temptation is often to give immediate attention to an issue that demands it. This reaction is, of course, justified when the issue is serious or urgent. If students discover that they are having very few problems with subject-verb agreement in their writing, and yet the teacher is spending most of their time reviewing this concept, the Pareto diagram will help both the teacher and the students make decisions about how to best use their time and resources.

Like many other classroom tools, the Pareto diagram helps students take more active roles in their learning and in reflecting how that learning takes place. It also represents a visual approach to sometimes abstract or complex issues. When it is used to reinforce positive behavior, the tool becomes an instrument for enhanced esteem and improved behaviors. It can be used with students of all abilities, levels, and ages.

Teachers, perhaps more than any other group, know that they often spend far more time on situations that involve small numbers of students than on those that affect the greatest number of students. If a child is causing a problem, regardless of how serious it is, attention must be given to that problem and diverted from the children who are not creating problems. By understanding how often this happens, teachers can go further with their analysis, perhaps using tools such as cause-and-effect diagrams or check sheets to gain additional insight about their classroom time.

The key classroom benefit is one of focus. The Pareto diagram will help students and teachers gain perspective on the importance of various events or behaviors, and to closely focus on improving the right things.

Example: Second-grade writing

Responding to a prompt, or specific writing topic, Madison Street School second-grade students (Ocala, Florida) were improving their writing in a variety of ways. Nonetheless, problems of correct expression continued to plague them. Since the school was examining reasons that its fourth-grade classes were not performing well on state-mandated proficiency tests, teachers were looking closely at ways in which they were preparing their students for writing of all kinds. Demand writing, or responding to a prompt, was one way; they also pursued a variety of other writing assignments that focused on descriptive and narrative expression.

After gathering data with check sheets (chapter 2), the students and the teachers and parents who were helping them combined their information and built a Pareto diagram to show which problems frequently recurred in written assignments. Students kept track of their errors over a period of several assignments and accumulated lists that totalled 493 different errors. Their Pareto diagram demonstrated that, as a class, the errors they made most frequently were related to spelling (see Figure 7.3).

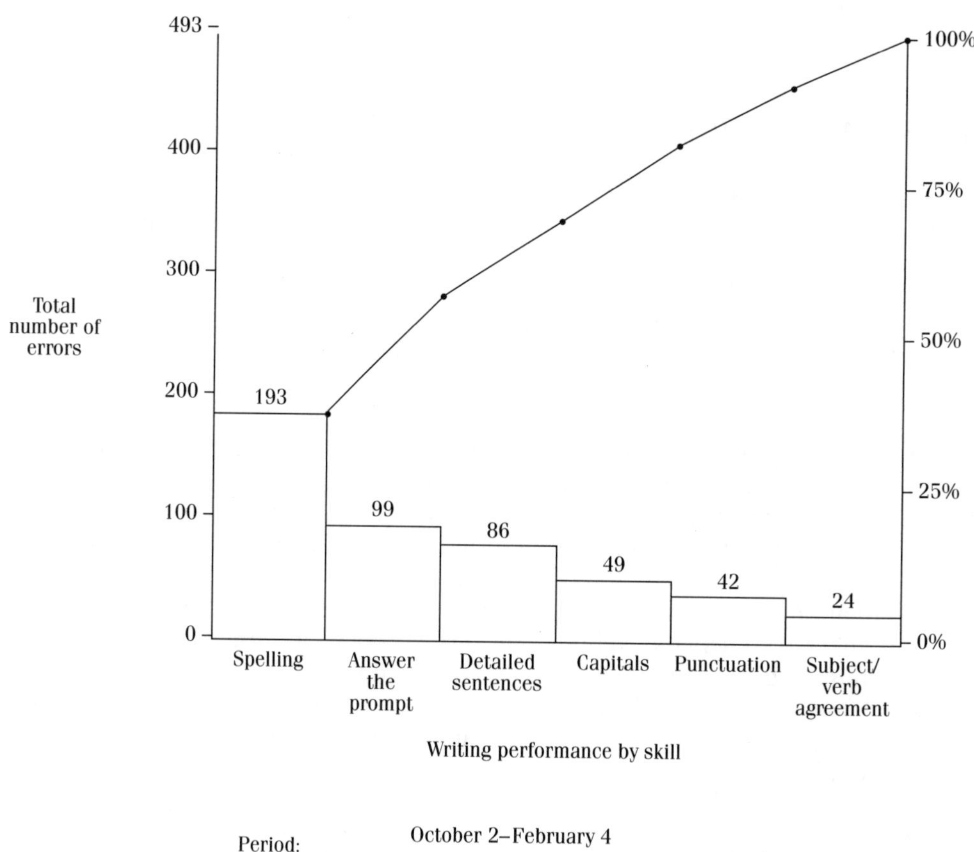

Figure 7.3: Second-grade writing performance Pareto diagram.

In the case of this group of teachers and students, the Pareto diagram did not stand alone, but represented an ongoing analysis of ways to improve writing. Students, teachers, and parents began to look for the reasons for poor spelling, creating a cause-and-effect diagram (chapter 3) and continuing to investigate ways in which student writing might improve. The Pareto analysis helped them to understand the frequency of their problems and to pursue the improvement of spelling.

Example: Constructive remarks

At Norton Middle School in Grove City, Ohio, a special education teacher was surprised by the kinds of negative comments students made to each other throughout the day. They had apparently learned that it was not cool to be supportive or constructive, but instead often spoke in cynical, insulting ways to each other.

Their teacher spoke to them about this habit, and although students were aware of it, they found it difficult to change their behavior. After all, the first one to make a constructive rather than a destructive comment was vulnerable to classmates' further insults, so students were reluctant to take the risk. They did agree to try to be positive, at least during the time they were in their learning skills class, and kept check sheets that recorded and classified the positive remarks heard.

By recording the incidents, students became more aware of the ways in which they communicated with each other. They became eager to record the incidence of positive communication and to try to substitute constructive remarks for negative ones. They were initially disappointed in the total numbers and actually tried to increase these—at first with artificial attempts, just to be counted ("Cool shoes!"); but as time went on, they saw the numbers of positive comments increase. At least within the confines of the class, students saw that they were much nicer people to be around. The Pareto diagram in Figure 7.4 reflects the data students gathered on check sheets.

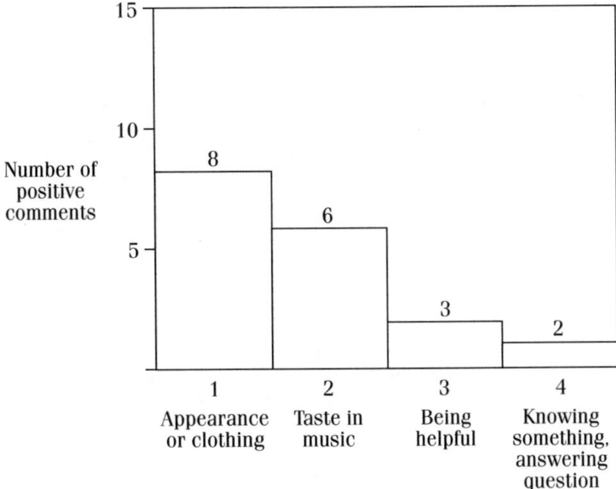

Figure 7.4: Positive comments heard in class Pareto diagram.

Example: Referrals for music camp

Priding itself on its strong instrumental music program, a Midwestern school district launched an ambitious promotion of a summer music camp that would further expand the opportunities for young musicians, not only from the district but also from other schools. The first year was a smashing success, but the second year's enrollment reflected a serious downturn.

Advertising and marketing promotions had been similar both years and had been extraordinarily expensive. A team of music teachers and administrators investigated sources of actual referrals to the program. They used Pareto to analyze the accumulated data and found that the greatest number of students the first year had come from those who were teaching at the summer camp. Many were taking private lessons from these teachers, who had recommended the camp.

The second year, the referrals had come from approximately the same sources, but the number of enrollments that had come from the music teachers had substantially declined. Separate diagrams were made for referrals for the two years' enrollment (Figures 7.5 and 7.6).

The two charts documented changes that had taken place between the first and second years of the camp. Most dramatically, the largest word-of-mouth referrals came first from teachers who were involved in the program, but later from parents whose children had been enrolled the first year.

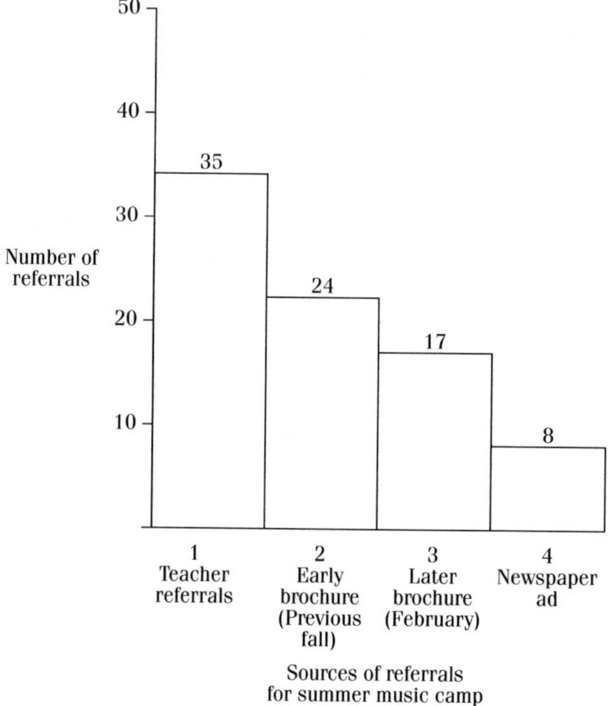

Figure 7.5: Referrals to summer music camp, year 1, Pareto diagram.

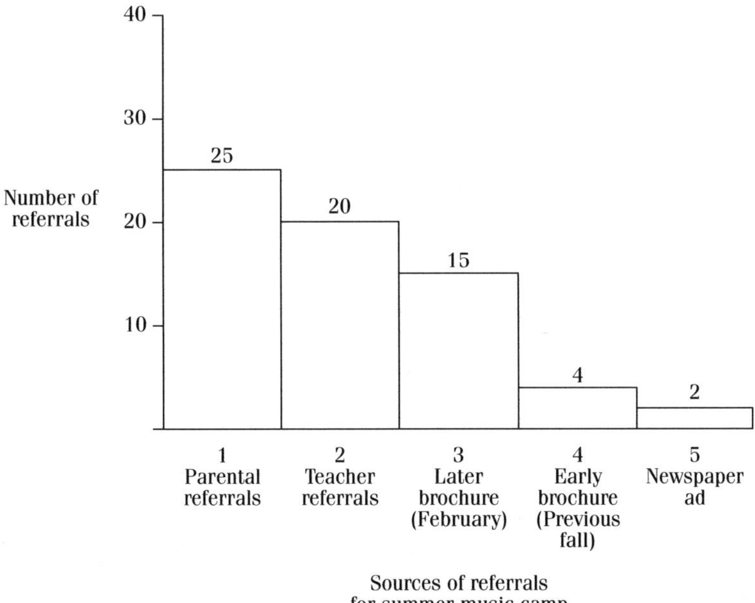

Figure 7.6: Sources of referrals to music camp, year 2, Pareto diagram.

What had begun as disappointment in the fact that teachers themselves were drawing fewer students, was translated into a positive statement about the success of the music camp. After all, parents would not be recommending it to others if their children had not had positive experiences. While the total enrollment had declined, it seemed clear that the program had been successful in its first year.

Decisions that were made about marketing for the third year focused on ways to encourage parents to contact others about the program and examined the relative merits of expensive strategies such as brochures and paid advertisements. The primary sources continued to be word of mouth, originating either with teachers or with parents, and these needed to be fostered and further developed to assure continued high enrollment.

Example: Math errors

Sixth graders at Silver Lane Elementary in Connecticut utilized Pareto analysis to demonstrate their mastery of concepts in math as part of the state's Mastery Testing Program. Like the Ohio class referred to in chapter 3, the Silver Lane students saw that their errors could be further categorized, providing more information about their difficulties and giving them enhanced direction in their improvement efforts.

Their first Pareto diagram, reflecting their scores on the four major areas, is shown in Figure 7.7. The percentages of students mastering each skill (on the left axis) indicated that the lowest number (53 percent) had mastered skills related to measurement and geometry. In order to pursue the analysis further, the students created a second Pareto diagram relating only to this skill area (see Figure 7.8).

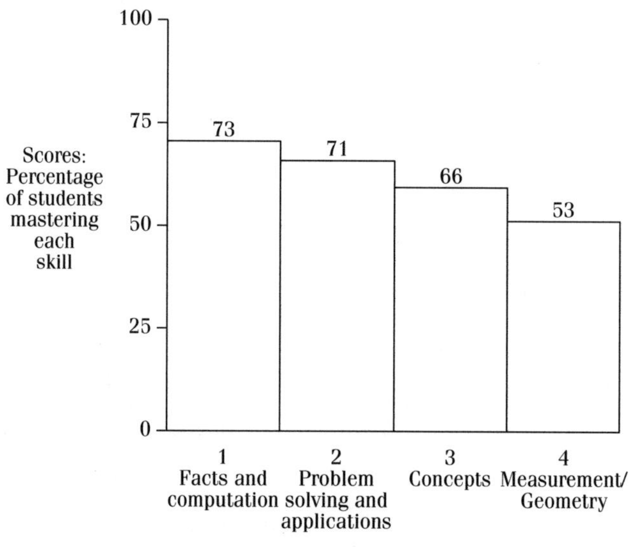

Figure 7.7: Mastery of math skills Pareto diagram.

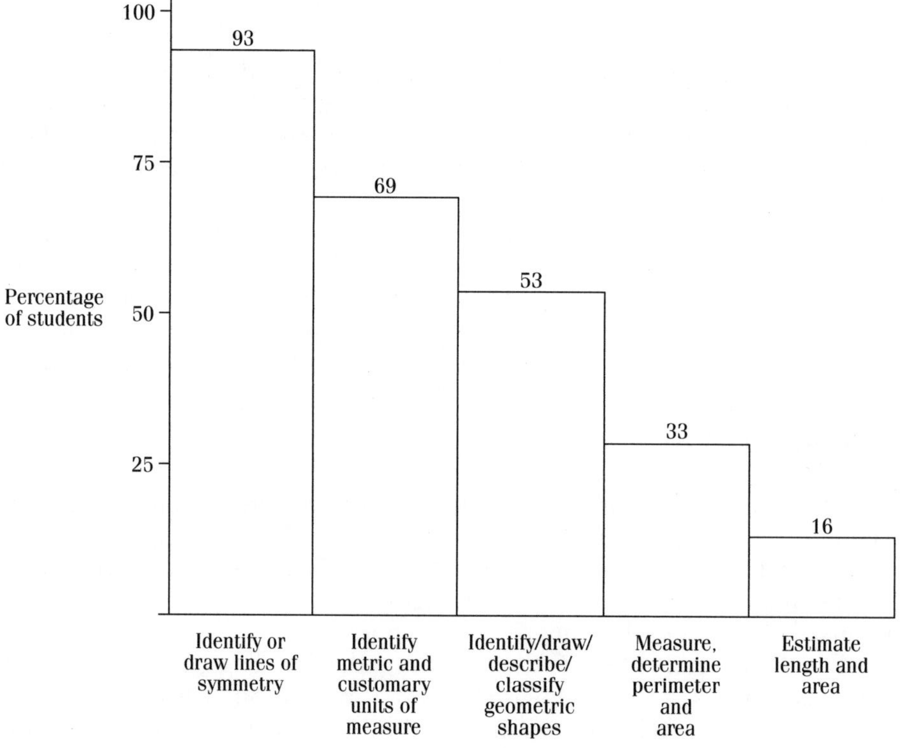

Figure 7.8: Measurement and geometry skills Pareto diagram.

Studying this diagram revealed that the students' two greatest sources of difficulty related to their skills in measuring (including determining perimeter and area) and estimating length and area. This information gave the students and their teacher specific direction in preparing for the proficiency test. More importantly, it gave them a sense of progress in learning math, since they knew that their review efforts were directed toward an area of greatest need.

As this example demonstrates, Pareto analysis can be repeatedly broken down. What might have first been asserted—"Our students have difficulty in math"—became "Our students need skills development in geometry." But finally, the conclusion is not that their skills are weak in geometry, but that they have difficulties with two specific areas within geometry. Knowing this, a teacher can design further study to ameliorate the problems, understanding with even greater precision where to direct improvement efforts, rather than simply beginning all over again with some kind of general math review. For example, these students might examine specific types of problems or skill areas related to measuring perimeters and estimating length.

Once the areas that create the greatest challenge for these students are addressed, not only will their grasp of measurement and geometry improve, but also the measurement of their overall math skills will reflect improvement.

Notable

Pareto analysis is best used concomitantly with other data-gathering and problem-solving tools. A check sheet, for example, feeds a Pareto diagram, and a control chart can deepen the analysis of the data. Understanding the purpose for using a particular tool will help determine which one can be most beneficial to the analysis.

For Pareto analysis to be most useful, it is important to gather as much data as possible. In this way, a Pareto chart can offer an opportunity to deeply probe into the meaning of that data. If, for example, only the information about the larger categories of math skills had been available (Figure 7.7), the specific knowledge about students' weakness in estimating length and area (Figure 7.8) would not have been accessible.

Remember that categories can be repeatedly broken down to get to the heart of an issue. Difficulties with estimating length and area might be analyzed with respect to whether students' greatest problems occur when they are estimating length of lines in millimeters or in inches.

Application

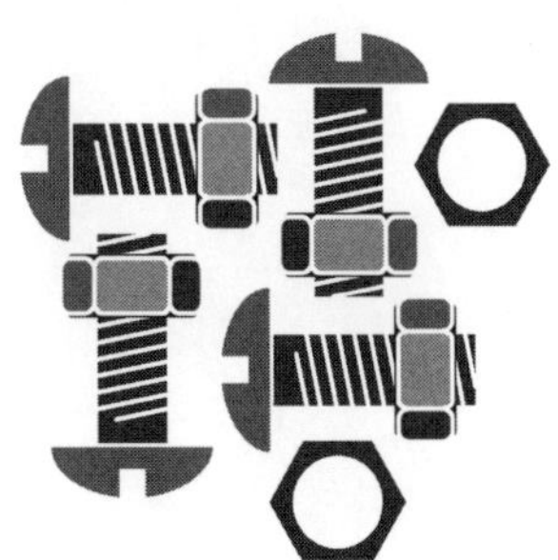

As an exercise in gathering data and creating your own Pareto chart, consider keeping track of the number of times students ask for help. Be sure to record something about the circumstances as well (time of day or class period, subject being studied, kinds of questions, and so on). Then chart these on a Pareto diagram.

To teach students how to use the tool itself, use M&Ms candies or other little packages of something that has a variety of colors or flavors. Give each small team one package and have the students open it and count the contents by color or other characteristic. Have them record their data on check sheets to be transferred to a Pareto diagram. For further analysis, have them provide a count of the total number of pieces in each package.

In addition to learning about Pareto analysis, the teams will see a good example of variation in the numbers of pieces in their packages. The candy is sold by weight or volume, not by individual number, so when they begin to feel cheated because they have fewer than another team, remind them of this.

The conclusion to this exercise is easy: The students can all eat their data.

References

Ball, M., M. J. Cleary, S. Leddick, C. Schwinn, D. Schwinn, and E. Torres. 1991. *Total quality transformation for K–12 education*. Dayton, Ohio: PQ Systems.

———. 1995. *Total quality tools for education (K–12)*. Dayton, Ohio: PQ Systems.

Chapter 8

Making Data Visible with Bar Charts

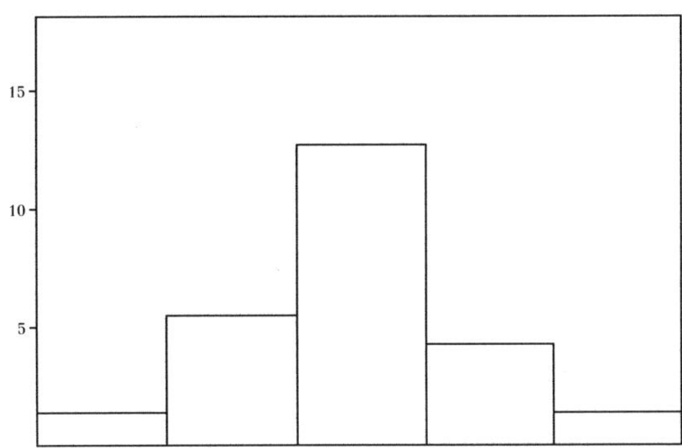

Introducing histograms

Histograms are everywhere. Like Pareto diagrams, these simple bar charts are a way of making information accessible. Everyone from *USA TODAY* to *The Wall Street Journal* uses them to create graphic interest to what might otherwise be boring data. Graphic artists make the bars into hamburgers or athletic shoes, depending on the subject matter, and the bars themselves have dimension and shadow to attract the eye.

Histograms do not have to have all these colorful attributes to be useful. They provide a way of seeing how often something happens (frequency of occurrence) and observing basic statistical concepts related to the central tendency, variability, and shape of the data set.

Data for histograms can be generated by check sheets (chapter 2) or other tools. The bar chart is made by determining the number of classes or subdivisions and what each class includes. *Frequency of occurrence* translates into how many students fall into each classification. A standard histogram for heights in a classroom is shown in Figure 8.1.

Analyzing the chart

Figure 8.2 illustrates different kinds of distributions. What is known as the bell curve, reflecting a normal distribution, is shown in the upper left-hand diagram (A). Other patterns can reflect non-normal distributions, such as B with two peaks, (bimodal), or data skewed to the left or the right (C and D, respectively). For further discussion and interpretation of such distributions and others, or for calculating standard deviation, consult a source related to the use of statistical tools such as PQ Systems' *Total Quality Tools* (1995).

The bell curve is formed out of a distribution that is considered normal, in statistical terms. The mean, median, and mode are equal in a normal distribution.

If the data are normally distributed, for whatever is being measured, the largest segment of the group will fall into the middle range. If the data do not seem to have a normal pattern, further analysis is in order. For example, if most members of the class never miss a question on tests for the entire term, a teacher might want to examine the reasons for this skewed data.

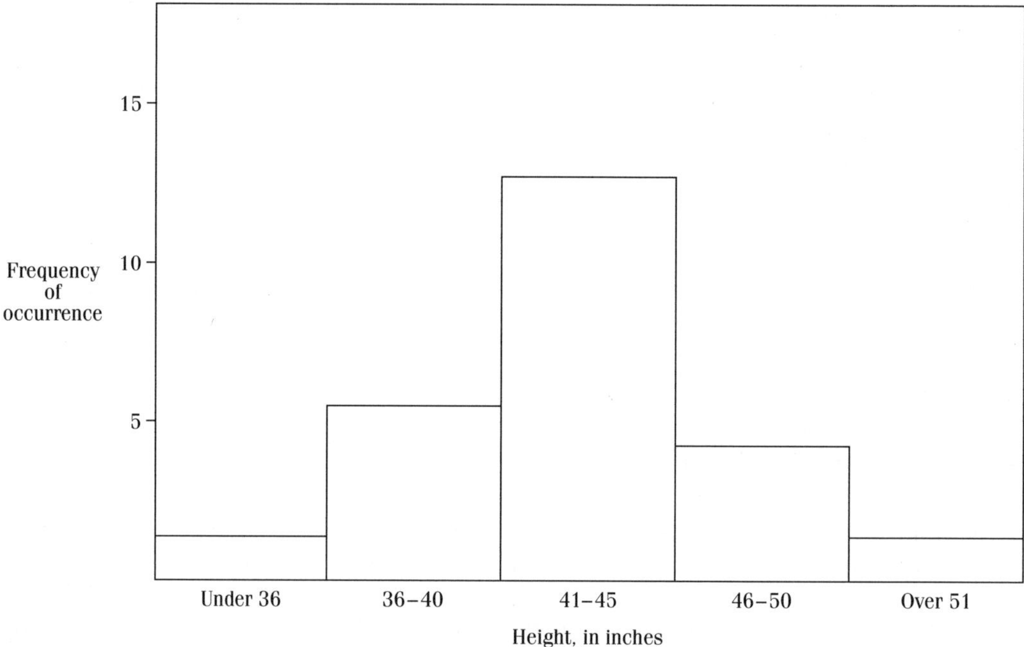

Figure 8.1: Student heights histogram.

The key to using histograms lies in understanding the data itself. Graphic portrayal of data supports interpretation of its meaning, making it more accessible, particularly to the visual learner. A histogram can be useful in identifying the classifications that have the greatest frequency of occurrence. Whether or not this information is useful depends on the questions that are asked about the histogram and its data. For example, if the numbers of injuries that occur on the playground were charted, it might be interesting to see that most of them occur between 11:30 A.M. and 1:30 P.M., which represents lunch time recess for several classes. Such information might lead to other analyses and finally to changing the playground system in some way to reduce the number of injuries at that time of the day.

Classroom benefits

Supporting skills of data gathering and analysis, the histogram also introduces some basic statistical concepts and utilizes simple math skills in its construction. The small child who weighs packages of candy can create a histogram from that data and derive these benefits from the exercise. Analysis of distributions enlarges students' grasp of statistical concepts.

Of course, when a process that is recorded on a histogram is closely related to learning, the benefits that accrue go beyond those of learning the statistical tool. Charting the actual weights of packages of candy, in the scheme of things, does not have the same importance as charting individual improvement toward mastering a musical composition on the piano or assessing what will need to be done to change a pattern of academic

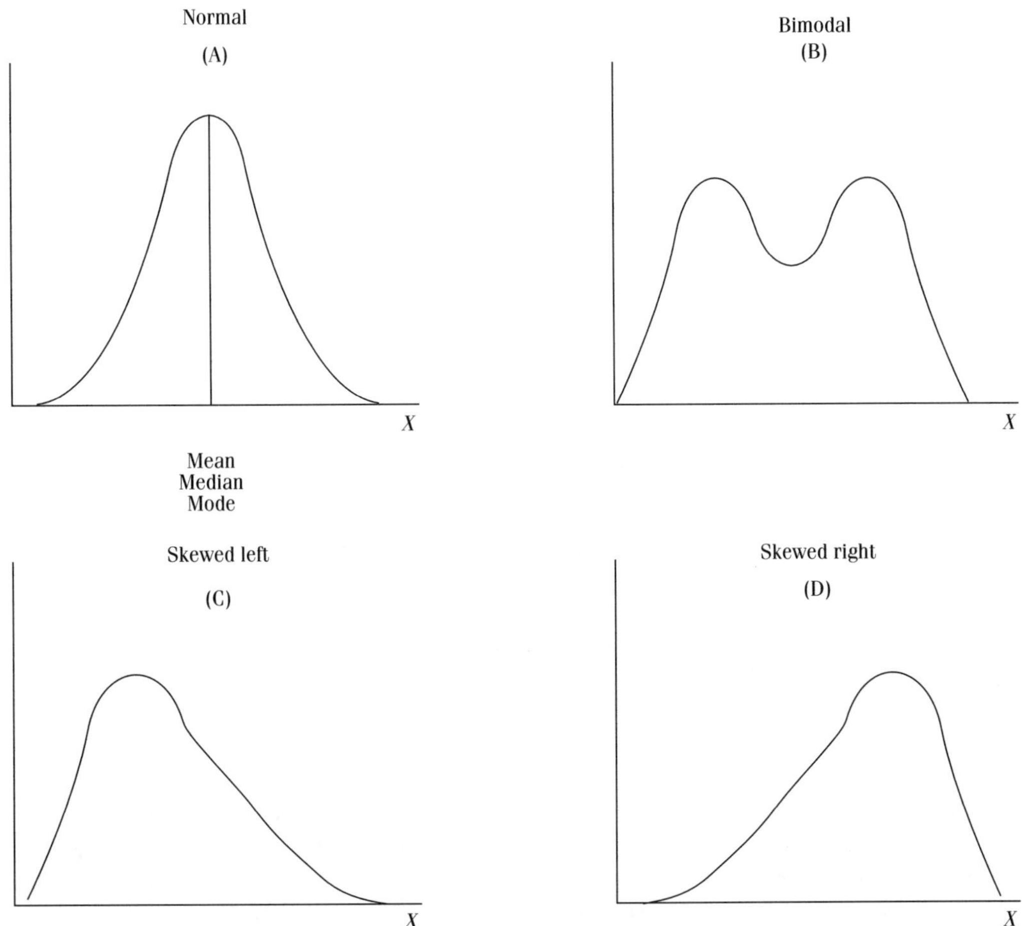

Figure 8.2: Common distribution patterns.

performance. But these benefits can be accrued in different ways by different ages in the classroom. The teacher's role in facilitating appropriate learning is, as usual, critical.

Example: Time study

An early-childhood teacher noticed that children in her classroom who already knew how to tie their shoelaces were taking longer and longer to do so, in spite of their established skills in this area. They seemed not to be in any hurry to do a good job with tying their laces, which often required re-tying because they had not been done correctly.

She asked children to tie their shoes while she timed the process, emphasizing concentration on the task and doing the best job they could. She recorded the times over a period of several weeks. Each time the children practiced shoelace tying, she recorded their cumulative times, from the beginning of the process until every shoelace had been properly tied (see Figure 8.3).

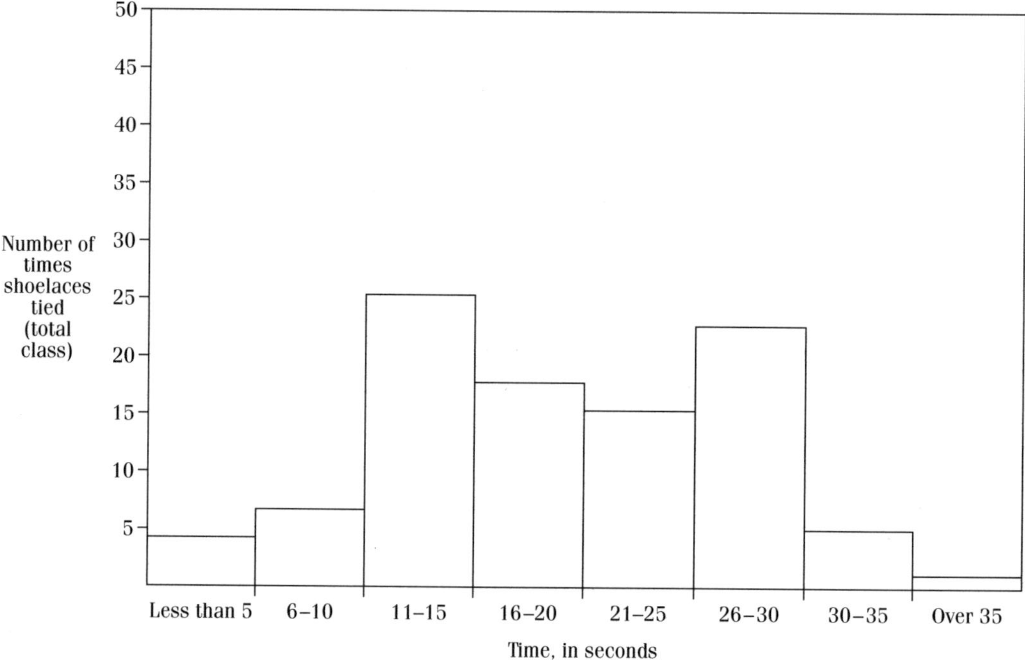

Figure 8.3: Shoelace times histogram.

The histogram reflected a bimodal distribution; in other words, it had two humps instead of a single curve. Most of the children's times fell into two categories.

Further investigation revealed that those in the faster category were primarily using the "run-around-the-tree" method of tying their laces, while the slower ones used the "two loops together" approach. The children themselves became more interested in the data at this point and decided to evaluate the method that was "best"; that is, not only faster but more likely to stay tied. They created histograms of times for the two classroom groups and found that there was less variation within each group, but the "run-around-the-tree" group was definitely faster.

While tying shoelaces may seem to be a trivial problem, anyone who has had to supervise 25 squirming four-year-olds while they tied shoelaces, found mittens, and put on jackets knows that such is the stuff of improvement at an early age. This teacher engaged the children in improving a process that was germane to their classroom learning, starting them on a path of responsibility even at a young age.

Example: Weighing in

In a science lab, third-grade students observed various characteristics, including weight and other measurements, of fruits they were studying. Histograms helped them organize the data they had collected about how much oranges were likely to weigh and the range of those weights.

Using a diet scale, students weighed the oranges they brought to class, making sure that the oranges were of different varieties and had come from different trees—or at least from different stores. The students first weighed the oranges with their skins on; then they squeezed the oranges and measured the juice that came from each one. In small teams, they gathered their data and averaged the amount of juice from 10 oranges each day. (Then they poured it all into a pitcher and drank their data with their morning snack!)

The students' histograms are shown in Figures 8.4 and 8.5. After the children examined the output, they began to ask questions about other variations that might be measured. Unwittingly, the histograms helped them to think further about oranges and other fruit, framing new questions about them, and reflecting on the ways they had gathered the oranges and measured them.

An additional benefit to this particular lab study was the carryover to home, where the students asked their parents to speculate about various weights and measurements. Then the students helped collect the data.

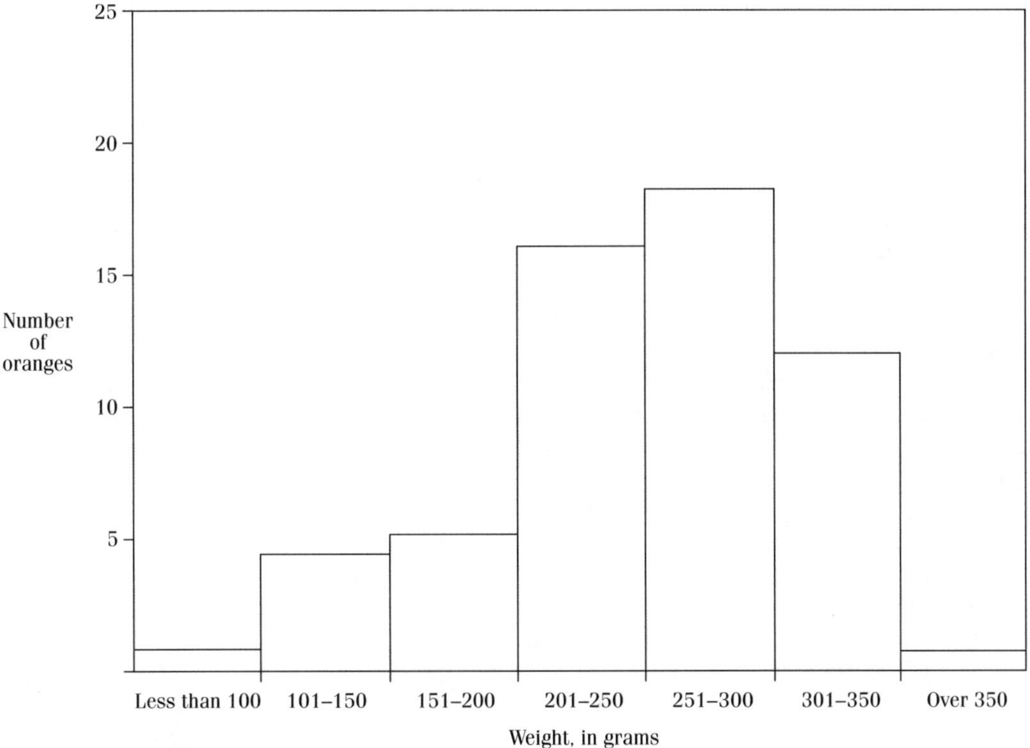

Figure 8.4: Weight of oranges histogram.

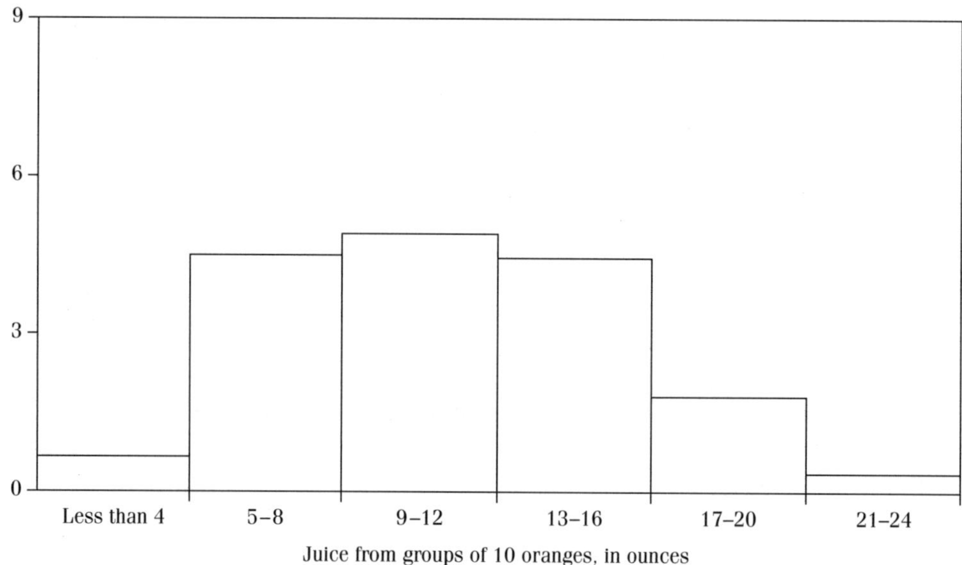

Figure 8.5: Amount of juice histogram.

Example: A bar chart that isn't a histogram

Although Pareto diagrams and histograms are both types of bar charts, not all bar charts are either of these. Using the data from Figure 2.6 (check sheet), a bar chart reveals even more dramatically than the check sheet how boys and girls were responding to questions in class. This is not a histogram because it does not have a continuum of numbers along the horizontal axis, representing classes or subdivisions of data. It is not a Pareto diagram, since the bars are not organized in descending order.

But it is a bar chart; and a highly useful one, at that. In this chart (Figure 8.6), the teacher selected only one category from the original data—the responses to questions or comments that students made in class discussions. The chart clearly revealed how much more frequently the boys were responding (or were being called on to respond) than the girls. This provided a clear basis for pursuing change in the classroom system and further study later.

Of course, the same format could be used to record only the number of times students participate, regardless of gender (Monday, 9 total; Tuesday, 8; and so on). This would simplify the chart and provide one kind of information. A number of teachers use the bar chart in this way and find it to be a good springboard for discussion with their students, in order to analyze classroom dynamics and their roles in it.

Figure 8.6 provides a way of looking at more than one characteristic of the data. That is, the bars reveal not only the number of times a student responds, but also whether that student is a boy or a girl. As noted, the more information, the more analysis will be possible, and this is a good example of that proviso.

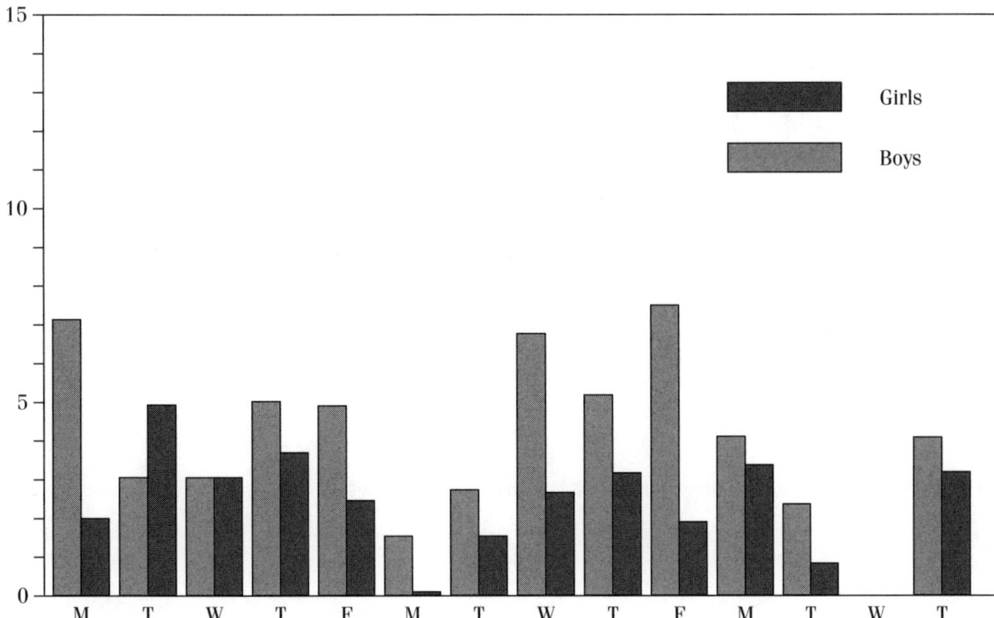

Figure 8.6: Responding to questions, by gender.

There are times when neither Pareto nor histogram analysis will provide the best source of information. Thus, it is important to remember that the plain-brown-wrapper bar chart is also available to support your purpose.

Notable

Science teachers help children collect data and record results in a variety of ways. Tools like histograms are useful in science labs, but applications extend to other areas as well. In this way barriers are broken down among disciplines, demonstrating that tools of science can be applied to a variety of learning opportunities. After all, students use their language tools to create lab reports and respond to other scientific demands. Carryover applications and skills reinforce the connections that must be made in order for learning to take place.

Once students understand how to create histograms and use them for interpretation of data, they can be encouraged to become more imaginative with them. Instead of simple bars, for example, they can draw a pile of oranges to reflect data about fruit or sketch little books to reflect the number of library books they have read in a term. Think about how many different disciplines can be represented in a single histogram.

It is important to remember that without accompanying statistical analysis to ensure that a system is stable, histograms cannot be used to predict future occurrences. But that's another story.

Application

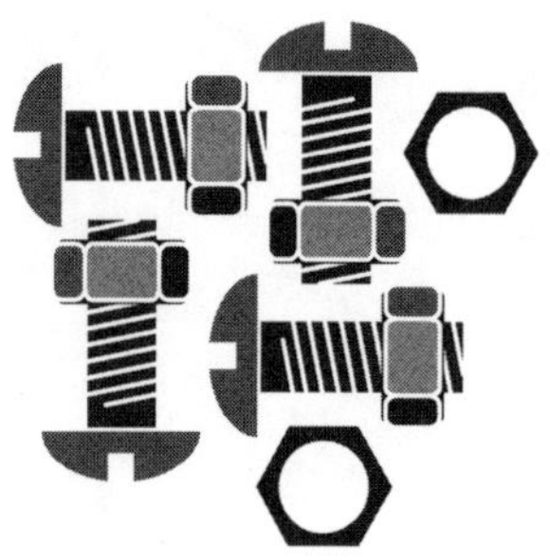

Create a simple histogram from the data available in your pantry. Check the expiration or "best used by" dates on a variety of products and chart the variety of dates that are represented. Or gather data about the birth dates of the children in your classroom. Most dates will fall within a predictable range, but the variation should reflect a distribution of dates that is normal. Remember that there should be a continuum of numbers along the bottom axis of your histogram.

Reference

PQ Systems. 1995. *Total quality tools for education (K–12)*. Dayton, Ohio: PQ Systems.

Chapter 9

Tracking a Run

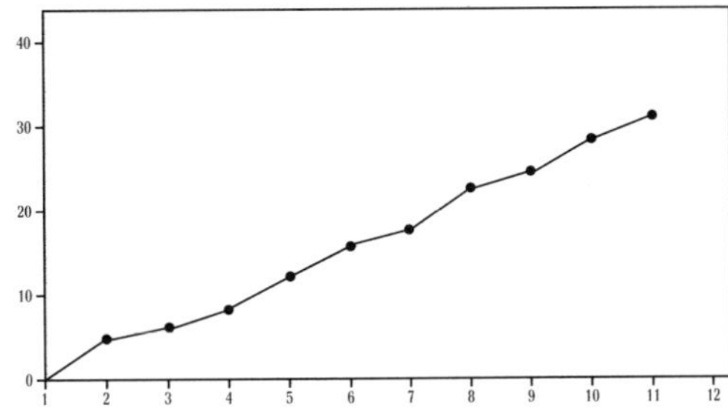

Introduction to run charts

Someone we know was receiving hang-up telephone calls on a regular basis. She became concerned after a robbery occurred in her neighborhood, preceded by a number of similar hang-up calls. When she reported her calls to the local law authorities, they responded with only polite interest to her vague assertion that she was getting "lots of hang-up calls."

Our friend began to collect data about the calls, keeping a simple check sheet next to her phone and then transferring the data to a run chart. When she showed the data to the police in this form, they were clearly more attentive to her concern, pursuing their investigation more aggressively and ultimately linking other break-ins to patterns of hang-up phone calls.

Run charts are useful because they track events as they happen, enabling users to recognize trends as they emerge and to pursue further analysis of hunches based on those trends. Stock market charting is a classic example of the run chart. Day-to-day market prices are charted over time, and patterns, such as the head-and-shoulders formation, begin to emerge.

Data or events that are recorded on run charts can be measurements such as the number of students who are tardy to class each day or the number of math problems that students failed to finish on a series of standardized tests. Run charts can also record proportions or percentages. For example, if students study 20 words each week for spelling tests, they might chart their percentages on these weekly tests over time.

The run chart's purpose in analysis is primarily visual. It can help to identify trends visually or to develop immediate insight about a run. If students are never tardy to art class on Wednesdays, but frequently tardy on other days, they and their teacher may suddenly realize that their tardiness is related to the length of the lunch period just before art class begins: On Wednesdays, they have a longer lunch period, so they are less likely to be late to class. Of course, trends often do not simply jump out of a run chart, but require further analysis to understand.

Run charts can provide the basis for further analysis as control charts (chapter 10), and data points are recorded on similar charts. This similarity facilitates further analysis and helps to scale the data appropriately. Run charts can be created on simple graph paper or ruled paper, as long as the increments are clear and the entry points legible. It is essential that events are recorded in the order in which they occur. Figure 9.1 shows a simple run chart.

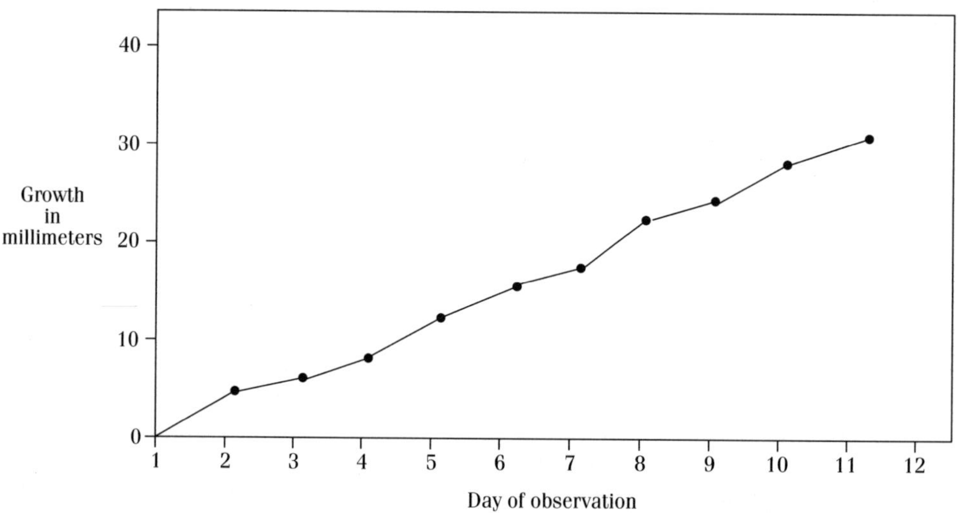

Figure 9.1: Run chart format.

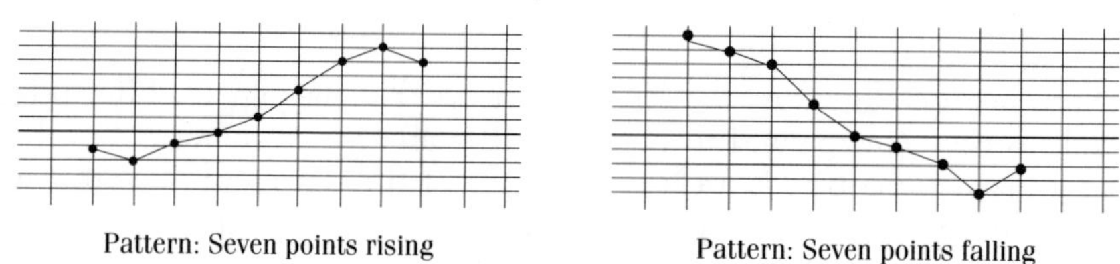

Figure 9.2: Number of students with incomplete homework.

Analyzing the chart

Run charts demonstrate the ease and clarity with which statistical methods enlighten understanding of processes. Basic patterns that have been identified as statistically important provide the basis for interpreting run charts.

Among the patterns that help to identify the need for further analysis are the following:

1. The appearance of runs of seven points in a row either rising or falling. For example, if the number of incomplete seventh-grade homework papers reflects either of the patterns in Figure 9.2, there is reason to question further.

In the first case, each day more students are failing to complete homework. This is not an isolated case, but what can be interpreted as a trend. Likewise, if each day, fewer students fail to complete their homework, it is reasonable to look further for the reasons.

2. Nonrandom patterns in the data (see Figure 9.3). Data that are entered on a run chart are generally random. There will always be some variation in a system (in this case, incomplete homework). When nonrandom patterns appear, however, such as a spike every Wednesday or a rhythm of up-and-down data points, there is cause for investigation. Likewise, if the data pattern remains the same day after day instead of fluctuating in regular ways, further analysis is in order.

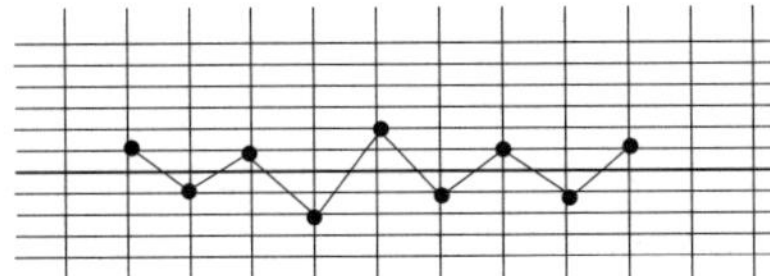

Figure 9.3: Nonrandom pattern.

Classroom benefits

Even the youngest children can keep run charts that help them to record aspects of their learning, behavior, or classroom experience. A teacher might encourage a youngster who is having trouble keeping quiet while someone is reading keep track of his or her own behavior each day. The child can see trends, sometimes with the help of the teacher. If it is the child who realizes that his behavior is worst when he sits next to his best friend—rather than the teacher who points this out—the likelihood that the behavior will improve is enhanced by this self-discovery.

Run charts at all levels reinforce the teaching of specific skills of data analysis, accurate charting, keen observation, and interpretation of events. They help children base their opinions on recorded data rather than on superficial observation or whim. And, of course, run charts enhance the opportunity for children to take responsibility for their own learning and behavior.

Example: Special education

Students in a primary-grade learning disabilities class with serious difficulty in identifying individual letters in words created run charts of their progress. Because their challenges had been so dramatic, they had not developed a sense of this progress until they used run charts, since incremental progress of only a few correctly identified letters at a time was hard for them to perceive. The run chart created visual documentation of their progress and, in fact, may have contributed to continued success, according to their teacher.

One of the students not only recorded the number of errors, but also stratified her data to indicate the kind of errors she was experiencing (see Figure 9.4). The chart reflected the class average and her own individual record. A second run chart indicated percentages, rather than numbers (see Figure 9.5).

With a supplemental list, the children could see not only when they had made errors, but also what kind of error each data point represented. These data can be recorded on a check sheet, or a list can be maintained at the bottom of the run chart itself. See control chart formats in chapter 10.

Example: English as a second language

High school students in a special class designed to help foreign-born students and non-native speakers improve their language saw a great deal of variation in their performance on tests in different subjects. Their overall grade averages were low because of poor performance in just one or two subjects. A run chart, shown in Figure 9.6, helped them to begin to organize their observations about this variation.

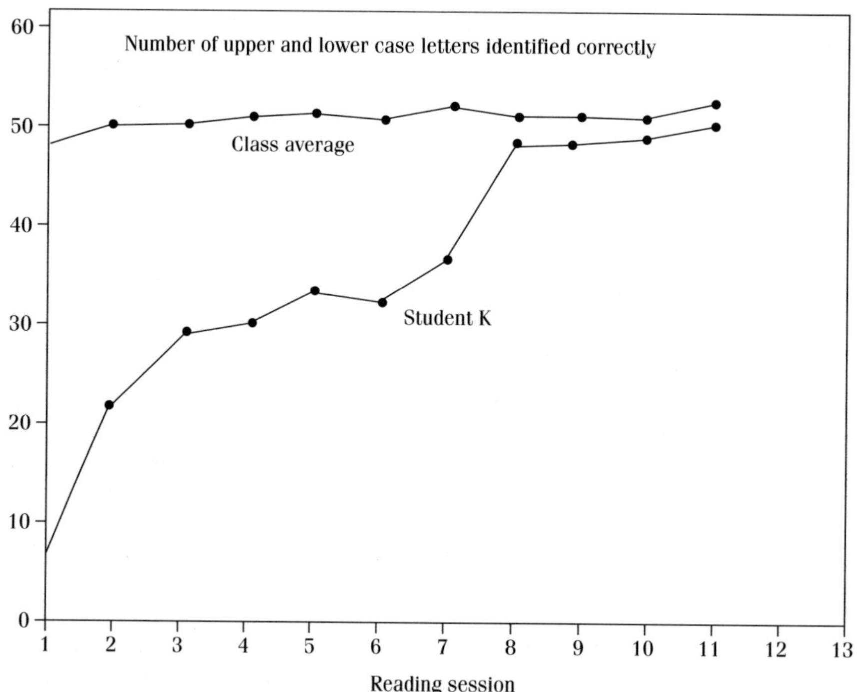

Figure 9.4: Letters identified correctly run chart.

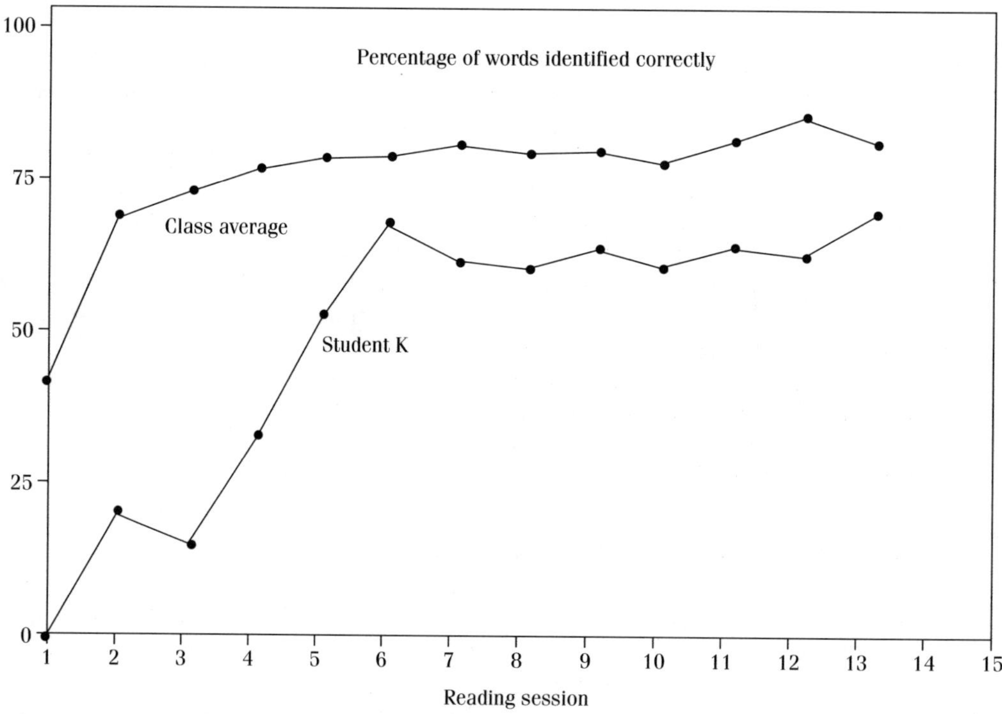

Figure 9.5: Percentages of correct words run chart.

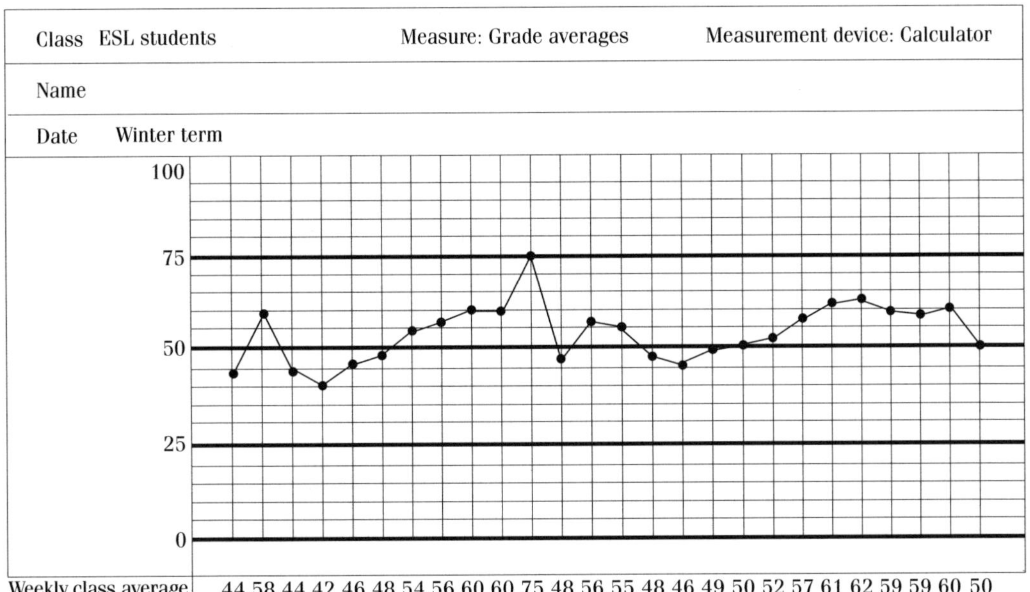

Figure 9.6: Overall average test grades for ESL students run chart.

After they had collected their data, the students and their teacher examined the chart further and began to see that most of their difficulty on tests was in nonlanguage classes. They pursued the analysis with the use of a scatter diagram (chapter 6), analyzing the relationship between success in English and high grades on tests in various subjects.

Ultimately, the teacher began to realize that, regardless of their success with the English language, most students were having the worst grades in Algebra II and geometry—both taught by the same teacher. This teacher believed that non-native speakers should "earn" their place in his classes and held them to higher standards than the native speakers of English. The ESL teacher was able to work directly with this teacher to try to reverse the trend to ensure that the ESL students would be evaluated by the same standards as the native speakers.

What began with an analysis of data led to a somewhat circuitous discovery of unanticipated bias. One never knows where data gathering will lead.

Example: Vocabulary

A group of fourth graders studying a unit on mammals accumulated a number of context-specific words and expressions they believed were critical to their understanding of mammals. They elected to demonstrate their mastery of these terms by responding to flash cards and by using the terms correctly in their research projects. They had already kept track of their own mastery for several weeks prior to beginning the flash card process.

In the flash card exercise, pairs of students quizzed each other three times a week until they felt confident about their mastery of the terms. Run charts of their flash card responses looked like Figure 9.7, where one student's progress is recorded.

This student was able to see a pattern that appeared to reflect dramatic and sustained improvement after the class had adopted the flash card method of reviewing vocabulary

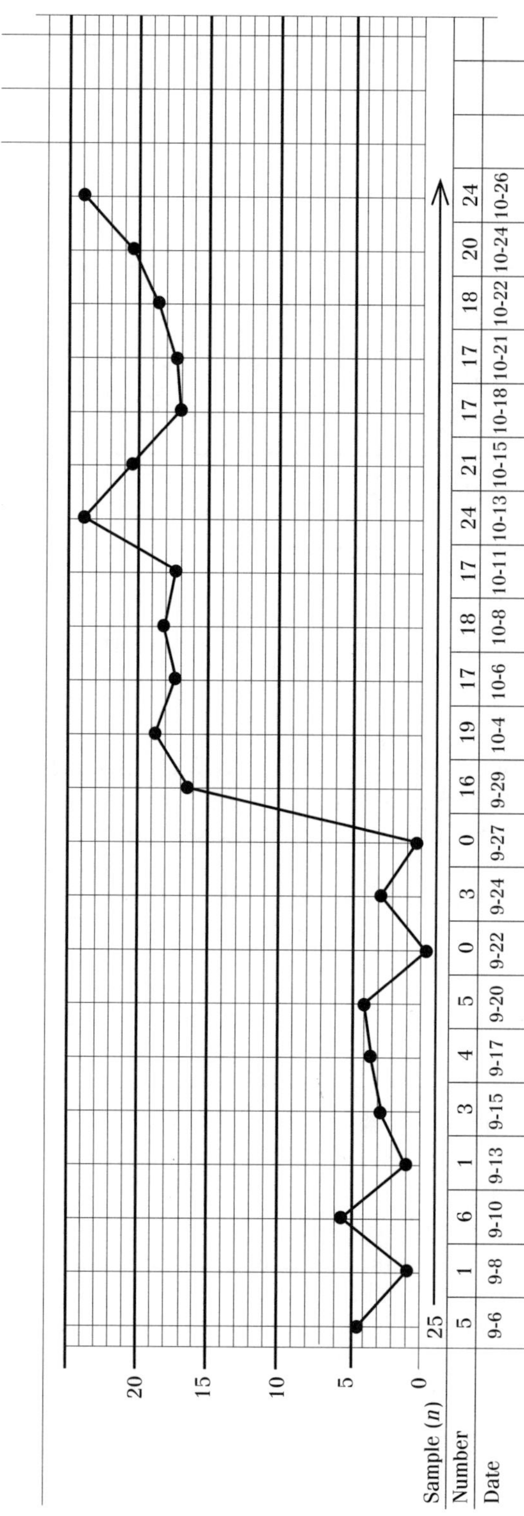

Figure 9.7: Mammal unit vocabulary identification run chart.

words. A run chart can reveal patterns such as this, but a control chart (chapter 10) is the appropriate tool to use to assess whether students can predict continued success with the new method.

Example: Plant growth

An activity for middle school science classes demonstrates the process of gathering and recording data. A sixth-grade science class at Norton Middle School in Grove City, Ohio, plotted data from this type of experiment on run charts.

The experiment involved planting beans: Pot A had one bean, Pot B, 3 beans, and Pot C, 6 beans. Their growth was observed and measured over a 10-day period, and the average growth for each pot (not each seed) was recorded. If students measured this growth each day and recorded the data on run charts, the differences in the progress of each pot's bean growth might appear as in Figure 9.8.

In this case, since the observations were recorded at the same time each day and reflected the same kind of measurements, an alternative might be to use one run chart with three separate lines to reflect the bean growth, as the fourth chart in Figure 9.8 demonstrates. Regardless of whether the data points are recorded on three separate charts or a single run chart, the comparisons among the growth patterns of the three pots are clear and suggest certain analytical conclusions. As in any scientific experiment, this example demonstrates the importance of gathering data and recording it in a systematic way.

Example: Returning work to students

Teachers who assign homework, projects, and papers and insist that students keep deadlines, but then fail to get that work returned in a timely way, represent a source of frustration and even anxiety for students. One teacher who was having difficulty returning work to students promptly—and held a reputation for this pattern over a period of years—used a run chart to keep track of his record. He was only vaguely aware of the fact that students were waiting two weeks and more for feedback about their work. He decided to keep track of the work he assigned for one term and the number of days it took to evaluate that work and return it to students.

His run chart, shown in Figure 9.9, reflected a pattern of delay in returning student work. Looking at this pattern, even without further analysis, enhanced his determination to change it. Chapter 10 will illustrate how using a control chart helped the teacher analyze the pattern further, but the run chart was useful in taking initial steps to recognize the problem.

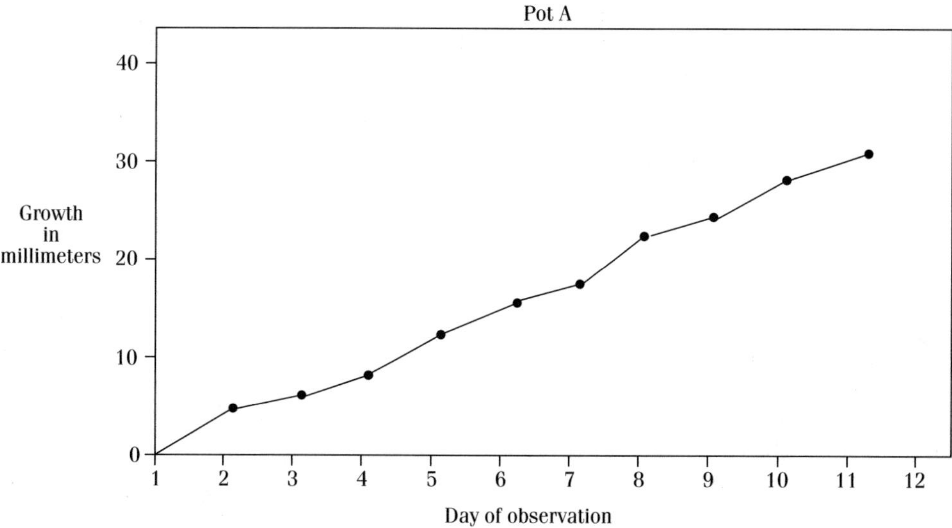

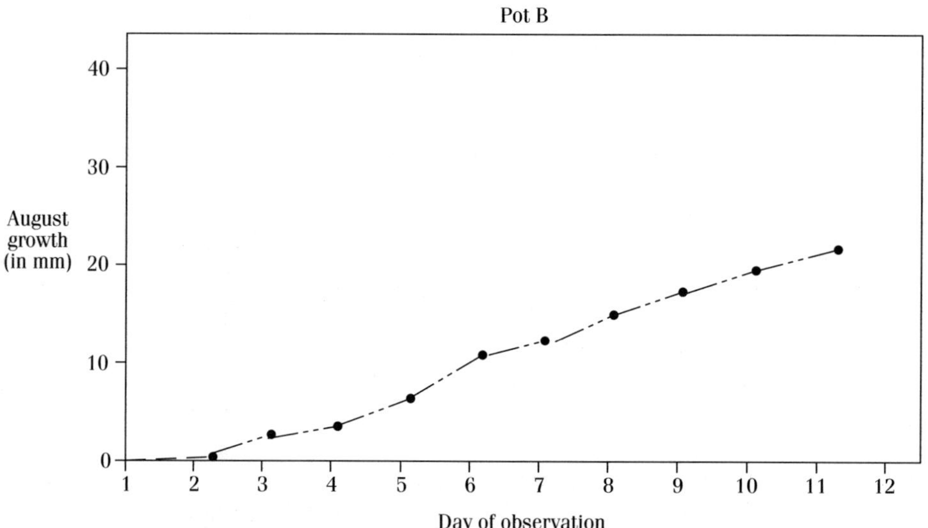

Figure 9.8: Bean growth data.

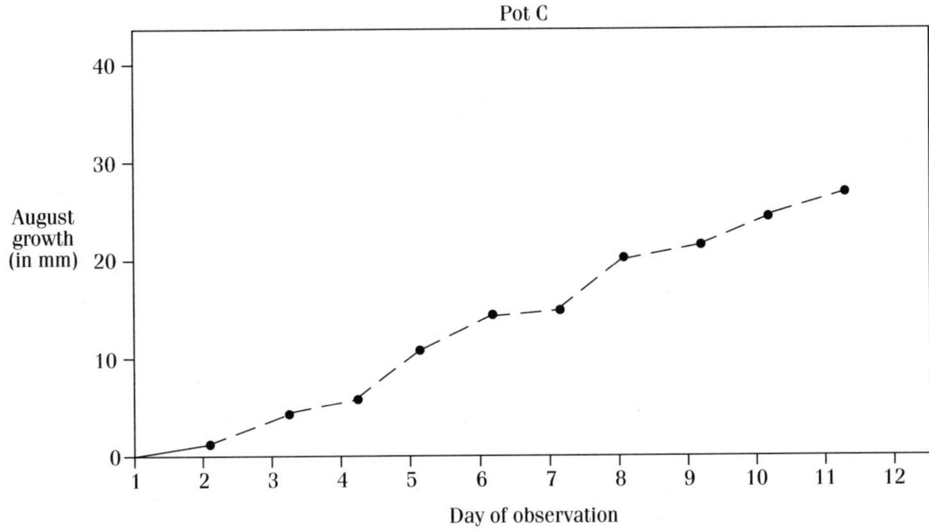

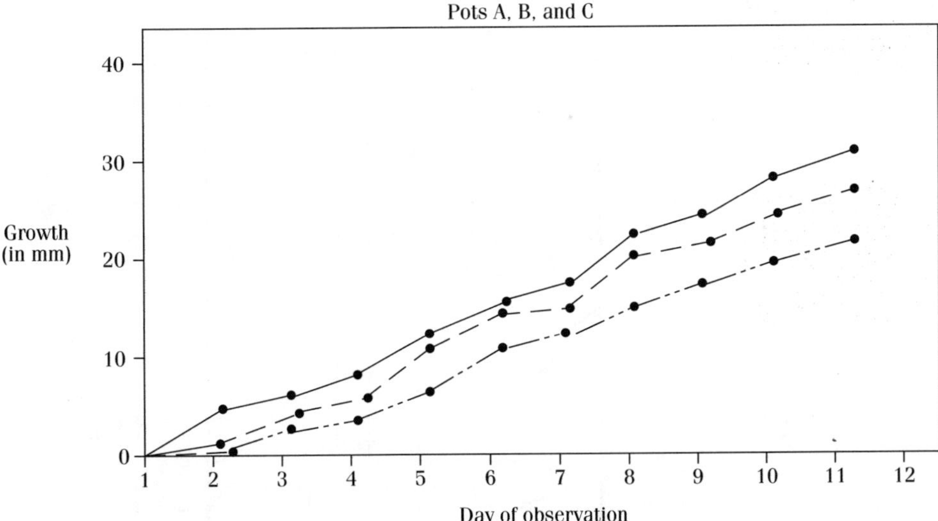

Figure 9.8: *Continued.*

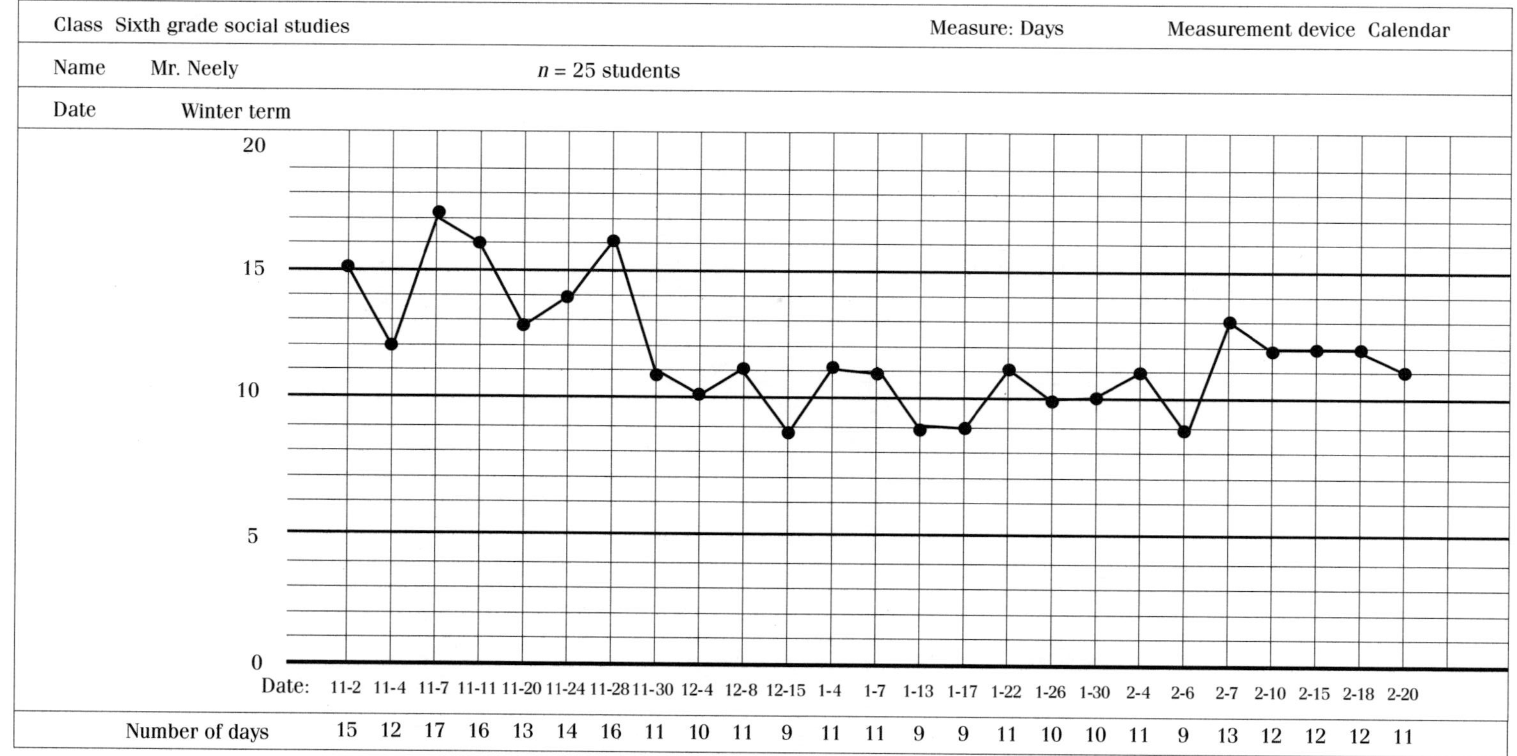

Figure 9.9: Returning student work run chart.

Notable

You may have noticed that the run charts in this chapter have not all had the same appearance. Some are simple graphs with few labels and broad scaling, while others have been constructed with lots of lines and space for additional information that can be used in creating control charts from the data. What is important in a run chart is not the way it looks, but whether it has clarity with respect to the particular data for analysis and whether it offers enough information for further analysis of that data.

Run charts can keep track of any kind of process that is repeated over time. These charts are a respectable statistical tool for data recording and analysis, and they may reflect a high level of sophistication in this analysis. Computer software programs help create control charts from these run charts, automatically determining the control limits that give insights about the stability of a particular process. Run charts can also be useful when they are created by hand as simple lines that capture certain information and reflect the patterns that are formed.

Application

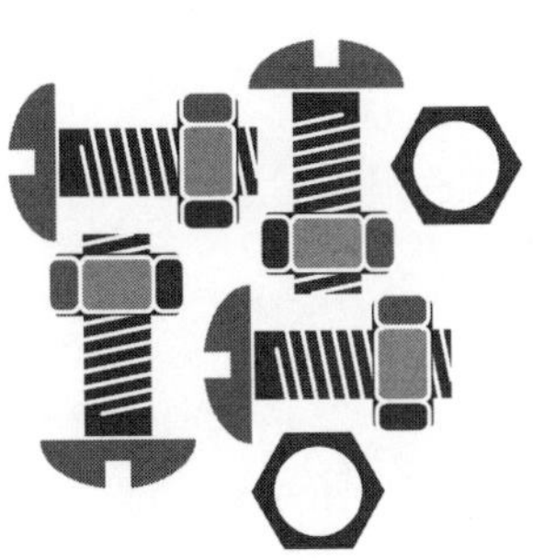

We hope you will not have a need to record hang-up phone calls in the same way our friend did in the beginning of this chapter, but you might try run charts by collecting data about other kinds of calls you get—marketing surveys, vinyl-siding sales, solicitations, and so on. Chapter 10 will look at control charts, which provide even greater analysis of data than that offered by run charts. In the classroom, try helping students record scientific data (like that of the beans and their growth) on run charts.

Chapter 10

Recognizing Stability

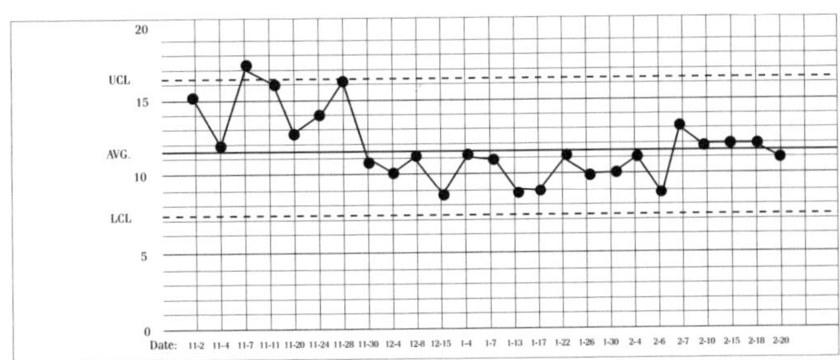

Introduction to control charts

"What do you mean, my class is out of control?"

Teachers may not like to hear that a process is out of control with their students, but control charts can help educators to discover that an out-of-control condition is not necessarily bad. In fact, out-of-control events may be quite positive. *Out of control* indicates that something is changing rather than remaining stable.

In this case, *out of control* is a statistical term referring to the stability of a system. It acknowledges that there is variation in every process. In other words, regardless of how well something is working, it will not always function at exactly the same level. If every student answers every test question correctly for an entire term, one would begin to wonder about the process itself or whether a well-defined system of cheating is in place!

Control charts help determine when to react to variation and when that variation is simply part of the normal running of things. They assess the *stability* of a particular process, or how predictable that process is. If a school bus arrives every day between 7:35 A.M. and 7:45 A.M., that arrival may represent a stable process. The bus cannot be expected to arrive precisely at the same minute day after day, because of the natural, or common, variation that occurs at each stage of its operation.

Like the bus arrival, other processes are also stable enough to be predictable. Other processes vary wildly and have no element of stability or predictability. There is a tendency to either overreact or underreact to variation. A parent whose daughter has been earning As on every spelling test believes that something dreadful has happened when she suddenly gets a B. On the other hand, a teacher who sees a steadily declining pattern of performance or behavior for a student may ignore it, believing that things will turn around soon.

A control chart looks a great deal like a run chart, with an important distinction. Control limits, both upper and lower, are drawn as dashed lines at the appropriate levels, and the mean occurs where a heavy line appears on the chart. These limits are determined statistically from the data reflected on the charts. The limits are not arbitrarily assigned. Simple formulas are used to create control limits, using the statistical mean of the numbers that are charted (see glossary). Software programs that do this automatically are available as well. It is important to remember that an out-of-control point is outside the control limits, not simply above or below the average or mean for the numbers charted.

Analyzing the chart

As in the case of run charts, it is the patterns that emerge on control charts that form the basis of any analysis. Patterns that are important to notice include those associated with run charts (chapter 9), as well as those related to further statistical analysis and associated only with control charts. The notable patterns are as follows:

1. A run of seven points above the data's center point (mean) or seven points below the mean (see Figure 9.2). This pattern provides notice that something is changing. By the same token, a run of seven points in a row going in either direction—up or down—is also a signal that something should be analyzed further. If the number of late homework assignments for a class steadily increases or steadily declines, the situation is worthy of further analysis. Incidentally, when it has declined to the point that the numbers are below the lower control limits, this out-of-control is positive, rather than negative. But it must still be examined for meaning.
2. A point that lies outside either the upper or lower control limits. If class attendance was charted using the number of students present, the figures would, for the most part, fall within control limits. A point that is higher than the calculated control limits reflects attendance that is considerably above the average, and a point below the lower control limits suggests the opposite. Sometimes there are reasonable explanations for these points. For example, attendance was much higher when students anticipated a field trip; or a chicken pox outbreak created low attendance on a given day.
3. As in the case of run charts, patterns in the data should be examined. Normally data points will assume a somewhat random pattern, assuming that they have been collected in the same way each time. Like life, they will have their ups and downs, but these are not precisely predictable on a day-to-day basis. If there is a recurring cyclical pattern, however, further analysis is required. If a group's current events quiz scores are always substantially down on Wednesdays, this pattern should be examined.

Other nonrandom patterns that demand attention occur when a series of points are all too close to the average, creating a nearly straight line, or too far from the average. Something has happened to create such patterns, and it deserves attention.

Classroom benefits

Children's growth and development is a long-term proposition. When they, or their teachers, learn to overreact to a single data point rather than seeing that point as part of a longer sequence, they waste important energy in figuring something out that does not need resolving. At the same time, examining patterns over a period of time and analyzing the blips as they occur give young people confidence not only in the system they are part of, but also in their ability to analyze this system.

Using control charts can support students' acquisition of analytical and mathematical skills. Even if they lack the skills to apply the formula themselves, they are able to understand statistical stability and the importance of reacting when it is important to react, rather than responding willy-nilly.

Control chart analysis can extend outside the classroom. A child who thought his bicycle tires were flatter in the morning than in the afternoon was adding air to the tires every morning and then finding that the tires expanded in the afternoon. Afraid that continuing to add air might create too much pressure in the tires, he decided to collect data on the air pressure over a period of several weeks. Indeed, there was variability in the pressure between certain times of day; but even this variability fell within the control limits. The child was able to figure out that the temperature of the ambient air created slightly higher or lower tire pressure, but as long as it remained in control, there was no reason to do anything.

Example: Second-grade writing

Those second graders that did the check sheets and cause-and-effect diagrams with their writing assignments also entered their class' data on control charts. Before making any changes in the way they approached these writing assignments, the students collected data relating to the number of errors, noting at the same time the kinds of errors on each assignment. This information came from the check sheets.

The first control chart, shown in Figure 10.1, reflected a process that was not in control. When the students examined the two out-of-control points in December, they found that everyone had done better with respect to the error rate, primarily because they were so excited about the writing assignment itself, which related to the upcoming holidays. On the other hand, the students surmised that the point above the control limits on January 4 had occurred because they had just returned from an extended holiday break and were not ready to give their full attention to the writing assignment.

Later, after the students decided that using dictionaries as they were doing their writing would cause a decline in the number of spelling errors, they changed their system of doing the writing prompts by adding dictionaries to the process. Then they gathered data on the new way of doing things and monitored the process with new control charts.

Any of the run charts in chapter 9 could be converted to a control chart if enough data were available to create accurate means and control limits. Usually 25 observations are considered necessary before these limits will have statistical integrity.

Example: Developmental reading class

Teachers of developmental reading classes in an Ocala, Florida, school used control charts to record and analyze the problems their students were having with spelling. Although the number of errors was important, it was also critical to determine the kinds of errors students were making, in order to address specific problem areas.

The control chart, shown in Figure 10.2, indicated what appeared to be a great deal of up-and-down variation in the numbers of errors the students made. After control limits were applied, however, it was clear that the system was stable; that is, the errors, for the most part fell, within calculated limits. One exception, on November 19, was attributed to a special cause: Dress rehearsal for the Thanksgiving program was held that afternoon, and the students believed that they would not be having a spelling test that day.

Of course, the fact that the system is stable, and that most of the variation is somewhat predictable, does not mean that it is good enough. The objective, at this point, is to

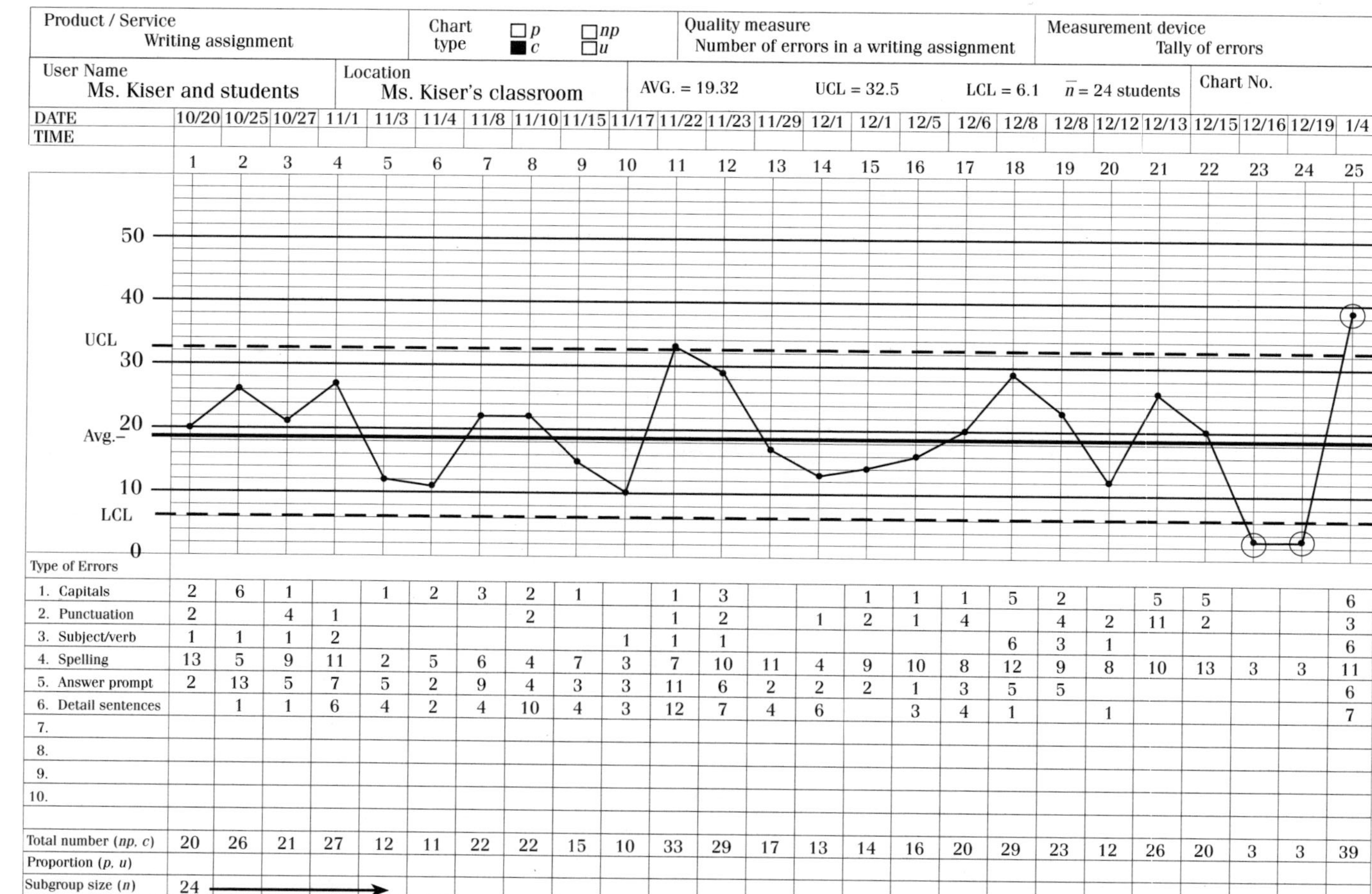

Product / Service: Writing assignment	Chart type: ☐ p ■ c ☐ np ☐ u	Quality measure: Number of errors in a writing assignment	Measurement device: Tally of errors
User Name: Ms. Kiser and students	Location: Ms. Kiser's classroom	AVG. = 19.32 UCL = 32.5 LCL = 6.1 $\bar{n}$ = 24 students	Chart No.

DATE	10/20	10/25	10/27	11/1	11/3	11/4	11/8	11/10	11/15	11/17	11/22	11/23	11/29	12/1	12/1	12/5	12/6	12/8	12/8	12/12	12/13	12/15	12/16	12/19	1/4
TIME																									
	1	2	3	4	5	6	7	8	9	10	11	12	13	14	15	16	17	18	19	20	21	22	23	24	25
Type of Errors																									
1. Capitals	2	6	1		1	2	3	2	1		1	3			1	1	1	5	2		5	5			6
2. Punctuation	2		4	1				2			1	2		1	2	1	4		4	2	11	2			3
3. Subject/verb	1	1	1	2						1	1	1						6	3	1					6
4. Spelling	13	5	9	11	2	5	6	4	7	3	7	10	11	4	9	10	8	12	9	8	10	13	3	3	11
5. Answer prompt	2	13	5	7	5	2	9	4	3	3	11	6	2	2	2	1	3	5	5						6
6. Detail sentences		1	1	6	4	2	4	10	4	3	12	7	4	6		3	4	1		1					7
7.																									
8.																									
9.																									
10.																									
Total number (*np, c*)	20	26	21	27	12	11	22	22	15	10	33	29	17	13	14	16	20	29	23	12	26	20	3	3	39
Proportion (*p, u*)																									
Subgroup size (*n*)	24 →																								

Figure 10.1: Attributes control chart, writing errors.

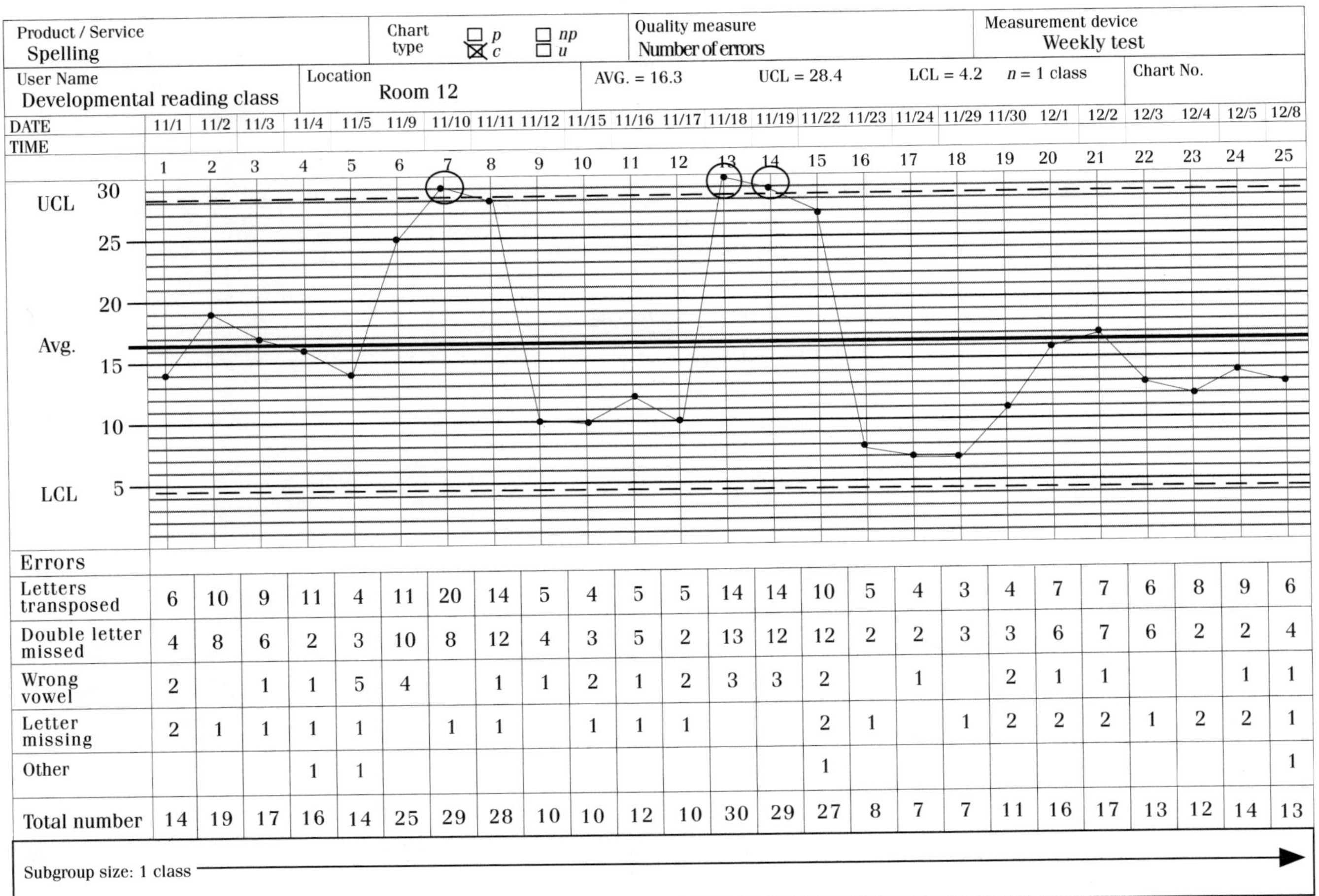

DATE	11/1	11/2	11/3	11/4	11/5	11/9	11/10	11/11	11/12	11/15	11/16	11/17	11/18	11/19	11/22	11/23	11/24	11/29	11/30	12/1	12/2	12/3	12/4	12/5	12/8
TIME																									
	1	2	3	4	5	6	7	8	9	10	11	12	13	14	15	16	17	18	19	20	21	22	23	24	25
Errors																									
Letters transposed	6	10	9	11	4	11	20	14	5	4	5	5	14	14	10	5	4	3	4	7	7	6	8	9	6
Double letter missed	4	8	6	2	3	10	8	12	4	3	5	2	13	12	12	2	2	3	3	6	7	6	2	2	4
Wrong vowel	2		1	1	5	4		1	1	2	1	2	3	3	2		1		2	1	1			1	1
Letter missing	2	1	1	1	1		1	1		1	1	1			2	1		1	2	2	2	1	2	2	1
Other				1	1										1										1
Total number	14	19	17	16	14	25	29	28	10	10	12	10	30	29	27	8	7	7	11	16	17	13	12	14	13

Figure 10.2: Spelling errors control chart.

further reduce variation, and ultimately the control limits will become closer together as a result of less variation.

In this case, the students created Pareto diagrams reflecting the specific kinds of errors they were experiencing and decided to work on letter transposition, which was the greatest source of difficulty for them. They speculated that spelling the words aloud during drills and practices would help to reduce this problem, and they set out to test their hypothesis.

After another month's data had been collected, the errors in transposition had actually been reduced, and the overall spelling improved as well. A second control chart was later created to study the process further and continued attention was given to problems as they were identified.

Example: Individual progress

Students can chart their individual progress by means of control charts, or teachers can maintain charts for each child. For the developmental reading class referred to in chapter 9, teachers kept individual charts, which they were able to discuss with students and share with their parents. Charts for one of the children are shown in Figures 10.3 and 10.4. They show his ability to identify upper- and lowercase letters in a reading exercise.

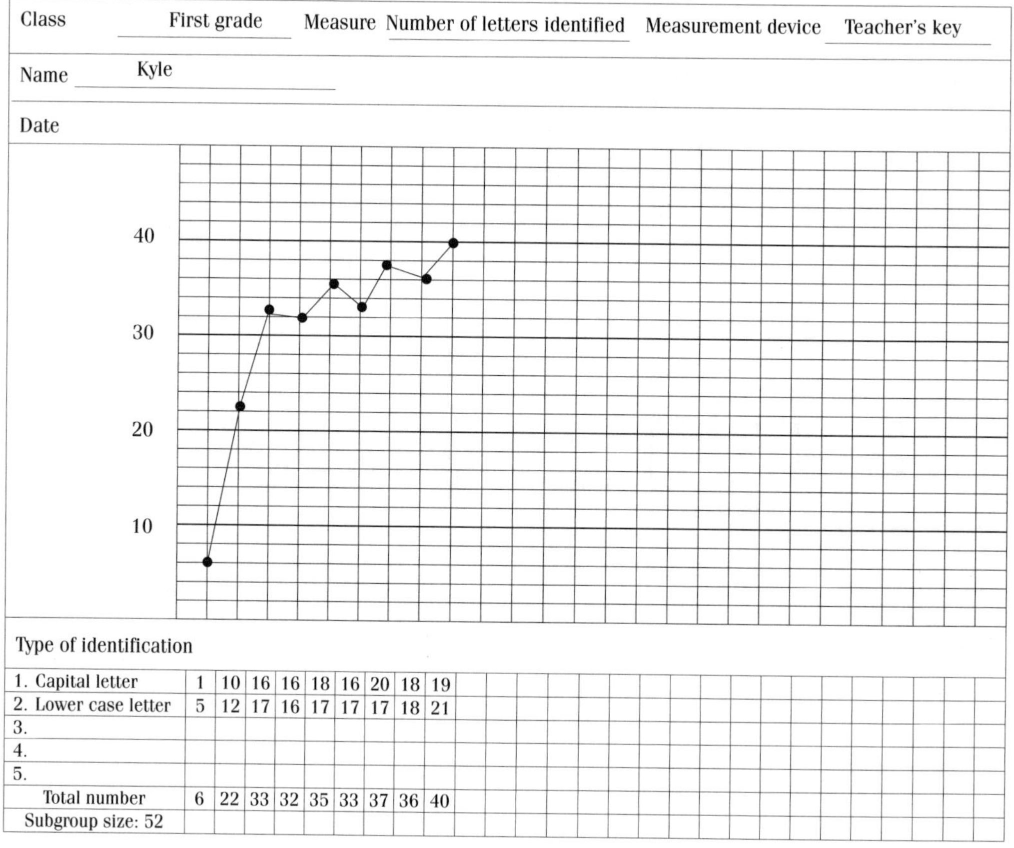

Type of identification									
1. Capital letter	1	10	16	16	18	16	20	18	19
2. Lower case letter	5	12	17	16	17	17	17	18	21
3.									
4.									
5.									
Total number	6	22	33	32	35	33	37	36	40
Subgroup size: 52									

Figure 10.3: Letter identification run chart.

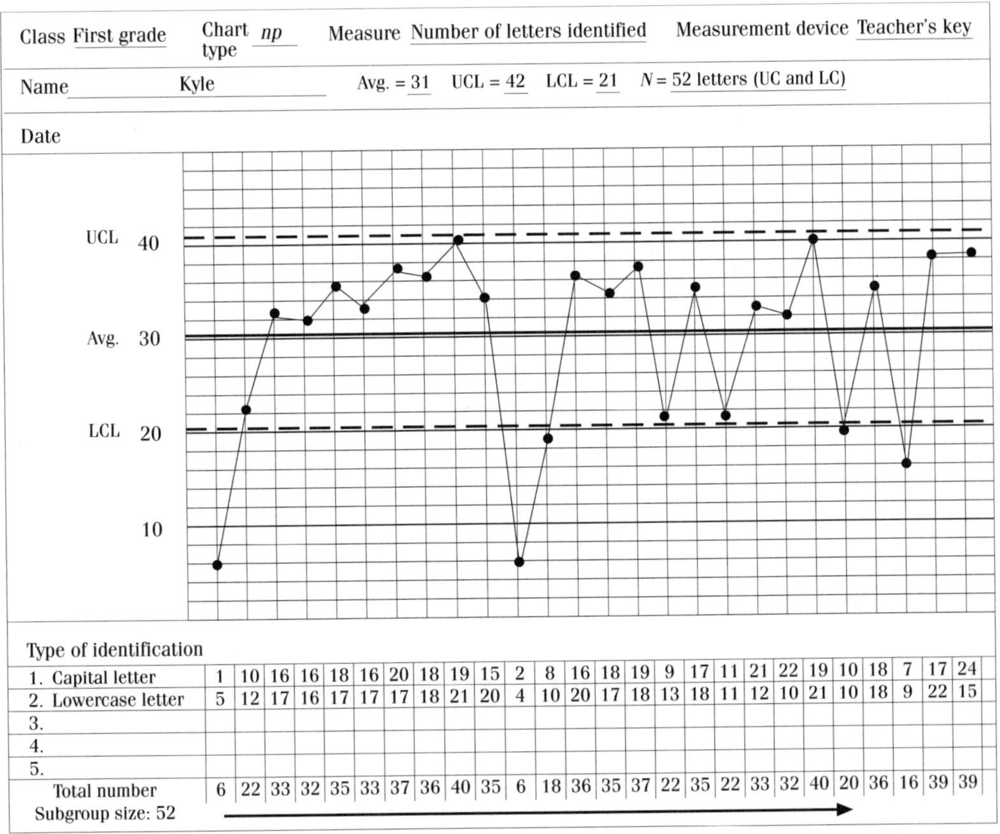

Type of identification																										
1. Capital letter	1	10	16	16	18	16	20	18	19	15	2	8	16	18	19	9	17	11	21	22	19	10	18	7	17	24
2. Lowercase letter	5	12	17	16	17	17	17	18	21	20	4	10	20	17	18	13	18	11	12	10	21	10	18	9	22	15
3.																										
4.																										
5.																										
Total number	6	22	33	32	35	33	37	36	40	35	6	18	36	35	37	22	35	22	33	32	40	20	36	16	39	39

Figure 10.4: Letter identification control chart.

A run chart first captured data relating to this child's reading (see Figure 10.3). After enough data points had been recorded, control limits were calculated, demonstrating the pattern of identification that this child was experiencing. With several points out of control, further analysis was devoted to understanding the reasons for the wide range in the child's ability to identify letters at different times (see Figure 10.4). Other tools, such as cause-and-effect diagrams, supported this analysis, and ultimately the teachers determined that the child was easily distracted during the reading sessions. With fewer distractions he was able to identify more letters and have fewer mix-ups between uppercase and lowercase letters. Analysis of the control charts had identified the sessions when out-of-control points occurred and enabled the teachers to pinpoint the circumstances on each of those days that had contributed to these incidents.

Example: Returning student papers

Recall the run chart that Mr. Neely made in order to analyze his return of papers and projects to his students (Figure 9.8). By determining control limits, using the appropriate statistical formula and evaluating the range of the data—how far apart each of the data points lies from the prior one—Neely was able to see that the system was not stable (see Figure 10.5). Too

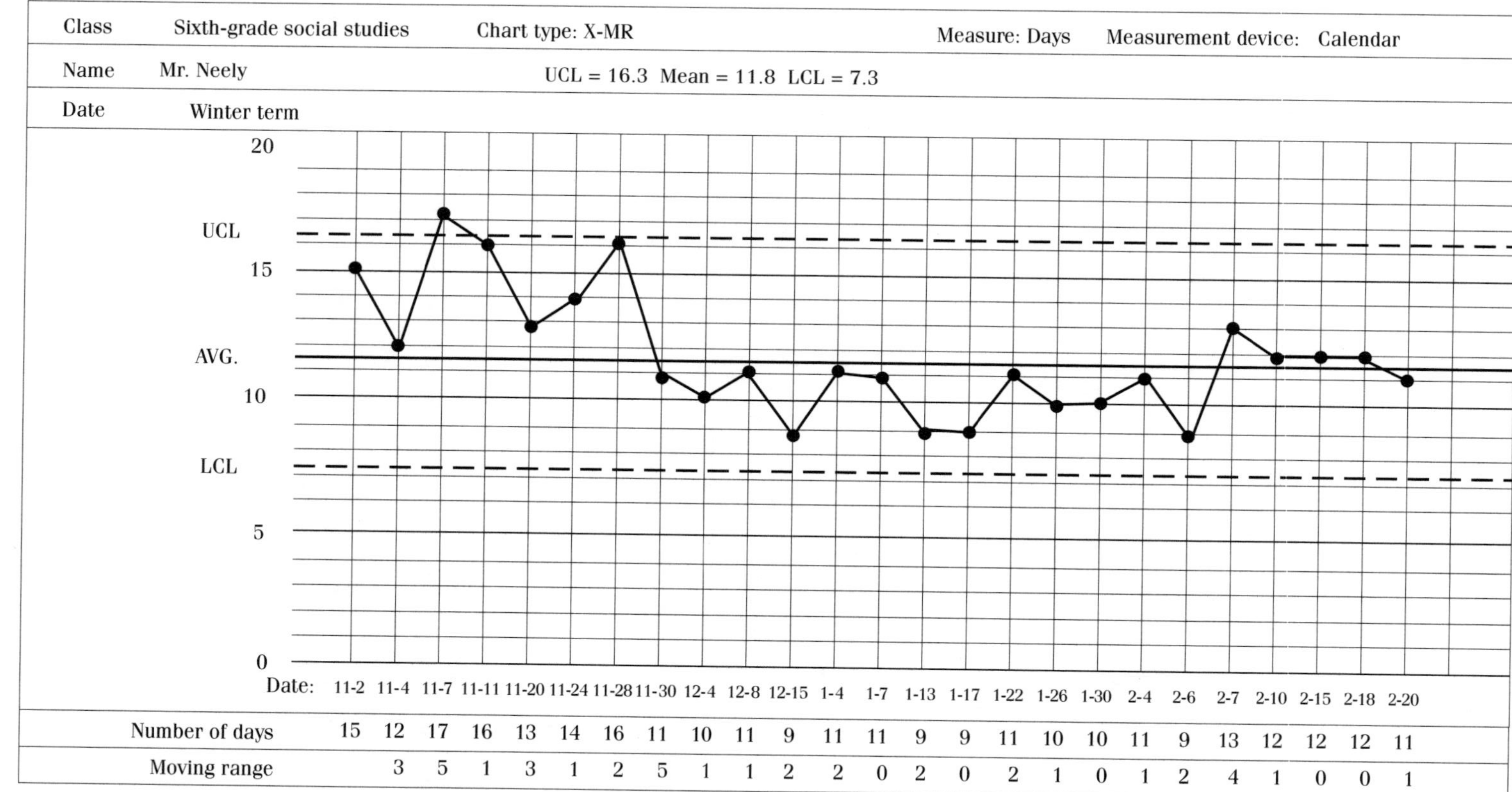

Figure 10.5: Returning student work control chart.

much variation existed in the process of returning student work. He was faced with a process that was indeed out of control, and he knew that even if it were stable, the average number of days as well as the range between the events would need to be reduced.

The data analysis made him think about his system of assigning and collecting work. Using the control chart information as well as insight gleaned from a Pareto analysis of the types of assignments that took the longest time to return, Neely was able to determine that he was spending far too much time on small assignments such as daily quizzes and homework, so his attention to major projects and papers was delayed.

He discussed this analysis with his sixth graders, who thought of examples when they, too, invested too much time in things that mattered less than other work that was more significant. After their teacher had changed the system of assigning and collecting work, they helped him collect data and analyze it, resulting not only in a better system and reduced cycle time, but also in their engagement in the issue and their analysis of their own behaviors. What had begun as an investigation of an administrative process—getting paperwork turned around—evolved into a source of satisfaction and improvement for both teacher and students.

Notable

While it may seem that control charts are most useful for recording discrepancies or errors, they are also helpful in monitoring many different processes. Once a measurement of a process is determined—for example, by count or by proportion for one kind of data—the data can be recorded on a control chart for further analysis.

The formulas that are required to create control limits are available in the glossary of this book. An even easier approach is to create control charts on a computer software program that will calculate control limits and draw all those tedious lines for you.

Application

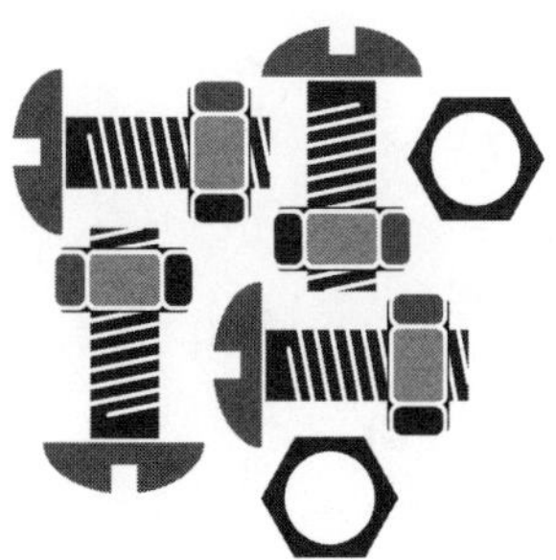

If you developed a run chart in the "Application" section of chapter 9, you might want to collect more data and use the same exercise for a control chart. Or think of other sources of data: the amount of time it takes your students to gather their things and put on their coats at the end of the day, or the number of interruptions caused in your class by announcements, fire drills, or schedule changes, or the number of successful free throws in girls' basketball drills.

Chapter 11

Creating Webs of Meaning

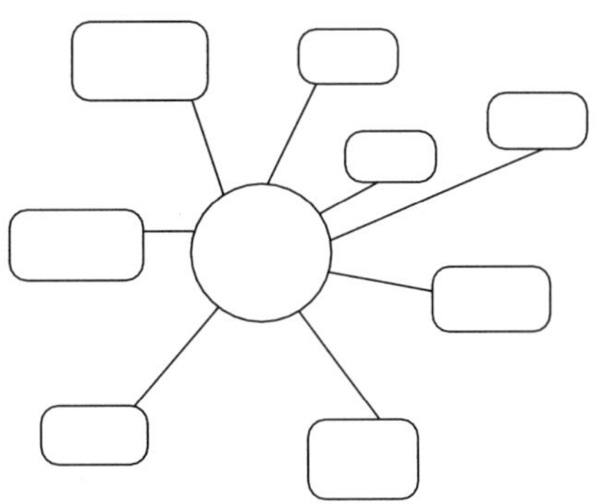

Introducing spider diagrams

Spider diagrams are named for their distinctive shape. They begin with one idea and link related ideas that sprout threads to other ideas, which become their own webs. The center may be seen as the spider itself (see Figure 11.1). Like affinity analysis and nominal group technique, spider diagrams are used to organize brainstorming. They are especially useful in creating a focus at increasing levels of detail, helping students to hone their analytical thinking skills.

Mind maps, of which spider diagrams are a variation, represent graphical expressions of radiant thinking, unlocking the immense potential of the brain to make connections (Buzan and Buzan 1994). Each person makes those connections with a unique set of images and words, demonstrating the capacity to hold onto literally trillions of associations.

Typically a group exercise, the spider diagram can also be used by individual students to stimulate their own thinking. The synergistic power of the brainstorming that comes from a group is lost, however, when the effort becomes an individual one.

To create a spider diagram requires only a single word or concept, written on a chalkboard with a circle around it. As students become accustomed to using spider diagrams, they will respond as soon as they see this body and begin to think of ways they can string it to related words and ideas. The exercise can be a free association, leading wherever the students' minds take them, or it can represent increasingly detailed concepts related to the original idea.

In a spider exercise seeking topics for written work, an example of the first might lead students from homework to assignments to rules to laws to gun control; thus making an enormous leap from the original idea. In the second model, homework might lead to math (or other kinds of homework), homework strategies, environments, favorite places to do homework, and a description of a student's desk, honing in on topics related directly to the original topic.

Analyzing the chart

Students can review all the nodes on the spider web, looking for the ones that are most appropriate or appealing for their use. If they are creating a diagram of approaches to drawing animals, for example, they might each focus on a different one to begin their artwork. A student who selects the strategy "use a photograph of my cat" may decide to begin with a photo to draw a cat and then will modify the drawing from that point. Another,

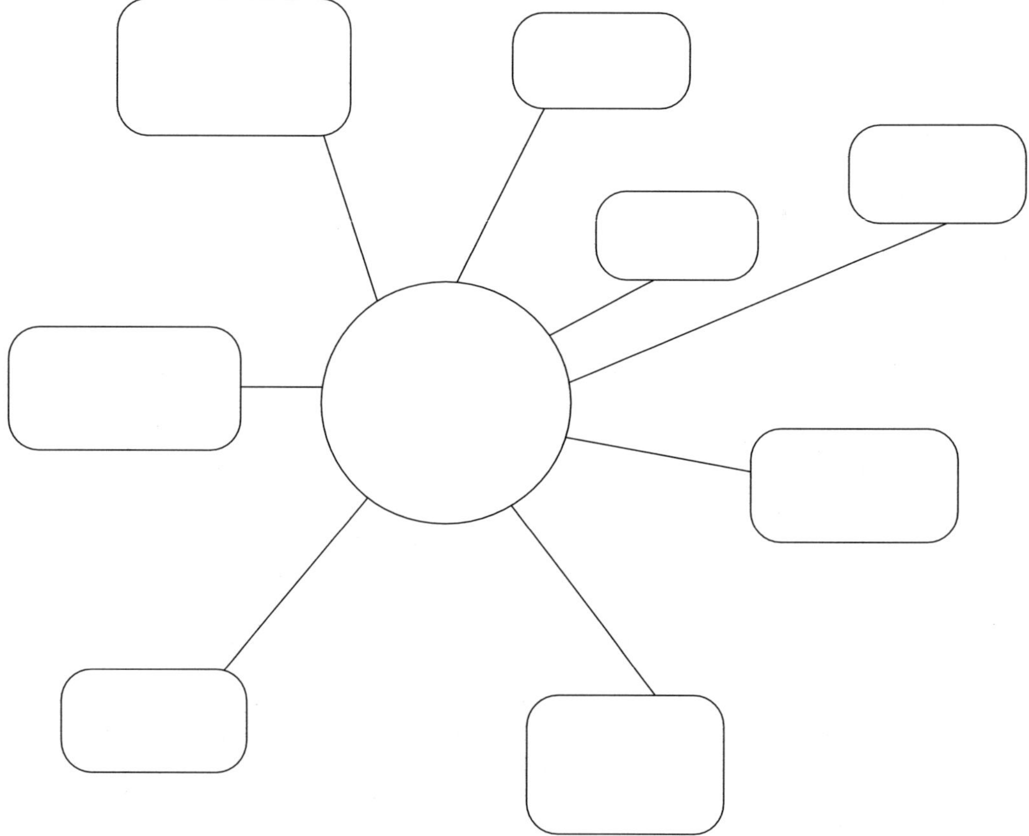

Figure 11.1: Spider diagram with potential connecting webs.

who wants to create an animation, might begin with a computer drawing tool to animate a series of drawings of a dog.

Classroom benefits

The benefit of stimulating creative expansion of an idea can be translated to all studies. While it seems most apt for creative arts and writing, it is not limited in its usefulness. For example, students might use the spider diagram to organize their thinking about an historical event or scientific phenomenon. In any case, the connections that are made between sometimes disparate ideas support the expansion of learning that is based on making such connections. Indeed, the neurosciences suggest that real learning takes place only through such connections and that nothing is ever really learned until it is connected with prior knowledge (Caine and Caine 1991). It is as if the brain creates its own spider diagram. In this sense, like brainstorming and other creativity tools, the usefulness of a spider diagram lies not in the finished chart, but in the process of developing it.

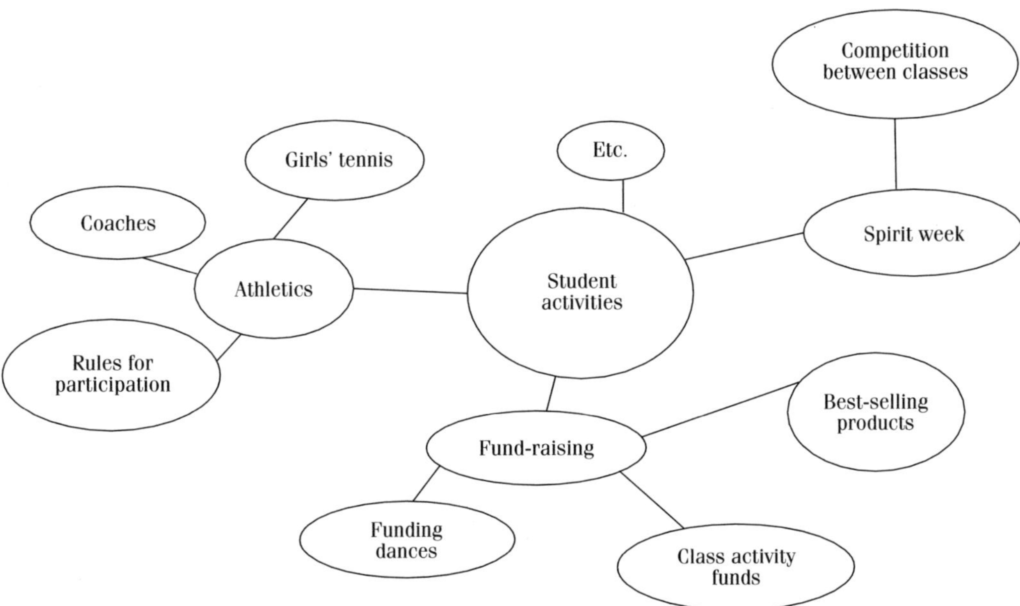

Figure 11.2: News ideas spider diagram.

Example: Journalism stories

Sixth graders were putting together a newspaper to be distributed to middle school students. They used a spider diagram, shown in Figure 11.2, to think about articles related to student activities.

In this case, brainstorming and diagramming students' thoughts generated several useful story ideas, all related to student activities. Since they will need a variety of stories, the spider exercise can be repeated with another focus, or the original one can be opened further with a word-association approach to the first concept. For example, a second diagram could be organized around the entry "what sells best," generating other ideas for news stories that are associated with that idea.

Example: Historical fiction

In a biography unit, intermediate-grade students went to an ancient cemetery and examined the gravestones for inscriptions, did rubbings of some of them, and took notes on the birth and death dates of others. When the students returned to their classrooms, they selected individuals whose graves they had seen and created stories about the lives of those people.

They stimulated their creative juices with spider diagrams. Students wrote the names of their historical person at the center of each of their diagrams. Together, they brainstormed various ways they could capture the essence of the lives they were writing about, as well as the spirit of the times in which each had lived. One student's spider diagram appears in Figure 11.3.

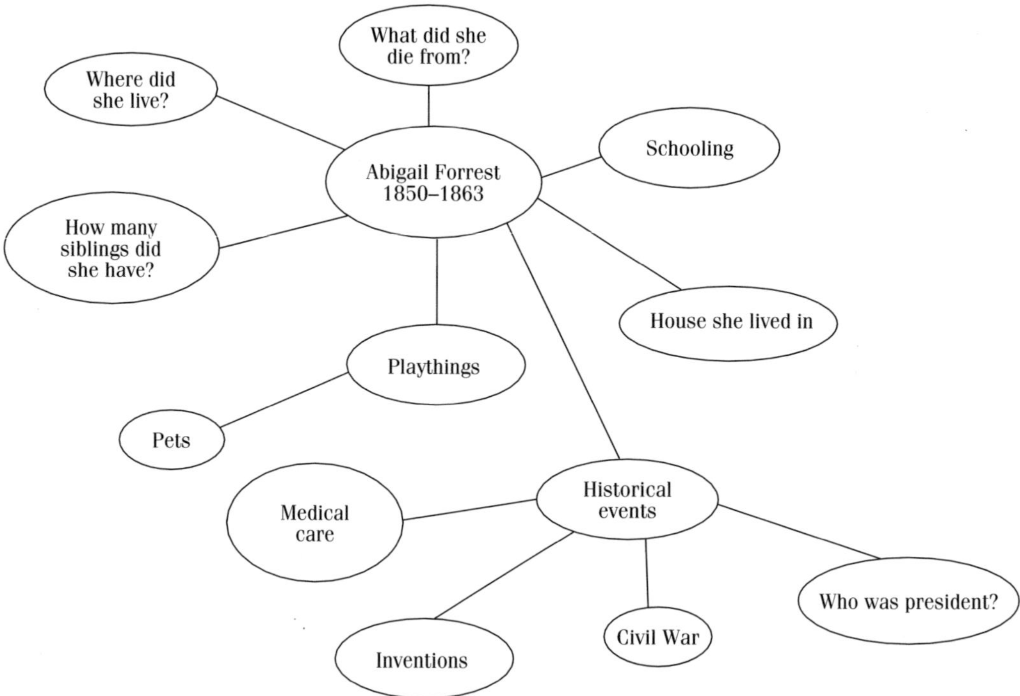

Figure 11.3: Historical biography spider diagram.

In this case, one web—the historical context of Abigail's life—made connections to specific historical and cultural developments that the student chose to pursue in his writing. His creative biography of Abigail related to a childhood disease she contracted, and the ensuing medical drama that took place because of the limitations of the medical profession and the distance of her family's home from adequate care.

The spider diagram helped the student to carry the idea much further than the original framework of creating a fictional biography of a real person. While this had been an interesting assignment in itself, it no doubt would have encouraged superficial and trite stories that presented only the chronological events in the person's life.

Example: Butterfly facts

Affinity-type thinking can be brought to bear in creating a spider diagram, as this case related to a butterfly exhibit at Cincinnati's Krohn Conservatory illustrates. Preparing to visit the exhibit, a group of children in a summer camp created a spider diagram (Figure 11.4) to show what they anticipated they might learn from their visit. Their leader wanted the children to be able to make some connections between their summer learning about butterflies and this experience. In fact, the spider diagram helped them to frame questions that later enriched their visit to the conservatory (chapter 15).

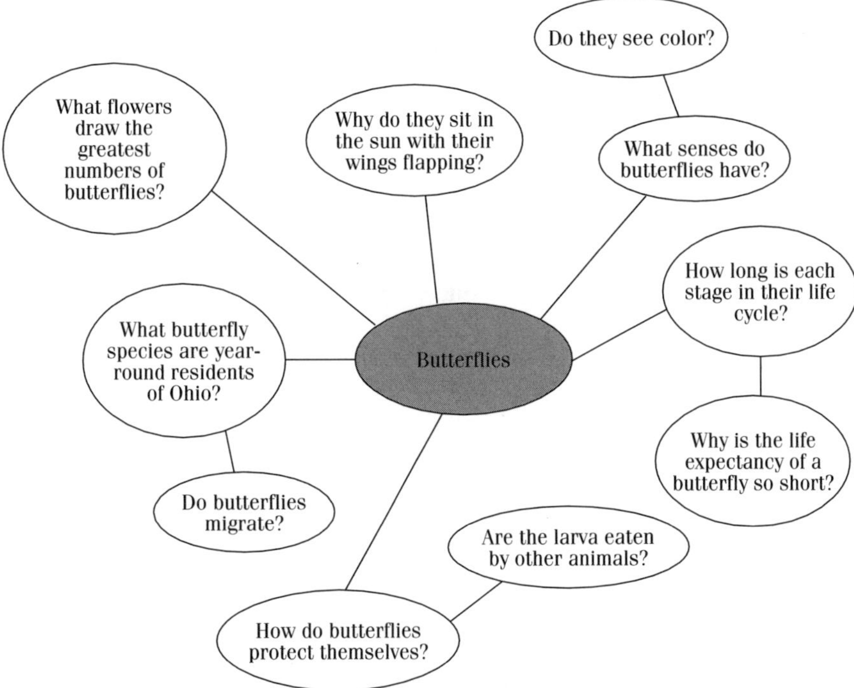

Figure 11.4: Field trip preparation; butterflies spider diagram.

Notable

As noted, spider diagrams are related to other tools. Although they are similar to relations diagrams, spider diagrams represent a slightly different approach to understanding connections among ideas or questions. Spider diagrams offer variety to the classroom teacher's panoply of strategies for enlarging students' thinking.

Small children can gain practice in making such connections by cutting out pictures from magazines and pasting them in spider-diagram format, demonstrating their relationships.

Application

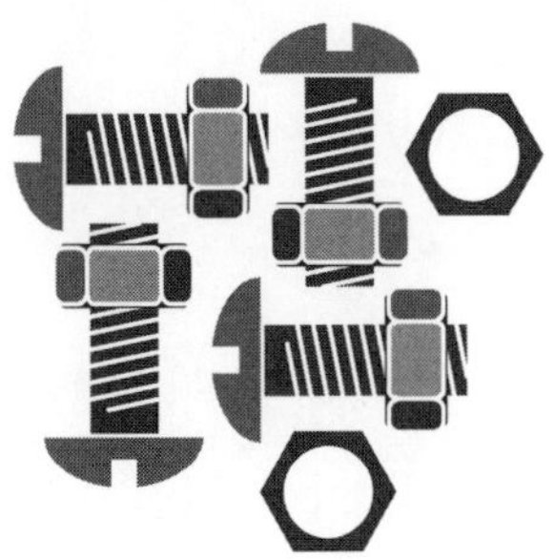

If you have never used spider diagrams to generate enthusiasm for an idea or project, you'll find that they are easy to use and that children respond eagerly to the challenge of developing extended webs. A natural use for spider diagrams lies in the area of creating topics for writing or speaking. Try developing an extemporaneous speaking experience by providing a topic (butterflies, for example) for the first speaker, then having other students begin to speak on a related, but not identical, topic after the first speaker has talked for a given time period.

Passing the topic on for further development or a related tangent is a fun way for students to jump into a public speaking opportunity.

References

Buzan, Tony, and Barry Buzan. 1994. *The mind map book: How to use radiant thinking to maximize your brain's untapped potential*. New York: Dutton.

Caine, Renata Nummela, and Geoffrey Caine. 1991. *Making connections: Teaching and the human brain*. Alexandria, Va.: Association for Supervision and Curriculum Development.

Chapter 12

Looking It All Over at the End of the Day

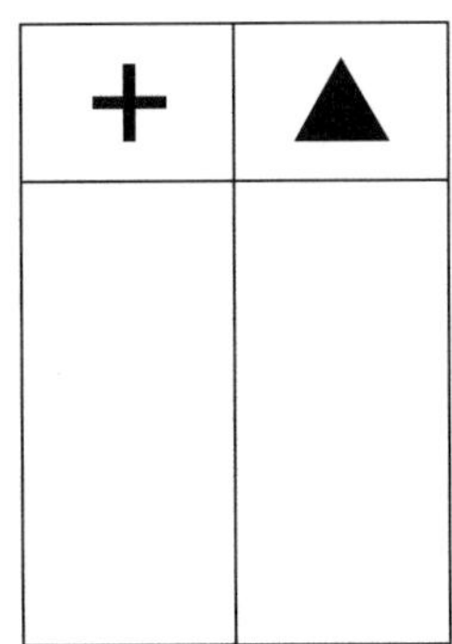

Introducing plus-delta charts

Although this book's primary purpose is to demonstrate specific classroom tools and their variety of uses, it is important to remember that these tools must be used in the context of a purpose. If students are using flowcharts simply to learn about flowcharts, they are missing a tremendous opportunity for the benefits to their wider learning that can ensue.

A sweeping assumption might be that whatever happens in the classroom has the purpose of promoting and enhancing learning. Unless that purpose is clear, however, students may begin to feel that much of what they do has nothing to do with their own learning. Its purpose may seem to be only administrative. For example, if students were asked why teachers record attendance, they would probably assume that it is for the purpose of the administration—to ensure state reimbursements, to protect themselves from lawsuits, and/or to have accurate information about enrollment.

Students need to be frequently reminded how important it is that they are in school. They are missed when they are absent; the dynamics of the class and its learning are changed when individual students are missing; their classmates need them to support the learning in the classroom; and so on. Tardiness and absenteeism, when they are only administrative negatives, become opportunities for discipline rather than reinforcement of the learning process.

Even the most apparently mundane tasks such as record keeping, however, can be tied to the purpose of the classroom. The facilitator of learning must continue to remind students of the why and so what of their classroom life until they reach the point that they can assess the purpose for themselves.

The plus-delta chart can help to keep students focused on the reasons they are in the classroom and to engage them in their learning. With regular review of the learning process, students will begin to feel that they are not mere observers, but have genuine input into how the classroom can reinforce learning.

The simplest of the tools in this collection, the plus-delta chart can be created anywhere: flip chart, chalkboard, overhead transparency, or even on a sheet of newspaper pulled from the recycling pile.

Constructing a plus-delta chart, like many other tools, relies on students' willingness to brainstorm with their classmates. At the end of a class period or a thematic unit or even a chapter, students are asked to list the things that went well with that particular unit. These are listed down one side of a large sheet of paper.

The second phase involves a consideration of what could have been better about the lesson, activity, or unit. *Delta,* the symbol for an increment of a variable, represents those

+ Pluses	Δ Deltas
Friendly staff	Orienteering was hard; would be better in a.m.
Having different teams for different activities	Lunch too early
Good mix in cabin assignments	More time needed for individual projects
Varied work rotations	Talent show would have been better if we'd had time to prepare
Having choice of morning activities	

Figure 12.1: Outdoor adventure plus-delta.

items that might be done differently if the experience were repeated. An example of a plus-delta chart created after a three-day middle school outdoor adventure is shown in Figure 12.1.

Analyzing the chart

Plus-delta charts provide a way for the facilitator of the exercise or learning to improve the experience when it is repeated. This may mean doing something different the very next day, or it may require reflection for the next year's class. In other words, one of its purposes is to have an opportunity to improve the experience if it is repeated.

A more subtle purpose, however, is to engage those who have been involved in the experience in evaluating their own learning. This is where the tool supports the larger purpose of the classroom: to enhance learning itself. When a kindergartner points out that he could have finished cutting out his lion more successfully if the left-handed scissors had been available when he began the project, that student is helping himself to review what he may need before he begins a similar project next time.

Classroom benefits

Students of all ages love to review what they have done and talk about what they might have done differently. Plus-delta charts help to structure that kind of review and improve the dialogue students will have with each other and their teacher about their learning.

Metacognition, or the understanding of one's learning process as it is going on, is a vital phase of knowledge building. A tool such as plus-delta supports this phase by promoting self-reflection and review of the learning process.

By facilitating the kind of reflection that the kindergartner had about the left-handed scissors, the teacher is helping that child to mature in his approach to learning tasks. Of course, plus-delta charts cannot do this by themselves without a supportive environment and a wide variety of other techniques and approaches. But maybe it can be a beginning.

Example: Leaf reports

Leaf reports represent one of those subtle but critical cultural ties that everyone shares. It may be safe to say that every elementary school child in the history of the American education system has put together a leaf report, with pressed and dried leaves representing the available regional trees. The variety of these reports lies not only in the differences between transitional forest areas and arid plains, but also in the way the assignment is structured. For some, it is a one-page-per-leaf project, with leaves glued and identified. For a school in Ohio, the leaf project has taken on the dimensions of a unifying task that dominates the students' autumn study for several weeks.

In this school, students begin their research with a walk around the neighborhood, asking questions and identifying trees. Their initial investigation of the scientific aspects of their leaves widens to music class, where they sing about trees, and art class, where a natural history illustrator visits to show them how leaves are drawn for scientific journals. Students examine the forestation patterns of their state, adopt trees to observe in up-close-and-personal ways, and write poems and stories about trees and forests.

At the conclusion of the project, a plus-delta chart helps students to reflect on the entire six-week unit. Throughout the project, too, they use plus-delta charts to review what they are learning and how they are managing that learning.

Here are some entries for a review of an oral report project.

+ Pluses	**Δ Deltas**
I liked hearing about other's adopted trees.	I couldn't see some of the drawings; make them bigger.
Using the microphone for reports was fun.	Someone needed to move the microphone down for short kids.
It was good to have only two reports per day.	By the time reports were over, no leaves were left on the trees; schedule reports closer together.
Earlier reports helped me to prepare my presentation.	I used a computer to draw my leaves.
Passing around reports was helpful.	Some of the reports were too long; we needed to have time limits.

Example: Chapter test

A West Virginia community college math teacher who uses flowcharts to review processes and concepts promotes plus-delta evaluation along with the flowchart discussion. For example, in evaluating what went well in learning signed number processes, students review the flowcharts that they had made earlier in the process (chapter 1). In a sense, they are reviewing the usefulness of the flowchart itself as well as the elements of their own learning. In addition, students assess the pace and sequence of the concepts that have comprised the course content, becoming increasingly accustomed to evaluating their own learning.

+ Pluses	Δ Deltas
Good review of process	Hard to read the chart
Clarified all the steps	Went too fast
Visual	Timing: Last day better
Shared by everyone	

Figure 12.2: Math flowcharts plus-delta.

Since they were creating plus-delta charts at several points in the course, the analysis of particular processes helped students prepare for the next process by focusing on what had gone well and what could have been improved. Figure 12.2 reflects their analysis of the math flowchart process.

Of course, each plus-delta evaluation will be unique, depending on the insights of those who pursue it. In this case, the chart itself will have further usefulness to the instructor as she prepares course plans for the following year. Knowing what has gone well in the instruction phase as well as in the student learning enables the instructor to anticipate areas of greater or lesser difficulty and to modify the approach accordingly.

Notable

It is important to remember that plus-delta charts are useful for reviewing and evaluating a process. Individual students or teachers might also use the technique to evaluate their own learning in a particular situation, but they are never to be used for personal criticism in a group setting. Imagine how devastating it would be for a student to have classmates list his or her leaf report as something that should be changed!

When students have an opportunity to review the processes that make up their learning, either separately or at the end of a large unit, they have amazing insights about those processes and are willing to share their ideas in an open, secure setting. You will find that it also brings out their idealism. As cynical as they may be about some things, students are interested in making experiences better for the next generation of learners. This optimism is certainly something to be encouraged.

In the case of the community college math example, the plus-delta chart had further application for the instructor in future planning. Many times, however, the chart has served its usefulness as soon as it is completed. A quick and dirty plus-delta evaluation of a single class, for example, helps to reinforce the learning that has taken place and to establish each student's role in that learning. Creation of such a chart should not be a protracted exercise, and in no case should it be extended to the next day's class period. Evaluation of the learning process is an ongoing exercise, with continuously developing aspects to examine. Getting stuck on evaluating a single class or concept interminably will cause the plus-delta exercise to become tedious and to outlive its usefulness.

Application

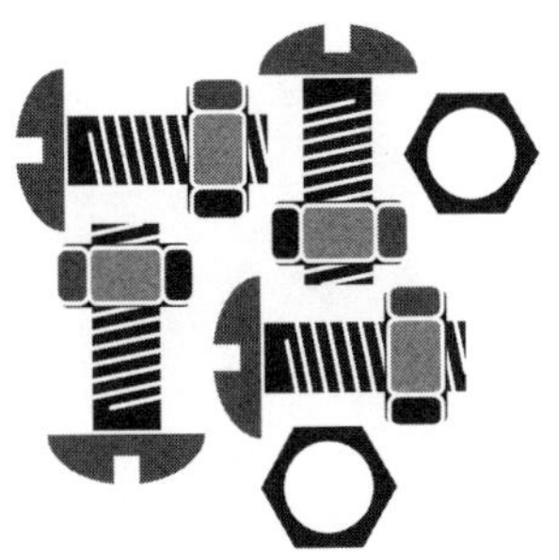

A dinner table practice in the Cleary household as our four boys were growing up was to review "good things and bad things" that could be shared during the meal—the events or situations that had brought joy or frustration during the day. Although not a structured plus-delta exercise, such conversation had some of the same effect for both parents and children. It provided an appropriate review of the day for each person, an opportunity to share in each other's successes and disappointments, and even, at times, some discussion about how things might have gone differently. Remember, of course, that the purpose of plus-delta charts is not to record good and bad things, but rather to focus on what might have been done differently to improve a process.

Try this at your dinner table as a trial run of the plus-delta exercise—but don't feel you need a flip chart in this case! Another more structured application might be found at the end of a project or field trip, or even at the conclusion of a single class. Allow several minutes to do the exercise, but try not to let the plus-delta become the focus of the class or activity.

Chapter 13

Facing Off Forces

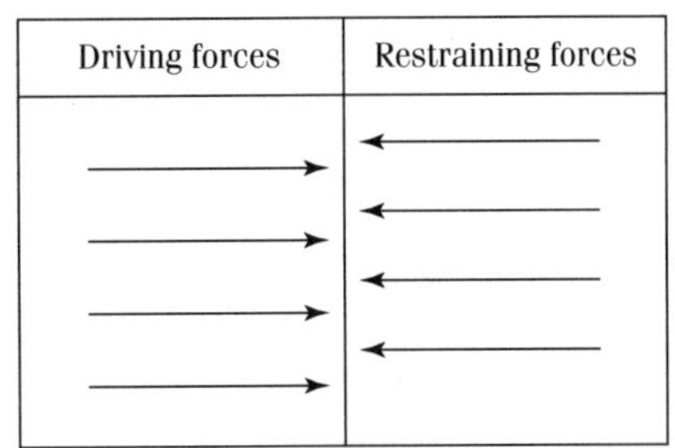

Introducing force-field analysis

Decision making is sometimes enhanced by creating lists of advantages and disadvantages. Parents and teachers have often encouraged young people to take this approach; for example, listing the pluses and minuses associated with a decision to audition for the school orchestra.

Sometimes, however, the reaction to making such a list is simply, "So what?" Even the longest list of advantages does not necessarily outweigh a single significant disadvantage such as "I'd have to practice, instead of going to the movies." So the tool, regardless of how highly recommended it may be, has only limited usefulness.

Another strategy that can be used in such a quandary is force-field analysis. This tool focuses not just on the pluses and minuses of a potential change or desirable outcome, but on the factors that actually drive the change as well as those that may restrain it.

The tool was developed by psychologist Kurt Lewin, known for his research on leadership and problem solving. Lewin (1986) saw the tool as helpful in the process of managing change.

Force-field analysis may be constructed simply as two lists—one of driving forces and one of restraining forces. Its visual potential is enhanced, however, when it is created with a line between the lists and opposing arrows for each item on the lists. Figure 13.1 provides a simple illustration.

The lists for both driving and restraining forces are generated through brainstorming, which encourages every member of the group to contribute in an open and creative atmosphere where no ideas are criticized or eliminated. Usually it is easy to think of driving forces or restraining forces alone, and this is the way the ideas should be generated, rather that trying to list both at once, in order to create the most complete list of each.

Once ideas have been generated and lists constructed, it is appropriate to post the ideas in the force-field format and analyze the results.

Analyzing the chart

One approach to force-field analysis is to match driving forces to restraining forces, wherever this can be done. Sometimes forces can cancel each other out, or at least mitigate each other's effects. For example, in a force-field analysis of the fact that so many fish are dying in a classroom aquarium, and trying to determine what might be done to keep them alive, students might observe that the food given every day as a driving force for keeping them alive and eating too much as a restraining force are actually related. It may seem that feeding the fish keeps them alive, but giving them too much food will kill them.

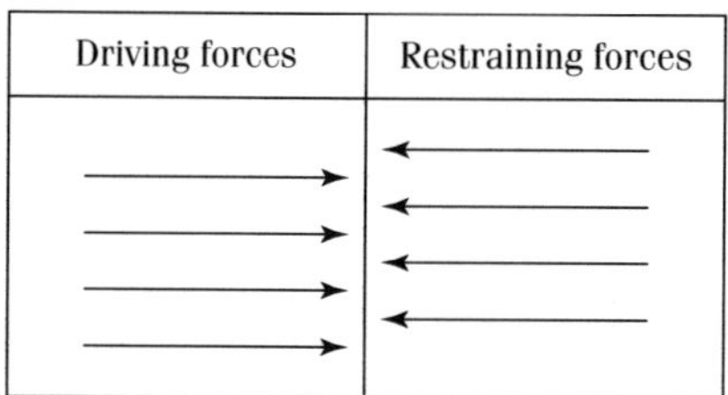

Figure 13.1: Force-field template.

Some of the forces may not seem to match, but instead present challenges of their own. At this point, it is important to entertain further dialogue about the forces and their interaction. Lewin suggested a variety of approaches to this analysis. Driving forces might be enhanced or increased; restraining forces might be diminished; or both might be done. It is interesting to see that sometimes items can reinforce each other's effect.

After sorting out and prioritizing the forces, students discuss their relative importance. Too much food, for example, may seem more important than the fact that people are looking at the fish all the time. At the bottom of the chart, they can list actions to be taken (also known as *implementation plans*), based on what the force-field analysis has revealed. An action item related to the fish example might be to measure food that is given.

Force-field analysis is especially useful when changing a situation promises to be complex or difficult. It helps to visualize the factors that are involved and to clarify the relative impact of these factors.

Example: Including Native American chants in music

An example of a force-field list made in this way is the following approach to including Native American chants in a study of music history. A group of teachers and a curriculum director were involved in this analysis, brought about in response to a focus on the importance of including various cultures in the curriculum.

In pairing driving forces to restraining forces, certain matches can be made (see Figure 13.2). The item, "could integrate with study of American history" can be matched with the item, "difficult to understand without a context." Actually, these opposing forces cancel each other out. Further discussion, however, might elicit the idea of action to ensure that the native chants are taught in conjunction with an American history unit on native cultures.

Driving and restraining forces can sometimes be seen as interchangeable, or at least creating similar impact. A driving force such as "Would help learn about rhythm" might be construed as a restraining force if it is determined that the native chants should be appreciated for more than their rhythms alone. This is where the analysis comes in; the sheer number of items is not the important consideration in force-field study, but rather the analysis of these items.

In this example, it is clear from the action items that the emotional content of the issue had been mitigated. When the teachers began the discussions, many of them felt that the curriculum decision had already been made and that they would be forced to

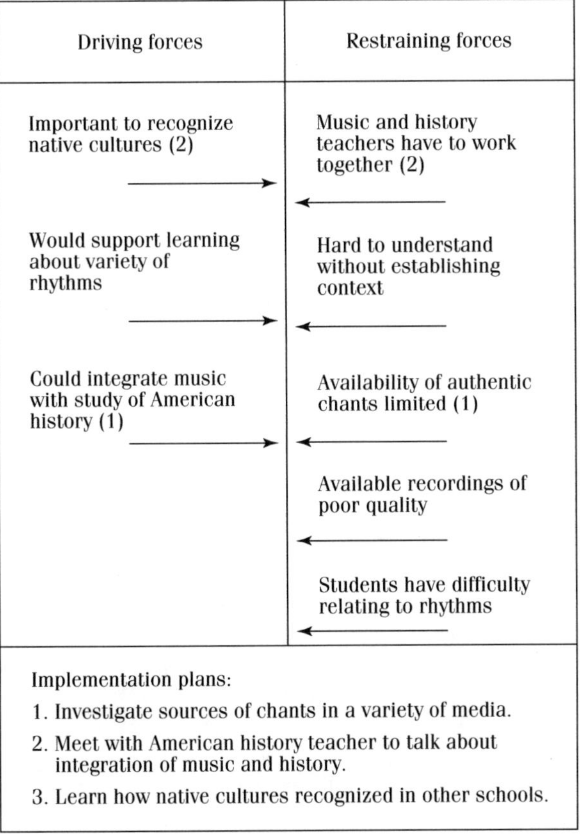

Figure 13.2: Native chants force-field analysis.

include Native American music in their classes. Instead, they were able to see the benefit of considering the addition and then to initiate actions that do not represent givens in terms of the outcome but rather provide a way to expand their understanding and make a decision based on information.

Example: Homework

Why do homework? Even fairly young students have sometimes developed an aversion to doing homework and a concomitant recognition of the fact that they must do it for a variety of reasons. Fourth graders were involved in force-field analysis related to doing homework (Figure 13.3).

This may be seen as a trivial analysis, since student comments are somewhat predictable. The outcome of the exercise was not only to focus on the shared problem of homework, but also, in the case of the teacher, to identify how much of the motivation for doing the work is external—for money, praise, or avoidance of pain. The teacher began to focus on the second action item, enlisting the students' help in determining ways to make the homework more relevant to their learning.

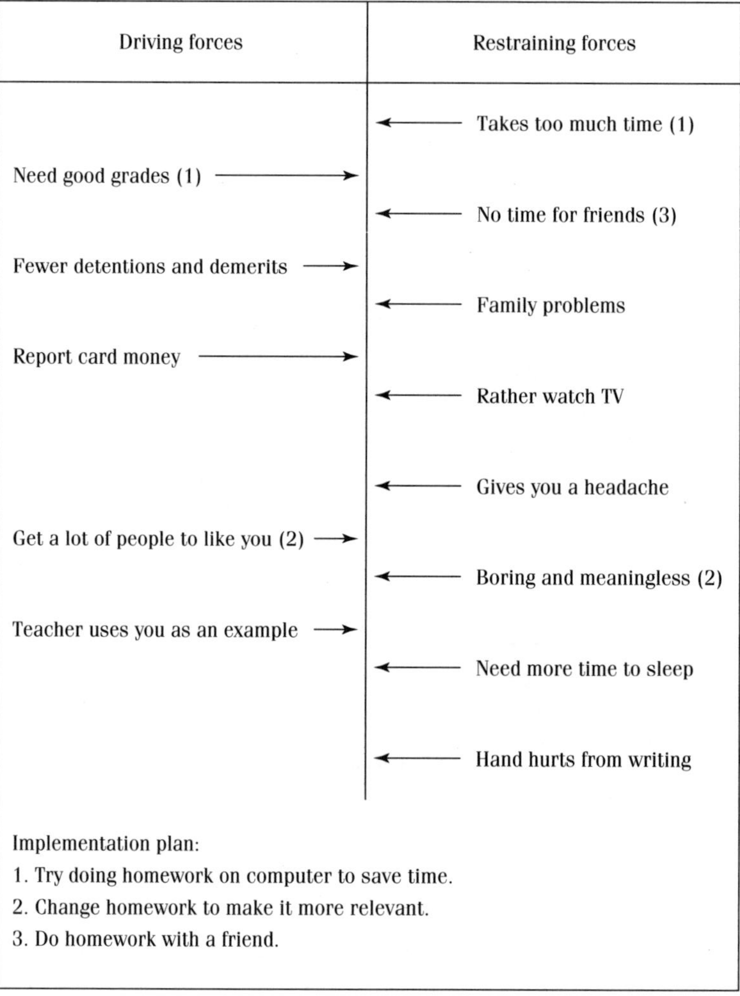

Figure 13.3: Homework analysis force field.

Example: Science class

Although force-field analysis usually addresses an issue involving change, creative teachers can always come up with new applications. An elementary science teacher used force-field analysis with students who were studying the emergence of butterflies from cocoons (see Figure 13.4).

In this case, the force field helped students identify the delicate balance in the process rather than to focus on action items or an implementation plan to bring about change. This is an interesting approach to force field. The analysis opened up opportunities for further study and questions. How does a larval butterfly get its nourishment? What are the

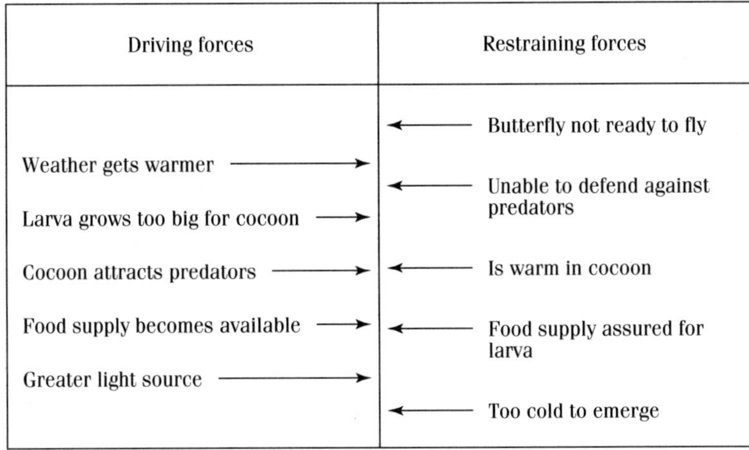

Figure 13.4: Cocoons and butterflies force field.

predators for butterflies, both in and outside the cocoon? These and other questions were discussed during the analysis.

Example: Journalism class

Force-field analysis helped students in an independent school's journalism class to think creatively about changing the course from an emphasis on print journalism to broadcast media. Brainstorming elicited the driving and restraining forces shown in Figure 13.5 and helped student focus on specific action items that would address the course focus.

Some of the driving forces balanced, or cancelled, restraining forces. For example, the fact that equipment was considered obsolete was balanced by the availability of at least some equipment.

Action items that were garnered from further brainstorming included the following:

1. Bring equipment to the classroom to try it out.
2. Identify available resources for classroom use through library research.
3. Introduce technical skills by using the expertise of a visitor from a local access channel.
4. Through a field trip, see and understand how a local television newsroom produces the news.

The older the students, the more appropriate their input will be. Even for young children, providing choices about what and how they will study will enhance their involvement in the outcome and improve their learning.

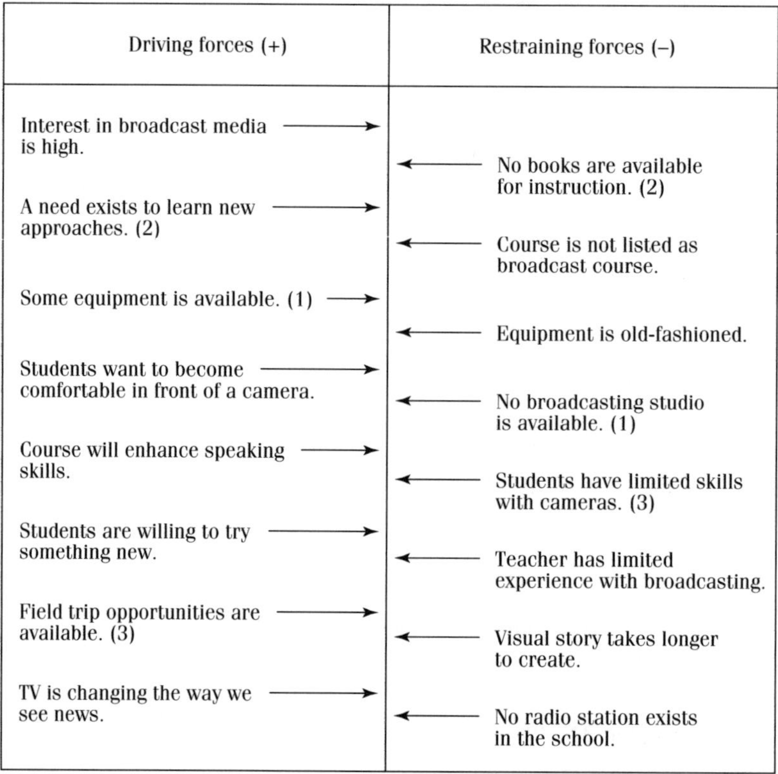

Figure 13.5: Changing focus of course from print journalism to broadcast.

Notable

Teachers who use force-field analysis to address issues of change swear by the tool and find amazing ways to apply it; from crisis situations involving playground incidents to students' complaints that their lockers are too small. It is important to reiterate the fact that force field is more than addition and subtraction of identified factors, but involves analysis of these factors and ways they can lead to specific actions.

Like adults, children love to feel that they are taking action to address a problem or change. When the action is based on rational and deliberate analysis rather than a just-do-anything approach, it is far more likely to prepare students for future analysis of problems or changes.

Application

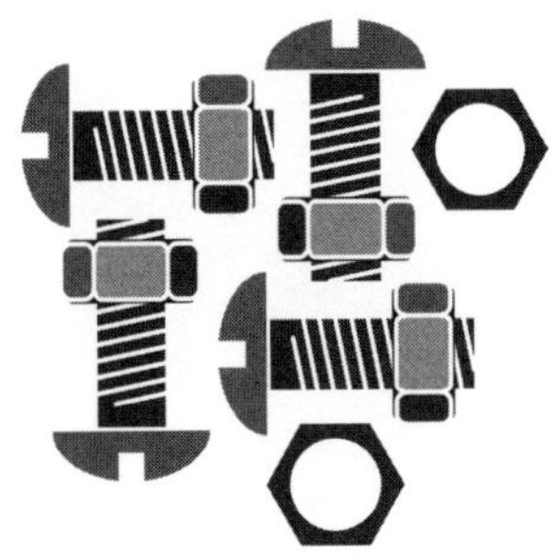

Force-field analysis is often used by groups of teachers. Think of a nagging, unresolved issue facing your team: Scheduling, supervision, planning time, and responsibility for discipline are issues faced by nearly every group of teachers and administrators. Often, a great deal of time is spent in discussing issues with little hope of resolution; but force-field analysis can help to move a group in a positive direction. Pick one of these troubling items or another that plagues your team and try a force-field analysis to help yourselves move forward toward resolution of the issues involved.

Reference

Lewin, Kurt. 1986. *The Lewin legacy: Field theory in current practice*. Berlin and New York: Springer-Verlag.

Chapter 14

Narrowing the Focus

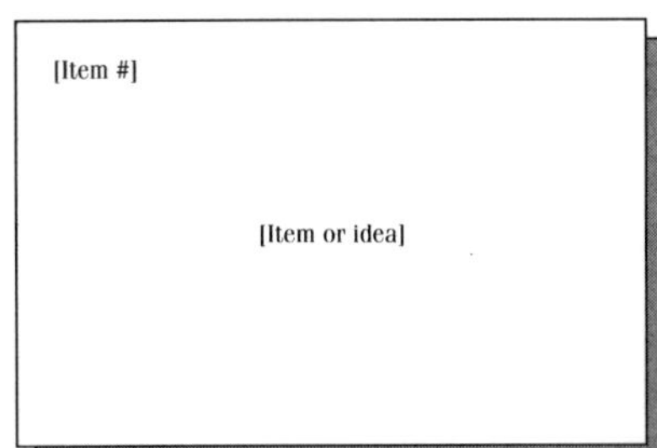

Introducing nominal group technique

"If the routine jobs are constantly decreasing and the jobs requiring creativeness are increasing, then clearly a burden falls on the educational system—the burden of sending children out to earn their living equipped with original, creative, and inquiring minds in addition to high levels of knowledge" (Jay 1968, 99).

Brainstorming, or generating ideas in a fertile environment for sharing, supports this kind of creativeness. Often, brainstorming alone is enough to generate a variety of ideas and serve the purpose of a classroom exercise. Sometimes, however, it becomes important to go beyond these ideas and identify those that will actually be pursued; or those that are most important; or the ideas that the team members like best.

One approach might be to simply vote on the ideas that have been generated during brainstorming. If a group of children has brainstormed about appropriate treats for a holiday party, voting will eliminate some of the treats. The process of voting, however, often creates a sense of competition—my ideas versus your ideas. Voting can even stimulate lobbying from members of the group for support of their own ideas. If the class decides by voting that Tootsie Rolls are not going to be served, the child who suggested that idea is likely to feel as if he or she has lost in the election process.

A less-destructive way to settle on one idea from a large list is that of nominal group technique, an instrument often used for planning and group process. By using this tool, a group reaches consensus rather than compromise. That is, individuals are much less likely to feel as if their ideas are not worthy of pursuit, since a final list reflects selections that the entire group can agree to, even when these have not been their own ideas. If input is considered from all members of a group, they are more likely to feel ownership of the final outcome.

Generating ideas

Brainstorming allows for the generation of large numbers of ideas. Its power lies in the creative energy it harnesses, so that participants are not afraid to offer ideas that may be judged stupid or impractical by other members of the group. In fact, if brainstorming is done correctly, the ideas are not subject to any judgment—positive or negative—from other group members. Everyone participates equally, since each group member speaks one at a time in an orderly way.

When controversy or conflict is likely to deter the generation of ideas in brainstorming, a Crawford slip process can be used. In this technique, individuals write their ideas on small slips of paper rather than expressing them orally. When they are finished,

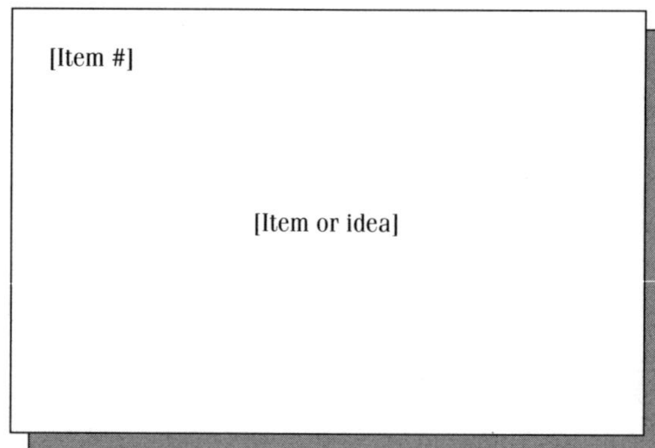

Figure 14.1: Crawford slip method notecard.

participants will have a small stack of these slips, each one representing a single idea (see Figure 14.1). If this method is used, the ideas can be collected by a facilitator and then listed so that everyone can see them, and the nominal group technique can proceed.

When the brainstorming is finished and the ideas are all visible to the entire group, there is a sense that every item has equal status with every other item, since it emerged from the creative contribution of one of the team members. Everyone may feel quite satisfied with the list, and at times the entire list is worthy of consideration. For example, this is true if the purpose is to think of as many different examples of a concept as possible.

Often, however, it is necessary to narrow down the list or to select a few of the ideas for further consideration or action. This need provides an opportunity to discuss each idea, not to develop support for it, but to clarify it and elicit reactions to it. It is also important to eliminate duplication of ideas. If an essentially identical idea is expressed in two different ways, the final voting may be split unnecessarily. It is important, however, that the people who suggested an idea agree that there is duplication. An idea should never be eliminated without this agreement.

Analyzing the output

As in an election based only on popular appeal, voting on a series of ideas is likely to become only a popularity contest, where people vote for their favorites, regardless of the criteria. To avoid this approach, a group must agree on the criteria that will be used for selecting items with the most importance or highest priority.

A list of criteria related to an analysis of ways to expand the influence of the school newspaper included the following items. The criteria stipulated that the final idea must

1. Be feasible.
2. Fall within fund-raising potential or existing budget.
3. Be consistent with the purpose of the school newspaper.
4. Involve student actions, not just administrative input.

By focusing on the constraints that must be exercised, these criteria help to eliminate some of the ideas that have been listed. Why not list these constraints before the original brainstorming exercise?

In order to generate the best and most creative ideas, it is useful to pursue a solution that is not within the confines of past thinking or rules, but gets out of the box of tradition or expectation. So the first values in brainstorming are creativity and imagination.

The criteria for selection help to limit the ideas with respect to practical potential—a second value that is important if the ideas are to be implemented. This value should be introduced only after the creative energy of the group has elicited a wide variety of ideas.

The final stage of nominal group technique is that of voting and ranking the ideas. The group determines how many ideas should appear on the list, and each individual selects that number of top priorities. For example, if five items are to be selected, each participant would use five cards or slips of paper, with one item per card and a number corresponding to that person's ranking of the item. If someone were to consider item 3, "Develop Web site," for example, as the idea that conforms best to the criteria and offers the best possibility for solving the problem, the number in the lower corner would be 5, or the greatest weight it could get (see Figure 14.2).

In tallying the results, each person's votes are written next to the item on the list, so everyone can see them all. Figure 14.3 shows that item 3, "Develop Web site" has been ranked second by one person, third by another, and fourth by another participant, in addition to the 5 vote noted in Figure 14.2.

The ensuing discussion will focus on the choices that have been made, with appropriate analysis of the rankings given. It might be that an item with the votes indicated in Figure 14.3 has more support than another item, even though it was not everyone's first choice. Group members look for inconsistencies among voters' rankings (from high to low), items that reflect great support, and items that have received too few votes. These items are then discussed. Usually, group members do not all select the same first choice, but there may be a handful of ideas with which they can all be comfortable. The objective of nominal group technique is to identify these items, discuss the objections that may arise from analysis, and determine whether the group has reached consensus. By showing

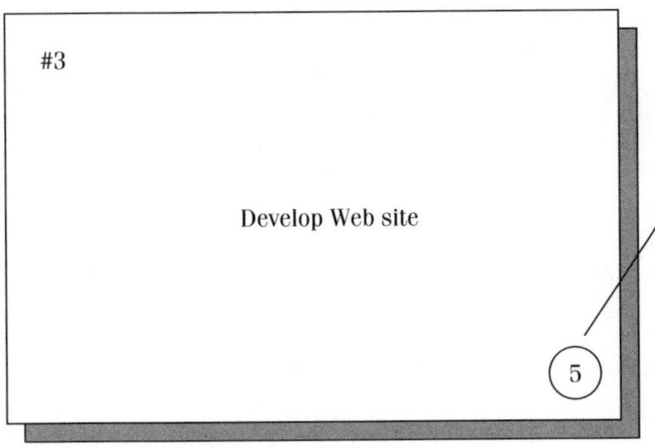

Figure 14.2: Preliminary voting on rank.

1. Mail to alumni. 4-2-2
2. Use variety in stories. 3-4-4
3. Develop Web site. 4-3-2-5
4. Invite guest writers. 1
5. Have parents buy ads. 3-2-5-5
6. Use more artwork. 4-2-4
7. Get a photographer. 4-4-3-5
8. Have more sports stories. 2-1
9. Put suggestion box in hall. 2
10. Write student profiles. 2-3
11. Do features on hobbies. 2-2
12. Have computer tips. 1
13. Review music. 4-4-5-5
14. Review movies. 3-4-4-5
15. Make newspaper bigger. 1-2-1
16. Change design. 3-2-2-3
17. Use color. 1-1-4-3
18. List student e-mail addresses. 1-1-3-2

Figure 14.3: Nominal group technique voting.

every vote (not just a cumulative tally), nominal group technique helps participants discern the kind of support each item has. "Can I live with it?" is the final operative question for each group member to ask. If the answer is yes, the final choice represents an idea that may not be everyone's first choice, but nonetheless is something that every person can agree to and support.

If every member cannot support the items selected by the preliminary vote, a second vote is taken, and a third if necessary, until participants can all support the item selected. The idea at this stage is not to win, but to explore a variety of approaches to each idea.

Example: Planning a menu

An astronomy camp-out provided an opportunity for a group of 10 fifth graders to plan the event and prepare the details (including budgets) for meals, sleeping arrangements, and activities. Each fifth grader had, it seemed, a different idea about what would make a good dinner menu. To avoid voting on every food item, the group decided that it should select the main entree and that a smaller group would decide what foods would accompany that entree.

Brainstorming elicited the following list.

1. Pizza
2. Tacos
3. Hamburgers
4. Chinese food
5. Barbecued ribs
6. Spaghetti
7. Egg rolls
8. Lasagna
9. Hot dogs
10. Macaroni and cheese
11. Chili

12. Lobster
13. Pasta
14. Crab cakes
15. Roast beef
16. Pork chops
17. Fried shrimp

After generating the list and numbering the items on it, the students discussed each item, eliciting clarification that included how each food might be prepared. A number of the fifth graders knew of a good recipe for several items on the list. Some of the discussion focused on allergies and food preferences, including religious dietary constraints. Although their focus was on selecting menu items, it is clear that they learned a great deal about each other in the process of this discussion.

The selection criteria that the group determined included these four constraints.

1. Easy to fix outdoors.
2. Does not violate religious dietary restrictions.
3. Fits in the budget.
4. No one is allergic to it.

This list eliminated a number of items, and the preliminary vote narrowed the field substantially. In selecting the final menu, the fifth graders felt good about the choices they had made. Even those who were not looking forward to preparing and eating the selected food items felt that they had a role in selecting them and had a greater appreciation for the many factors that had been considered in the choices.

Example: School dismissal

The group of fourth graders who made the flowchart related to school dismissal (see Figure 1.1) had generated a very broad list of suggestions. Addressing ways to provide more time during the day to do homework, they listed everything from dropping a subject to eliminating recess. Some of the ideas they thought of included the following:

- Drop music.
- Use less time for gym.
- Take less time to get started in the morning.
- Do homework during lunch.
- Let custodians clean up classroom.
- Have shorter class periods.
- Have longer class periods with homework included at the end.
- Have a shorter lunch period.
- Change the bus schedule.
- Do homework during computer class.

- Have art teacher come to our classroom to save time.
- Eliminate morning sharing.
- Take less time getting ready to leave.

The value of the exercise is clear when the students' final flowchart is examined. It is based on their selection of improving the dismissal process and thereby taking less time in getting ready to go home each day. As they reviewed their selection criteria, the fourth graders realized that they needed to make a change that they could do themselves. They could not effect change in the length of the school day, the bus schedule, or the lunchroom schedule, since these had impacts on other classes or constituencies.

Notable

Approaching the dismissal-time problem in a less creative way, the teacher could have just told the class that it would have to take less time getting ready to leave in the afternoon. The results are easy to imagine: Undoubtedly, nothing would change, and, in fact, most children would probably not recall hearing the teacher's admonitions about this issue. The difference is that when the teacher gives directions about what to do, the problem no longer belongs to the students, but is the teacher's. When students acknowledge a problem and want to address it, the power of their participation is clear. Brainstorming and nominal group technique help to make this transfer of responsibility take place.

Just as in the case of the other tools and strategies that have been presented, it is important to remember that the point of using the tool is not the tool itself, but to support the learning objective beyond that tool. The facilitator of the process (usually the teacher) must be alert in order to sense whether the tool is serving its purpose, or when it has become ponderous or artificial—and adjust accordingly.

Application

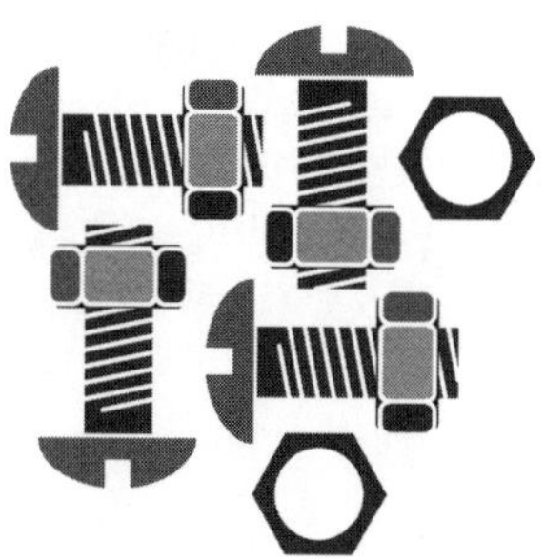

Undoubtedly you have used brainstorming in many different ways. The next time you have created a list of ideas with your class or colleagues, apply nominal group technique in order to narrow the list and select the group's final choices. One application might be to have students brainstorm the ways that they can demonstrate their mastery of a particular skill. They will come up with lots of ideas, particularly since they will know that the strategy-of-choice for demonstrating mastery is often an exam. Nominal group technique will eliminate those suggestions that will not work, and those that demand far too much time to execute, depending on selection criteria that are used. You and your class will end up with a list of viable projects, reports, and multimedia presentations that will serve nicely to show how well students have mastered a particular concept or skill.

Reference

Jay, Antony. 1968. *Management and Machiavelli: An inquiry into the politics of corporate life*. Hinsdale, Ill.: Dryden Press.

Chapter 15

Framing Appropriate Questions

Introducing questioning techniques

When a popular cable television channel for young people had an opportunity to ask a question of just-elected President Bill Clinton, many viewers were shocked to hear the question: Did the President, the interviewer wondered, prefer boxer shorts or jockey shorts?

Probably no one was more appalled by this question than that interviewer's band of former teachers. Remember, these were not spontaneous third graders, but high school and college journalists. The question reflected not only the current trend of in-your-face, brash journalism that is frequently seen on broadcast media, but from the point of view of the educational system, it represented a superficial and trivial approach to a unique opportunity to interview the President—a tremendous waste of a learning moment.

Traditionally, educational systems have been designed with the primary purpose of providing information to students, rather than emphasizing the skills of knowledge building and learning that the future will demand. As this need becomes clearer and schools jockey to equip their students for the next century, one of the essential tools in the panoply of strategies will be that of framing appropriate questions. Since students have traditionally been expected to answer rather than ask questions, this tool will become increasingly important.

Analyzing questions

What makes a good question?

Every teacher has had an experience such as taking a group of young people on a field trip with the advance admonition, "Be sure to ask some good questions," only to have eight-year-old Carla ask a docent in a local museum, "How much do they pay you to do these tours?" or "Why is your hair blue?" Anyone can spot wrong answers, but "it takes a creative mind to spot wrong questions" (Jay 1968, 101).

As technology enhances access to experts in all fields, asking appropriate questions will become increasingly critical. After setting up an on-line chat with a university professor who is an expert on Middle Eastern women and their roles, no teacher wants to hear a student ask a trivial or embarrassing question like "So, why do they wear those funny veils?"

How do students learn to frame good questions? As they facilitate this process, teachers will find that asking good questions not only prepares students for isolated interviewing opportunities with the director of the Peace Corps, but more importantly, helps them reflect on and expand their own learning.

Because of the nature of the tool, this chapter will focus on the characteristics of good questions and models for building learning, rather than reflecting the format of other chapters.

Classroom benefits

As part of a system of communication, questions have a variety of purposes, from expressing an understanding of someone's feelings (Are you feeling nervous about your upcoming speech?) to summarizing what someone has just said (Are you suggesting that we should have more children on the cleanup team?).

The questions that are fundamental to expanding knowledge are those that have been developed in the context of what is already known. To enlarge the already-learned by adding new knowledge is at the heart of the education process. This chapter will focus primarily on this kind of question.

A learning model developed by Marlene Scardemalia and Carl Bereiter (1993) puts questions at the heart of knowledge building. If a child is pursuing the study of cell structure, for example, he or she might begin with a statement-question such as "I wonder about. . . ." If the student has already studied cell structure, the areas of wondering will be more sophisticated than if there has been no prior knowledge. A very young child, for example, might begin with "I wonder how a cell works," while a seventh grader who is preparing a project for a science fair, will wonder whether cell structure is altered by breakdowns in the autoimmune system or how DNA mapping is related to more traditional understandings of cells.

From the time a question is formulated, learning can begin to expand in ways that are unique to a particular child and his or her background. A teacher can facilitate the process of formulating sound initial questions through a dialogue with a student about what is already known.

Questioning is a good way to help develop thoughtful young learners, who continue to think about what they see and hear, rather than dismissing it as an isolated fact or event. It also provides a way to enhance participation in class discussions and activities, creating an environment of mutually supportive learning.

Recalling again that students learn in different ways, oral questions support the learning styles of those who remember and learn best when they hear something. They may recall a question or a response from a discussion far more clearly than if they read it from a book.

Strategies

Cause-and-effect diagrams as starters

Many of the tools described throughout this book can be used to help young people develop questions. Cause-and-effect diagrams, for example, can focus on deep analysis. The five whys are often urged. If students have created a cause-and-effect diagram to reflect the causes of the Civil War, one of these causes might be, "the South's weakening economy." Students might develop questions along these lines.

1. *Why was the South's economy weakening?*
   There was less dependence on cotton internationally.
2. *Why had dependence on Southern cotton declined?*
   Fashions in Europe demanded more use of silk.
3. *Why were people using more silk?*
   Trade with Asia had increased.
4. *Why had trade to Asia expanded?*
   Asian trade increased through improved shipping technologies.
5. *Why had technology improved?*
   An emphasis on scientific method affected the shipping industry.

By means of persistent questioning, young historians can begin to see the tremendous interrelationship of world events, even when they may seem on first analysis to be isolated.

Spider diagrams and interview questions

Spider diagrams, relations charts, force-field analysis, and other tools can also be useful in developing questioning skills. In the case of spider diagrams, the expanding web represents increasingly focused topics. The same technique applies to questions.

A fifth-grade class was preparing mock interviews of historical figures, role-playing with classmates to gain insight about a particular era or historical event. The students used spider diagrams to create questions for their interviews and to anticipate the follow-up questions that they might need to ask. They had begun their study with a series of research projects, so the students had already garnered a great deal of information about the persons they planned to interview. This kind of information is critical if students are to get beyond simple, closed questions that will elicit only the most bare and superficial information.

A student who planned to interview Jane Addams started with a series of questions about the specific work Addams did at Hull House. Without the prior research, she might have framed questions such as, "Where was Hull House?" "What did you do there?" "Whom did you serve?" and so on. Instead, she was able to create interesting, provocative questions that would have provided good material for an interview on public radio. Her questions included the following:

- How did you formulate your vision for Hull House in its earliest stages?
- What inspired you to share your vision of a facility to care for people with these needs?
- Will you describe the financial challenges you had in beginning your work?
- Who were your supporters as you began to create the foundations of Hull House?
- What were your relations with the health care professionals in Chicago?

The student had used a spider diagram to create questions that were related, so she did not find herself jumping superficially from topic to topic when she conducted the actual interview.

Expanded tests

Tests, both written and oral, have a real place in classroom learning, especially when they are given with the spirit of stimulating and expanding that learning, rather than simply measuring acquisition of facts. There are times, however, when this technique supports learning as well.

Even the infamous multiple-choice test can become such a learning tool. The typical multiple-choice test, let it be said, is not only *not* a learning enhancer, but it also misleads students and limits expanded thinking. In its traditional mode, such a test often suggests to students that there is only one right answer. As is known from the complexity of life, this is rarely the case. Depending on perspective, there are often several ways to respond to a question.

W. Edwards Deming's suggestion about multiple-choice tests is a useful one. He encouraged teachers who give these tests to direct their students not to find the best answer to the question, but instead to respond by indicating the circumstances in which each of the answers given might be correct. Let's look at a simple factual question: When was the Declaration of Independence signed?

a) July 4, 1776 b) July 14, 1789 c) August 1776 d) June 1788

Students might respond correctly with *c* to elicit the factual connection between the question and an answer, recalling that although the document had been written by the Fourth of July, it took until August for signers to complete their work. For the other answers, they would have to become more creative. One approach might be to alter the question to fit the answers given; so for choice *b*, a question might be, "When was the Bastille stormed during the French Revolution?" or for choice *d*, "When did the final state ratify the Constitution?"

If the original question had been framed, "How are the following dates related to the development of colonial government?" students would be challenged to differentiate among them. One date, for example, might be the actual completion of the Declaration of Independence in Philadelphia. Another important date was when the Declaration was presented to King George III of England; another when it was permanently ensconced in its museum site; and so on. Such questions should be designed not to encourage isolated memorization of dates, but rather to enhance students' understanding of several related events and their interactions.

Teachers and students alike respond when they are given opportunities to use their brains. Such questions encourage creativity, build curiosity, and make connections among what might otherwise be unrelated facts.

Improving questioning

Teachers can model good questioning by understanding the kinds of questions they ask. A closed question, for example, can be answered with a simple yes-or-no response. Of course, sometimes this is required. "Emma, is the light off in the classroom?" is not a question that requires discussion or expansion. But closed questions can cut off communication, implying that there is nothing else to say. "Did the mixture fizz when you dropped the tablet into the test tube?" can be easily answered, with no need for further explanation.

Closed questions can be used deliberately to get information quickly or even to shut down a student who is likely to go on and on with an answer or who dominates a class. A school counselor, who has heard a student's excuses about what happened and why it was not that student's fault and a million tangents related to the incident, can productively pull such a student up short by saying, "But were you in the rest room when the paper was stuffed in the toilet?" This approach will limit the young person's response appropriately and help to focus the discussion.

An open question invites more insight and discussion. Reframing a previous question, the teacher who asks, "What happened when you put the tablet into the test tube?" is likely to get expanded responses from students and to open them to further discussion about what they had seen. In the case of the incident in the rest room, it might even be useful to begin by saying, "Tell me what happened in the rest room during recess." Although this is not structured as a question, it becomes an open question because it invites an expanded response. To stimulate children's observations related to classroom study, a comment like "Tell me what's happening to the leaves in your yard" opens the opportunity to discussion in ways that "Have the leaves fallen from your trees yet?" may not. Older children probably need this kind of encouragement far more than younger ones, who sometimes tell everything they know regardless of the question.

Communications experts advise ways to use questions to verify feelings and to demonstrate active listening. These are certainly important aspects of questioning in the classroom and elsewhere. Since the focus is on expanding learning and helping students to build knowledge, however, these issues will not be addressed here.

Tossing questions

A kind of classroom game that can encourage the habit of formulating questions begins with a teacher asking a question. Typically, the teacher's question elicits a flurry of hand waving from students eager to answer and a flutter of eyes cast downward from those who want to escape the question.

In this technique, the teacher asks a question, directing it to a particular student. That student can either answer the question and create a related question, or pass the original question on by calling on another student in the classroom. The second student can do the same, and so on, until everyone has been asked a question and been given an opportunity to respond or to frame a new question.

Evaluating the overall quality of the questions can be pursued as students become more comfortable with the game. A plus-delta chart may help to focus this evaluation.

At the very least, the strategy keeps students alert rather than waiting for the teacher's voice to draw them back to attention. At its best, the question-toss helps students to reinforce each other's learning. Initially, they may want to put a classmate on the spot or embarrass someone who is not likely to know an answer, but this will change. They will become increasingly comfortable both answering and asking questions, and will find that satisfaction comes from learning rather than from making their classmates uncomfortable. Some students will deliberately ask questions related to a classmate's own interest or even go easy on someone who becomes anxious about the question process.

Other questions

Analogies provide a good basis for new thinking. They help students to compare and contrast, and to recognize that all analogies eventually break down, since nothing is really identical to anything else. Asking how things are related creates a clear sense of how they are unrelated as well. Questions such as, "How is a blackboard like a computer?" or "How is the card catalog like a grocery store?" can engender discussion. Everyone in the group knows at least one similarity and one difference. The technique paves the way for more sophisticated analogies, enhancing comparison-contrast thinking. The more closely related ideas are, the more a student will focus on differences between them. The question, "How was the Spanish–American War like the Civil War?" will send their minds scurrying for information about both events.

Another approach involves asking for new perspectives. The question, "How would you feel about industry in the Northwest if you were a salmon?" demands a new orientation toward an issue. Writing teachers have often adopted this technique, asking students to create stories from a particular viewpoint or an unusual perspective.

Starting backward

Students are all familiar with the popular game-show approach of providing an answer and then asking for the appropriate question to match that answer. This strategy can create an opportunity not only for fun, but also to help students think about concepts from a variety of perspectives; both to create an answer and to formulate the question that might be answered by it.

While the temptation in playing this game might be to trivialize the learning in order to make the question difficult, this temptation is diminished when competition is minimized. If students are playing in order to expand their learning or review what they know, rather than simply to win, they are likely to develop thoughtful answers and questions.

The news interview as stimulus

Students who are learning how to develop stories or news articles based on interviews find that they must prepare in advance in order to take full advantage of the opportunity that is presented in an interview. As they do so, they are likely to create a number of questions that are not necessarily related, and the result will be a collection of isolated information, but very little learning.

Encouraging students to practice interviews where they may start with only one question and must pursue a line of questioning with a series of follow-up comments or questions helps them to develop deeper analysis in their stories.

By beginning with a single event, such as, "What has been your role in securing a crossing guard for our school?" students can build on the answer that is given. If enough preparation has been given to developing that single question, students will be able to anticipate some of the answers that will be given and may be able to think of several potential follow-up questions even in advance of the interview.

The best follow-up questions, however, are those that are genuinely elicited by the interview itself. These demand close attention to the responses that are given, and thoughtful analysis of how those responses can provide further strands in the fabric of an interesting story.

Application

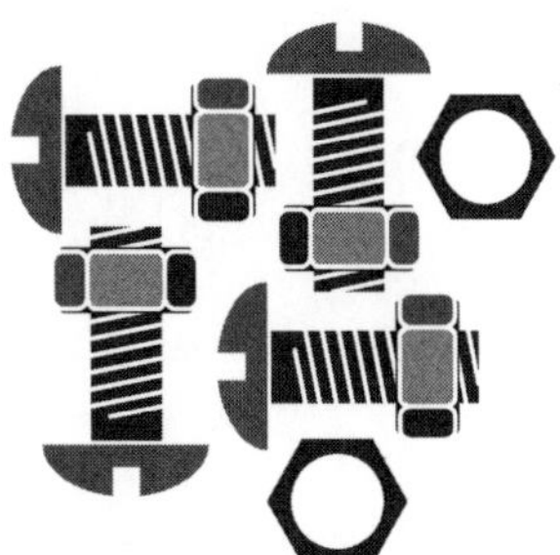

Try one of the strategies that have been mentioned here, either with your entire class or in a small group of students. Think of other strategies you have tried that build on the important role of questioning. Try using the electronic network to make contact with people who can answer your questions.

References

Jay, Antony. 1968. *Management and Machiavelli: An inquiry into the politics of corporate life*. Hinsdale, Ill.: Dryden Press.

Scardemalia, Marlene, and Carl Bereiter. 1993. *Surpassing ourselves: An inquiry into the nature and implications of expertise*. Chicago: Open Court Press.

Chapter 16

Putting It All Together in One Place

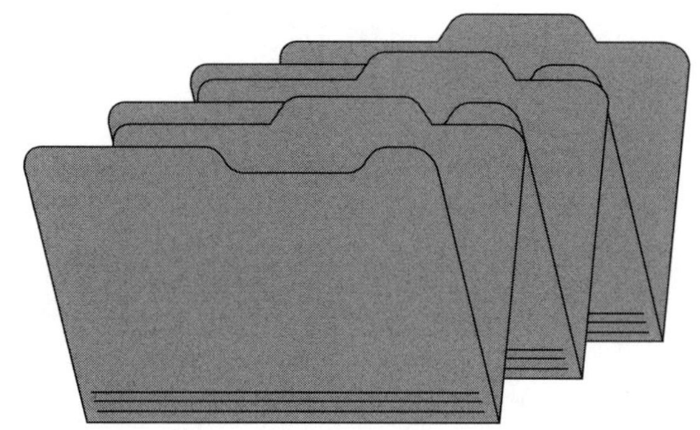

Introducing portfolio management

No, this chapter is not an introduction to financial investment strategy. It is a reminder of another tool that has become a mainstay of the teacher-student dialogue.

Student portfolios have become standard fixtures in classrooms, where the records represent new approaches to assessment as well as documentation of student work for reevaluation and reflection. Statewide use of portfolios as part of student assessment in Vermont has helped students to think more deeply and creatively about their work (O'Neil 1993). What goes into these portfolios, and how are they used?

Early childhood portfolios often contain photographs as well as samples of children's work. In secondary education, portfolios represent a way to document improvement in the writing process. Teachers who encourage their students to revise their writing until they are satisfied with it use portfolios to keep various versions of each paper. At the end of a term, the contents of the portfolio provide a basis for dialogue between student and teacher to assess progress, recall roadblocks, and celebrate learning.

Portfolios offer a way to document progress for parents as well. During conferences parents review student work and activities throughout a term, with the student actually guiding the parents through the portfolio. This practice opens dialogue among student, teacher, and parents about learning successes and challenges, thus changing the dynamic of communication in significant ways.

Learning competency matrix

A number of the strategies that have been introduced in this book can support the use of portfolios and their purpose. Another, the learning competency matrix developed by David Langford, is a particularly useful tool in this endeavor (Langford and Cleary 1995). It is maintained by the students, depending on their evaluation of where they are in the learning process and that of their teachers.

Classroom benefits

Tools such as the learning matrix support portfolio communication and enhance the engagement of students in their learning processes. This tool is based on Bloom's (1956) learning taxonomy, familiar to educators for several decades. It represents an acknowledgment of the ways that learning evolves as a process, diminishing the sense that something is either learned or not learned. This binomial approach has sometimes characterized traditional understandings of learning.

By evaluating their learning and seeing it as part of a continuum, students become increasingly engaged in the process of learning itself. In effect, the learning shifts from a passive reception of information to an active quest for learning improvement.

Carl Jung commented that learning is "not a vessel to be filled, but a fire to be ignited." Traditional classrooms, with an emphasis on transfer of information, emphasized novice learning rather than expert learning (Scardemalia and Bereiter 1993). In expert learning, students repeatedly return to a once-learned concept, refining and modifying it, and incorporating it into other learning. Traditional learning is often fragmented and isolated; students study a chapter, take a test, and move on, with little occasion to connect the content of that chapter to other chapters or other disciplines.

A learning competency matrix underscores the evolving nature of learning. At first, students may only be able to recognize terminology related to a concept. From that beginning, the learning can progress to increased sophistication with the concept.

Example: American literature

With the variety of skills and concepts that are relevant in studying a work of literature, the competency matrix helps to address those skills and concepts in the larger context of learning. For example, *The Adventures of Huckleberry Finn* is not simply learned. Instead, by reading Mark Twain's novel students learn something new about character, as well as about larger themes such as justice, honesty, and compassion. The novel, of course, does not teach everything there is to know about these concepts. Before reading Mark Twain, learners have already been exposed to these ideas in a variety of formats, both in life experiences and through literature, and will continue to gain insight about these important concepts after finishing the novel. The book will only contribute to the understandings, not teach them in any final way.

The competency matrix helps students to understand that this is the case. Accrued understandings and skills are reflected in the students' assessment of learning. Knowing something may mean only recognizing it or being able to define it (level 1). But with increasing sophistication and enhanced understanding, that knowledge may develop to levels of analysis, synthesis, and evaluation of the ideas.

Anyone who read *Huck Finn* as a child and then returned to it as an adult understands, too, that simply reading a novel (or studying the Civil War in a text book) once does not complete one's knowledge about it. Returning to it later, after other experiences have contributed to one's maturity and understanding, will be a different experience entirely.

The competency matrix, shown in Figure 16.1, supports understanding learning as a continuum; that is, an ongoing process that is never finished. In the example, certain concepts and skills related to the study of Ernest Hemingway's stories are listed, based on a high school literature class. Students fill in the chart as they make progress in learning

Name ____________________

Beginning date ____________________

English 11: Hemingway stories

Outcomes	Competencies	Level I	Level II	Level III	Level IV	Level V	Level VI
		Knowledge	Understanding/ comprehension	Application	Analysis	Synthesis	Appreciation/ evaluation
	Dialogue						
	Purpose						
	Elements						
Identify characteristics of Hemingway's work	Creating dialogue						
	Building characters						
	Setting						
	Description						
	Technique						
Demonstrate understanding of code hero concept							
	Plot and structure						
	Story length						
	Organization						
	Character						
	Code hero						
	Women in stories						
	Relationships						
	Motivation						
	Style						
	Sentence length						
	Word choices						
	Vocabulary						
	Tone						

Figure 16.1: Story outcomes learning matrix.

each of these areas, thus developing a map of the learning. At this level, students and teacher collaborated in determining the concepts and competencies that were important to them in the course, and this can happen with younger students as well. An alternative approach is for the teacher to develop the list of outcomes for the students and then to discuss each of the anticipated outcomes in the context of developing competencies in each area. This exercise helps students to become aware of their own learning processes.

Example: Journalism

This example, cited in *Orchestrating Learning with Quality* (1995), demonstrates the matrix used in a journalism class. The outcomes that are listed on the left were determined by means of an affinity diagram. Students and their teacher discussed the importance of specific skills and concepts, and wrote a list of competencies they hoped to develop as the course progressed. Their matrix is illustrated in Figure 16.2.

Other portfolio enhancements

Among the tools that have been introduced in this book, a number are especially appropriate in supporting the purpose of the portfolio.

- *Flowcharts* can demonstrate the way in which a student goes about a particular task. The two examples given in chapter 1 that relate to long division and subtraction are particularly appropriate to this end. An evaluation of a learner's mastery of a skill can be demonstrated by asking the student to create a flowchart that reflects the way he or she goes about performing that skill. For example, "Create a flowchart for using the card catalog in the library," would cause the student to think about that process, record the best-known way to pursue it, and reveal areas that might need further discussion or refinement in understanding.
- *Check sheets* can translate into tests relating to a particular skill or concept. They can also be used to keep track of the contents of portfolios or of revised work that has gone into the portfolio.
- *Cause-and-effect diagrams* support and demonstrate analytical thinking skills and mastery of concepts. A child's version of the contributing causes of malaria, for example, will involve classifying and organizing concepts and analyzing causal relationships. Like the check sheet, a cause-and-effect diagram might represent a useful way to evaluate how well a student understands a concept. This demonstration would be an appropriate addition to a portfolio. Supporting the student's reflection on his or her own learning, a cause-and-effect diagram might be developed for the successes that the young person has had. Questions such as, "What has contributed to the fact that you sustained your piano practice every day throughout this term?" helps to review what has gone well and to record it for reference.
- The same can be said for *relations diagrams*. Although they tend to be highly useful in stimulating discussion in a group setting, an individual student can use the tool to assess relationships among complex events or concepts. The tool could be applied to historical

Name ____________________

Beginning date ____________________

Outcomes	Competencies	Level I	Level II	Level III	Level IV	Level V	Level VI
		Knowledge	Understanding/ comprehension	Application	Analysis	Synthesis	Appreciation/ evaluation
	Triangle: Elements of news						
	Fact and news						
	Elements of interest in news						
	Inverted pyramid						
Write news	**Leads**						
article	Purpose						
	Length						
	Content						
	5Ws and H						
Communicate	Kinds						
effectively	**Interviews**						
in writing	Setting up the interview						
	Questioning techniques						
	Quoting accurately						
	Using LT QT QT						
	Attribution						
	Headlines						
	Purpose						
	Style						
	Content						
	Editing news						
	Proofreading						
	Being concise						
	Developing clarity						

Figure 16.2: News writing learning matrix.

events or literary analysis, and can reflect the student's analytical thinking skills as well as provide a record for further analysis later.

• *Bar charts* support the visual learner by transferring concepts to a graphic format. As a child reflects on specific challenges, errors, or successes, Pareto or histogram analysis can represent these experiences. Such diagrams would communicate immediately to parents or others who might review a child's portfolio. If the student had been having a great deal of difficulty with spelling, for example, successive Pareto diagrams might demonstrate the areas that have represented the greatest source of trouble in writing. It may be that, although spelling is the most dramatic (especially from a parent's point of view), other problems may occur with more frequency.

• *Run charts* can provide graphic documentation of regular achievements, challenges, grades, and behaviors. Run charts help students review a term, by means of the portfolio, and seeing progress with respect to any of these areas.

• *Spider diagrams*, as chapter 11 pointed out, offer ways to further develop ideas. While this is successfully done in groups, the tool may provide a source for individual brainstorming and organization of ideas as well. It might become a part of the writing process: a spider diagram to probe ideas for expression, then the prewriting, writing, and revision efforts form a cohesive record of the work.

Notable

Convinced of the value of portfolios, the challenge of utilizing a variety of sources of content for those portfolios is an energizing one. Students, teachers, and parents find that a portfolio communicates best when it offers a variety of expressions—both words and graphics. The additional benefit of creating tools to help reflect on the learning process is reinforcing the kinesthetic and visual learning that takes place when many of these suggested tools are used.

References

Bloom, B., M. Englehart, E. Furst, W. Hill, and D. Krathwohl. 1956. *Taxonomy of educational objectives: The classification of educational goals*. New York: Longmans Green.

Langford, David P., and Barbara A. Cleary. 1995. *Orchestrating learning with quality*. Milwaukee: ASQC Quality Press.

O'Neil, John. 1993. The promise of portfolios. *Update* (Alexandria, Va.: Association for Supervision and Curriculum Development) (September): 7.

Scardemalia, Marlene, and Carl Bereiter. 1993. *Surpassing ourselves: An inquiry into the nature and implications of expertise*. Chicago: Open Court Press.

Chapter 17

Conclusions and Beginnings

Teachers are always at the cutting edge, whether they know it or not. Teachers are in the business of leading young learners to the frontiers of their own knowledge and then helping them map their away into the new frontiers where learning will take them.

This important life work demands a great deal of planning and strategizing with colleagues and students alike. It requires an ability to envision the future—at least as far as their students' lives and what they will need to meet the changing challenges of that future.

Maps are useful tools even when we think we know the way. Sometimes—especially when the way is difficult or uncertain—we may need other tools such as compasses or sextants. No matter how helpful these implements are, we never mistake them for the destination itself, and we continue to use them in ways that work toward that destination. If the map can be folded into a hat, why not? The purist may say that is not the purpose of a map, but understanding flexible use is a hallmark of creativity.

Tools and strategies of all kinds are important to classrooms. Teachers have always tried new ways to reach students, sharing their successes and challenges with colleagues, modifying techniques, and trying again to reach their students. Some of the tools and strategies in this book are tried-and-true techniques long used by teachers in a variety of situations. Spider diagrams are one of these: English teachers have used this tool for decades to generate thinking for a variety of writing and speaking assignments.

One of the caveats of the quality movement, which has popularized the use of many of these tools, is that quality improvement efforts must come from the top of an organization. Unless the system of education is changed, little can be expected in the way of improvement. Currently, many are indeed addressing the needs of the larger system of education and are finding success via systemic improvement efforts.

At the same time, improvement efforts must reach into the classroom if they are to have any lasting effect on the education of children. As we cautioned in the beginning of this book, using the tools alone is not sufficient. All strategies must be used in the context of purpose, or they are simply tricks to keep things going. The purpose of systemic improvement efforts must be to enhance the learning process. Within the smaller system of the classroom, the purpose is the same.

Classrooms are not isolated units with doors that can be shut against outside influences. Suggesting that teachers use strategies for improvement means understanding that even these individual efforts will have an impact on the larger system. And that is our hope. It may be that improvement in schools is not actually going to be a top-down process, but one that fulminates from the work of inspired teachers who believe in the purpose of their work and are willing to try strategies to confidently advance toward fulfillment of that purpose.

And while teachers are beginning to change the larger system of education of which they are a critical part, they are still managers of their own classroom systems. These are amenable to the processes of continuous improvement and to the changes that represent a recognition of the new challenges that face students.

Improvement theory

The theoretical foundations of quality improvement in organizations lie in understanding systems, variation, change, and the needs of those who benefit from the organization's work. These foundations apply to schools as well as to industry.

Shewhart's PDSA (plan-do-study-act) cycle, referred to in the introduction, provides the framework for improvement. Many educators, including some of those cited in this book, have utilized essential tools within that framework and have created projects for themselves and their students that reflect the continuous improvement that the cycle suggests. Figure 17.1 illustrates a storyboard that reflects such a project for the second-grade writing team involved in the Koalaty Kid Initiative.

The larger cycle involves using appropriate tools at each stage of the improvement process. For example, in defining the system that they wanted to address, the team members used flowcharts, Pareto analysis, and other tools. The storyboard shows their progress through seven interrelated steps, including a plan for continuous improvement. It demonstrates their creativity as well; notice that the survey instrument used with their young students offered puppy dogs in various stages of excitement.

Learning theory

The theoretical framework of continuous improvement can certainly support the educational process, it is clear. For educators, however, another theoretical framework scaffolds their daily strides toward improvement, and that is the understanding of learning and how it takes place. Recent research from the worlds of the neurosciences, psychology, and education has brought new insight into this process. This knowledge cannot be ignored, nor can theories of organizational development or process control supplant it in carrying out the purpose of the classroom and the educational system of which it is a part.

A major shift has taken place with respect to understanding the purpose of education. Even the metaphors that apply to the teaching-learning process have changed: from the *tabula rasa* or empty slate waiting to be filled, to a process of making connections in a never-ending spiral or gyre of learning and refinement. Renate and Geoffrey Caine (1991) have articulated ways in which the brain makes connections, asserting that nothing is really learned until it is connected with something previously known. The work of Howard Gardner (1983), addressing multiple "intelligences" in children, Donna Markova's review of learning styles (1992), and Jane Healy's (1987) arguments about the ways in which children learn all represent important contributions to understanding purpose in the classroom. Others—Herman Epstein (1978), Roger and David Johnson (1991), and Marlene Scardemalia (1993)—have focused on ways that learning takes place and how that learning can be supported. The landscape of learning has changed.

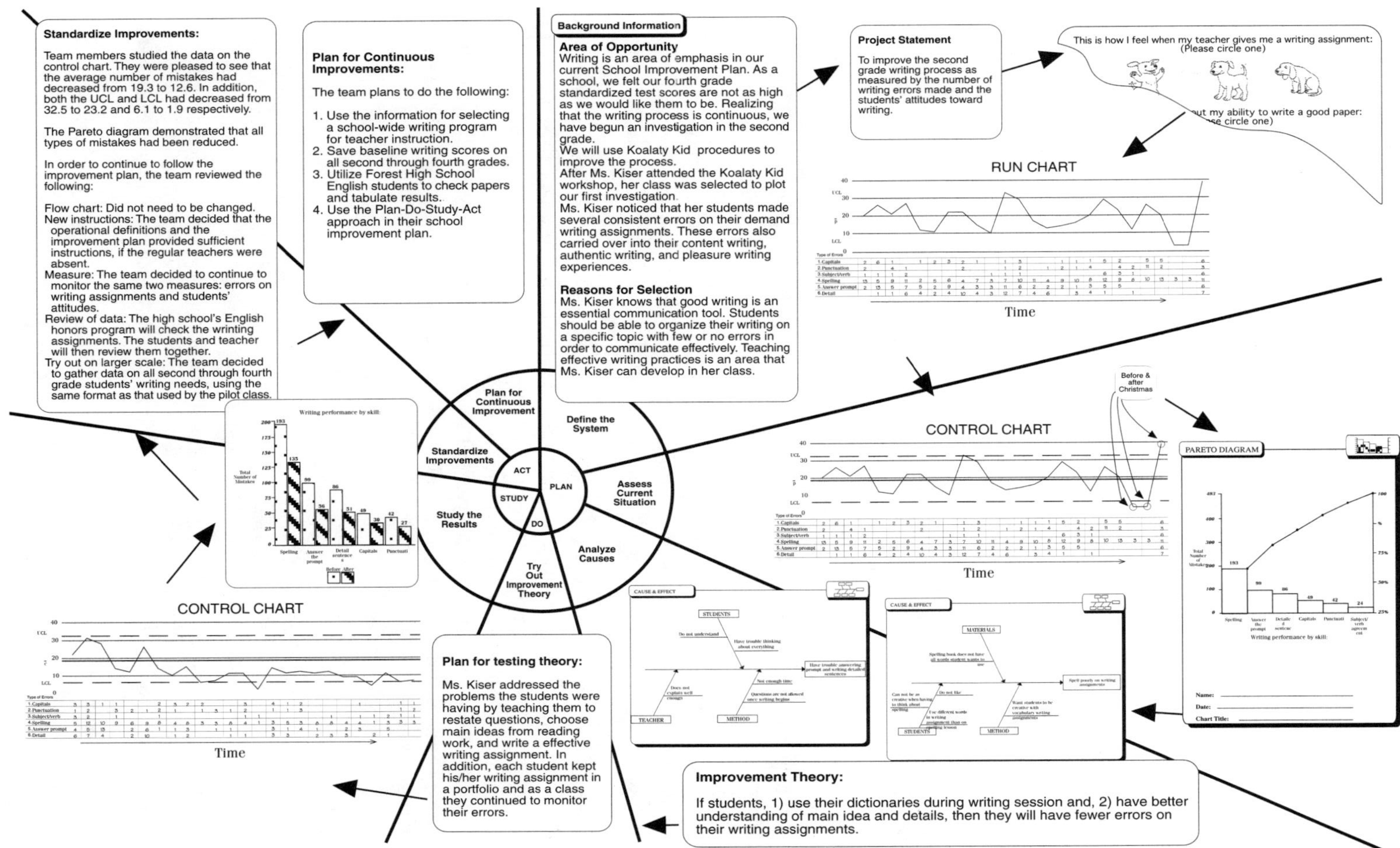

Figure 17.1: Second-grade writing team communication storyboard.

After the publication of his book confessing enormous failures in the U.S. approach to Vietnam, former Secretary of State Robert McNamara was asked on the *McNeil-Lehrer Newshour* how the nation's "best and brightest" could have continued a course that was so obviously flawed. Responding slowly, he acknowledged the reason: "We were prisoners of our own assumptions."

Educators, too, are sometimes prisoners of the assumptions about learning that have been widely held and long practiced. Many people assume that because they experienced a good education in decades past, the same methods and attitudes will continue to produce a good education for this generation of learners. Meanwhile, we have advanced in our understanding of learning and in our recognition that this generation must be prepared for challenges that we have never had to face. A different set of attitudes, strategies, and practices apply to a world that is essentially changed. As Kathleen Norris notes in her book *Dakota: A Spiritual Geography* (1995), "disconnecting from change does not recapture the past; it loses the future."

With new understandings about learning and the theoretical framework of improvement, the focus cannot be only on the tools and strategies for learning, important as these are. It must always be on the learning process itself and on the young learners who participate in it. We have confidence that teachers will continue to keep trying to do the best they can for their students. Teaching, as educator Joseph P. McDonald (1992) points out, is "not like building bridges between stable points, but like building flexible webs among constantly moving points." It is an inexact science because it must reach 20 or so different minds in perhaps as many different ways, moving them forward toward the frontiers of learning.

So what's next?

We urge you to try some of the suggested applications from these chapters and then to draw students into the process. As you proceed, consider how the tools and strategies are contributing to your purpose in the classroom. If they are not doing this, throw them out.

If you find them to be useful, experiment with new ways to try them. Encourage your students to understand the techniques that you are introducing and to think of other ways to use them. Don't be afraid to make a hat out of a map.

The best tools you have in the endeavor of leading your students into the next century are your own creativity, ingenuity, and experience. We hope you'll pull all these together, try some of the suggestions in this book, and see some progress in your students' learning process.

References

Caine, R. N., and G. Caine. 1991. *Making connections: Teaching and the human brain*. Alexandria, Va.: Association for Supervision and Curriculum Development.

Epstein, Herman. 1978. Growth spurts during brain development: Implications for educational policy and practice. In *Education and the brain: The 77th yearbook of the National Society for the Study of Education*, edited by J. S. Chall, and A. F. Mirsky. Chicago: National Society for the Study of Education.

Gardner, Howard. 1983. *Frames of mind: The theory of multiple intelligences*. New York: Basic Books.

Healy, Jane. 1987. *Your child's growing mind: A guide to learning and brain development*. New York: Touchstone Books and Simon and Schuster.

Johnson, David W., and Roger T. Johnson. 1991. *Learning together and alone: Cooperative, competitive, and individualistic learning*. 3d ed. Boston: Allyn and Bacon.

Langford, David P., and Barbara A. Cleary. 1995. *Orchestrating learning with quality*. Milwaukee: ASQC Quality Press.

Markova, D. 1992. *How your child is smart: A life-changing approach to learning*. Berkeley, Calif.: Conari Press.

McDonald, Joseph P. 1992. *Teaching: Making sense of an uncertain craft*. New York: Teacher's College Press, Columbia University.

Norris, Kathleen. 1995. *Dakota: A spiritual geography*. New York: Ticknor and Fields.

O'Neil, John. 1993. The promise of portfolios. *Update* (Alexandria, Va.: Association for Supervision and Curriculum Development) (September): 7.

Scardemalia, Marlene, and Carl Bereiter. 1993. *Surpassing ourselves: An inquiry into the nature and implications of expertise*. Chicago: Open Court Press.

Additional Reading

Armstrong, T. 1993. *Seven kinds of smart: Identifying and developing your many intelligences*. New York: Plume.

———. 1994. *Multiple intelligences in the classroom*. Alexandria, Va.: Association for Supervision and Curriculum Development.

Ball, M., M. J. Cleary, S. Leddick, C. Schwinn, D. Schwinn, and E. Torres. 1991. *Total quality transformation for K–12 education*. Dayton, Ohio: PQ Systems.

Bloom, B., M. Englehart, E. Furst, W. Hill, and D. Krathwohl. 1956. *Taxonomy of educational objectives: The classification of educational goals*. New York: Longmans Green.

Bruner, Jerome, J. Goodnow, and G. A. Austin. 1967. *Learning modalities. Toward a theory of instruction*. New York: John Wiley & Sons.

Buzan, Tony, and Barry Buzan. 1994. *The mind map book: How to use radiant thinking to maximize your brain's untapped potential*. New York: Dutton.

Caine, R. N., and G. Caine. 1990. Understanding a brain-based approach to learning and teaching. *Educational Leadership* 48, no. 2:66–70.

———. 1991. *Making connections: Teaching and the human brain*. Alexandria, Va.: Association for Supervision and Curriculum Development.

Chall, J. S., and A. F. Mirsky, eds. 1978. *Education and the brain: The 77th yearbook of the National Society for the Study of Education*. Chicago: National Society for the Study of Education.

Csikszentmihalyi, M. 1990. *Flow: The psychology of optimal experience*. New York: Harper & Row.

Deming, W. Edwards. 1986. *Out of the crisis*. Cambridge, Mass.: MIT Center for Advanced Engineering Study.

Dienstfrey, H. 1991. *Where the mind meets the body*. New York: HarperCollins.

Epstein, Herman. 1978. Growth spurts during brain development: Implications for educational policy and practice. In *Education and the brain: The 77th yearbook of the National Society for the Study of Education*, edited by J. S. Chall, and A. F. Mirsky. Chicago: National Society for the Study of Education.

Friedman, S., K. A. Klivington, and R. W. Peteson, eds. 1986. *The brain, cognition, and education*. New York: Academic Press and Harcourt Brace Jovanovich.

Gardner, Howard. 1983. *Frames of mind: The theory of multiple intelligences*. New York: Basic Books.

———. 1991. *The unschooled mind: How children think and how schools should teach*. New York: Basic Books.

———. 1993. *Creating minds*. New York: Basic Books.

Halford, G. S. 1993. *Children's understanding: The development of mental models*. Hillsdale, N.J.: Lawrence Erlbaum Associates.

Hart, L. 1975. *How the brain works: A new understanding of human learning, emotion, and thinking*. New York: Basic Books.

Healy, Jane. 1987. *Your child's growing mind: A guide to learning and brain development from birth to adolescence*. Garden City, N.Y.: Doubleday.

———. 1990. *Endangered minds: Why children don't think and what we can do about it*. New York: Touchstone Books.

Harmin, Merrill. 1994. *Inspiring active learning: A handbook for teachers*. Alexandria, Va.: Association for Supervision and Curriculum Development.

Jay, Antony. 1968. *Management & Machiavelli: An inquiry into the politics of corporate life*. Hinsdale, Ill.: Dryden Press.

Johnson, D. W., and R. T. Johnson. 1991. *Learning together and alone: Cooperative, competitive, and individualistic learning*. 3d ed. Boston: Allyn & Bacon.

Kohn, A. 1986. *No contest: The case against competition*. Boston: Houghton Mifflin.

———. 1993. *Punished by rewards: A's, praise, and other bribes*. Boston: Houghton Mifflin.

Leinhardt, Gaea. 1991. What research on learning tells us about teaching. *Educational Leadership* 49, no. 7:20–24.

MacLean, P. D. 1978. A mind of three minds: Educating the triune brain. In *The 77th yearbook of the National Society for the Study of Education*, edited by J. S. Chall, and A. F. Mirsky. Chicago: National Society for the Study of Education.

Markova, D. 1992. *How your child is smart: A life-changing approach to learning*. Berkeley, Calif.: Conari Press.

Nummela, R., and T. Rosengran. 1986. What's happening in students' brains may redefine teaching. *Educational Leadership* 43, no. 8:49–53.

Ornstein, R. 1986. *Multimind*. Boston: Houghton Mifflin.

Ornstein, R., and R. F. Thompson. 1982. *The amazing brain*. Boston: Houghton Mifflin.

Perrone, V., ed. 1991. *Expanding student assessment*. Alexandria, Va.: Association for Supervision and Curriculum Development.

Piaget, J. 1952. *The origins of intelligence in children*. Translated by M. Cook. New York: International Universities Press.

Scardemalia, Marlene, and Carl Bereiter. 1993. *Surpassing ourselves: An inquiry into the nature and implications of expertise*. Chicago: Open Court Press.

Slavin, R. 1983. *Cooperative learning*. New York: Longman.

Springer, S. P., and G. Deutsch. 1981. *Left brain, right brain*. New York: W.H. Freeman and Company.

Strom, R. D. 1971. *Teachers and the learning process*. Englewood Cliffs, N.J.: Prentice Hall.

Sylwester, Robert. 1986. Learning about learning: The neurosciences and the education profession. *Educational Horizons* (summer): 162–167.

———. 1995. *A celebration of neurons: An educator's guide to the human brain*. Alexandria, Va.: Association for Supervision and Curriculum Development.

Whitehead, A. N. 1929. *The aims of education and other essays*. New York: Macmillan.

Glossary

affinity diagram A tool that provides a way to organize the output of brainstorming sessions by grouping and categorizing it for further analysis. Categories are based on shared characteristics, and items are generated either by brainstorming or by Crawford slip method.

attributes control charts A family of control charts for plotting attributes data; includes p, np, c, and u charts.

attributes data Qualitative data collected on objects possessing a certain characteristic; for example, yes/no, good/bad, pass/fail, go/no go, and number of nonconformities. These data are counted, not measured.

average median The central location of subgroup medians on a $\tilde{X}$–R chart. Its symbol is $\bar{\tilde{X}}$.

average subgroup size An average of all the subgroups on the control chart. It is found by summing all the subgroup sizes and dividing by the number of subgroups taken (k). Its symbol is $\bar{n}$.

bar chart A graph with bars (rectangles) of different heights to show and compare data.

baseline data Data collected at the beginning of an improvement project. It is compared with future data collected on the same system to measure improvement.

bimodal Said of a distribution having two modes. On a histogram, this condition is reflected by two peaks or high points.

brainstorming A creative process performed by a group to generate ideas on a certain topic. The members of the group use their collective thinking power to gather information about a problem. Each idea is written down.

c chart An attributes control chart that is used to monitor the number of nonconformities, such as defects per subgroup. The subgroup size remains constant as the data are gathered.

cause-and-effect diagram A tool for individual or group problem solving that provides a way to generate and categorize causes for a given effect. Also known as a fishbone diagram or Ishikawa diagram.

centerline A solid horizontal line drawn on the control chart to represent the average or central location.

central location The location of the center of a set of data points. Mean, median, and mode are the statistics that describe it.

check sheet A device for gathering and organizing information. The check sheet format is a function of the situation for which it will be used.

common causes After data have been gathered and charted (see *control chart*), the causes of variation that are universal and ordinary, or inherent in the system. Common causes are *not* created by unusual circumstances (see *special causes*). Common causes of variation can be altered only by changing the system.

competency matrix (also *learning competency matrix*) A charting technique used to break down topic or subject areas into steps for accomplishing a specific learning outcome. Using Bloom's taxonomy, the matrix identifies tasks, knowledge levels, and depth of understanding of each subject area, so that a student and teacher can evaluate competency with a given skill or concept.

control chart A statistical tool useful for plotting data over time in order to determine whether a system is stable or not by evaluating its variation. (See *common cause* and *special cause* of variation.) May be variables control chart or attributes control chart (see *attributes* and *variables*).

control limits After data have been gathered and recorded on a control chart these limits, or lines, are calculated using a simple formula. The control limits are not imposed from without, but generated by the data. The formulas for individual moving range variables data are as follows:

$$\overline{X} = \frac{\Sigma X}{n} \qquad \text{UCL}_X = \overline{X} + (2.66 \times M\overline{R}) \qquad \text{UCL}_{MR} = M\overline{R} \times D_4$$

$$\overline{R} = \frac{\Sigma R}{n-1} \qquad \text{LCL}_X = \overline{X} - (2.66 \times M\overline{R}) \qquad \text{LCL}_{MR} = M\overline{R} \times D_3$$

cooperative learning A classroom approach that emphasizes teamwork and collaboration rather than individual performance and competition. Teams work toward a common learning opportunity, supporting each other in order to achieve a common vision.

correlated Two variables are said to be correlated if they have a relationship. In other words, one variable will change when a change occurs in the other variable, such as in a scatter diagram.

Crawford slip method A method for generating ideas, the Crawford slip method minimizes internal group influences. Ideas are written on cards in silence rather than said aloud as in traditional brainstorming. The slip method minimizes influences from the group and reduces fear when there is danger that this might exist in a group.

cumulative percent line On the Pareto diagram, the final line drawn to represent the cumulative percentage of the categories.

data-gathering plan A plan, usually in the form of a matrix, that describes the process of collecting specific data. The plan includes what data to collect, how they will be collected, how much to collect (subgroup size), how often to collect data (sample frequency), where to collect data, methods to use, and who will collect the data. The form also includes an area to record issues of stratification such as time, location, symptom, and type.

decision matrix In nominal group technique, an alternate technique for final selection of actions to be taken. A decision matrix is a worksheet of rows and columns, listing potential actions in the left column and selection criteria across the top row.

dependent variable In a scatter diagram, the variable that is expected to respond to changes in the independent variable. The dependent variable is plotted on the vertical axis of the scatter diagram.

deployment flowchart A picture of a process that includes who is responsible, or deployed, to carry out each task in the process.

driving forces Forces that currently exist and help to bring about change.

drop shadow A darkened shadow behind a symbol in the flowchart. It is used to zoom a step in the flowchart. It indicates that another flowchart exists for the zoomed step.

flowchart A graphic portrayal of a process, showing the steps that are involved in that process and their relationship to one another. A process flowchart shows the steps, in time order; a deployment flowchart includes a people coordinate, to illustrate who is responsible for each step in the process.

force-field analysis A planning tool that helps generate actions to implement a change. The tool is based on the idea that driving forces and restraining forces must be considered in any proposed change. Using this tool in problem solving, teams can choose to increase the driving forces or diminish the restraining forces.

frequency The number of times a specified event occurs.

frequency distribution The arrangement of data into classes or interval groups.

histogram A bar chart that represents the frequency distribution of data. The height of the bars corresponds to the number of items in the class and the width of the bar corresponds to a measurement interval.

implementation plan A set of actions designed to increase the chances that change will occur; the output of force-field analysis.

independent variable In a scatter diagram, the variable that is believed to influence the other. The independent variable is usually plotted on the horizontal axis.

LCL The lower control limit on a control chart.

learning competency matrix See *competency matrix.*

metacognition Consciousness or awareness of the thinking and learning process and of the ways in which the student learns best; knowing what one knows.

moving range The difference between consecutive subgroup values on an $X\text{–}M\overline{R}$ chart. The moving range is used as the measure for variability.

MR The symbol for the average moving range.

n The symbol for subgroup size. A subgroup of five items is denoted as $n = 5$.

negative cause-and-effect diagram A cause-and-effect diagram made for the opposite effect of what is preferred. Negative cause and effect is useful to generate many causes to be avoided if the positive effect is to be reached.

negative correlation In a scatter diagram, the relationship between two variables is such that as one increases, the other decreases.

nominal group technique A problem-solving tool used to help teams generate ideas and choose the best one. A list of items generated by brainstorming is considered against agreed-upon decision criteria, with team members selecting from four to eight ideas that meet these criteria and, in their opinions, should be considered.

non-normal distribution Any data set that does not show a normal bell-shaped distribution.

normal distribution A theoretical distribution of data that is bell-shaped and symmetrical. It is the underlying distribution for variables control charts.

***np* chart** An attributes control chart that plots the number of items possessing a characteristic of interest in a constant subgroup size.

operational definition A clear, concise, and detailed definition of a measure. It includes the characteristic of interest, measuring instrument, method of test, and decision criteria.

outlier On a histogram or scatter diagram, a point that does not fall into the pattern of the others.

out of control A system is said to be statistically out of control when data points fall outside statistically calculated control charts; when there is a run of seven points or more that are either above or below the center line; when a run of data points goes in the same direction (up or down); or when data patterns appear too close or too far from the average. Analysis is based on the data, not on subjective judgment.

***p* chart** An attributes control chart for plotting the proportion of items possessing a characteristic of interest.

Pareto diagram Like a histogram, a Pareto diagram can also be considered a type of bar chart. It provides additional information, however, by ranking related items with respect to frequency of occurrence, from greatest to least. This helps to separate items that are significant in terms of number of occurrences from those that are less significant. A cumulative percentage line appears above the bars. This tool was developed by Italian economist Vilfredo Pareto.

PDSA cycle Statistician Walter Shewhart's description of the improvement cycle, emphasized by W. Edwards Deming. The four stages of plan-do-study-act are essential to continuous improvement success and are the basis for a seven-step improvement process: (1) defining the system; (2) assessing current situation; (3) analyzing causes; (4) trying out an improvement theory; (5) studying the results; (6) standardizing the improvement; and (7) planning for continuous improvement.

people coordinate A series of connected boxes drawn horizontally across the top of the deployment flowchart. Each box contains the name of the person, department, or division involved in the process.

portfolio An alternative method of assessing student work by collecting samples of written expression or artwork for review with the student or parents. The method provides a basis for the student, teacher, and parent to see progress, identify best work, and develop pride in learning.

positive correlation A relationship between two variables such that as one increases, so does the other.

process flowchart A picture of the flow of materials through the sequence of steps required to make, move, store, and inspect items.

purpose The aim of a system or of an improvement. Purpose is determined through leadership and consensus and is closely related to the needs and expectations of the system's customers.

R The symbol for range.

range An estimate of spread in a set of data points; the difference between the highest and lowest values in the data set.

relations diagram A pictorial representation of a problem and the aspects that make up the problem. Relationships of the aspects can be analyzed, and root causes or primary drivers can be determined using a relations diagram.

restraining forces Organization forces that currently exist and resist change. These forces are identified in a force-field analysis.

root cause The main cause of a problem. In the relations diagram, the root cause is the element that has the most number of arrows leading out.

root effect The element of a problem that is affected most by the root cause. In the relations diagram, the root effect is the element with the greatest number of arrows leading in.

run chart A statistical tool that records data chronologically. Observations are entered on a chart over a period of time in order to observe a system's behavior with respect to trends and patterns. After data have been collected over a sufficient period of time, a control chart can be constructed from it, providing additional information about the system.

scaling Numbering or labeling the lines of a control chart or other graph in order to plot the points.

scaling factor The width or value of each division of the total length of an axis on a graph. Also called the *increment value* in scaling.

scatter diagram A statistical tool that plots the values of two variables on a graph in order to study the extent of the relationship between the two variables.

skewed Said of the shape of a distribution that tails off to one side. May be portrayed by a histogram.

special causes Variation that occurs because of a unique situation or unpredictable occurrence is said to be created by special causes. Variation that is created by factors that are universal to the system is considered common causes.

stable system A system free of special causes of variation; this system is also said to be in control. The variation within a stable system is due to common causes and is predictable.

standard deviation A statistic that describes the variation or spread within a data set.

statistical process control (SPC) The use of data and statistical tools to monitor processes over time. SPC helps to *prevent* problems in a system rather than merely *detecting* those that are occurring.

statistics Numerical data used to describe a process based on subgroup data. Mean, range, standard deviation, median, and mode are examples of statistical data.

stratify To arrange or divide data into various configurations in order to understand it further. A check sheet, for example, may record data by time, date, type, and so on.

subgroup One or more occurrences or measurements taken at one time; multiple subgroups are used to analyze the performance of a system. Also known as sample.

system A collection of processes and people that are aligned toward serving a common purpose or aim. A system includes inputs, outputs, feedback mechanisms, and customers. Defined by Laszlo as a collection of parts with an identifiable set of internal relationships as well as identifiable external relationships to other systems.

taxon learning Learning that depends on taxon memory, consisting of items that do not depend on specific physical contexts. Information is placed in taxon memory through memorization and practice, and is often associated with rote learning processes and physical learning (such as riding a bike). Taxon memory includes information or skills that can be recalled and used with little reference to meaning.

total quality management (TQM) A way of management that includes an emphasis on understanding systems, variation, and customer needs and a focus on making improvement after collecting data and analyzing responses to what that data suggest. TQM utilizes statistical and problem-solving tools to bring about planned change and continuous improvement in a system.

***u* chart** An attributes control chart that monitors the number of nonconformities per unit; can be used for variable subgroup sizes.

UCL The symbol for the upper control limit on a control chart.

unstable system A system that contains special and common causes of variation; this system is also said to be out of control. An unstable system is unpredictable and cannot be improved until the special causes of variation have been addressed.

variables control chart A family of control charts for plotting variables data; includes $\bar{X}$–R, $\tilde{X}$–R, $\bar{X}$–s, and X–MR.

variables data Quantitative data in the form of a measurement; for example, length, height, temperature, density, weight, and time.

variation A common characteristic of systems. Variation can be analyzed by means of appropriate statistical tools so that it can be reduced and improvement can ensue. Variation may be due to common causes or special causes.

$\bar{X}$ Represents the mean or average of a set of data points. This symbol is used to indicate the subgroup average on an $\bar{X}$–R control chart or the centerline on an X–MR control chart.

$\tilde{X}$ Symbol for the median, the middle point of a data set arranged from low to high.

X–MR control chart A variables control chart that uses the individual data reading from a subgroup of one to chart central location, and the range between consecutive subgroups to chart the system variability.

$\tilde{X}$–R control chart A variables control chart that uses the subgroup median to chart central location, and the subgroup range to chart system variability. Subgroup size must be larger than one and is typically an odd number less than 10.

$\bar{X}$–R control chart A variables control chart that uses the subgroup average to chart central location, and the subgroup range to chart variability. The subgroup size for this chart must be larger than one and is typically less than 10.

$\bar{X}$–s control chart A variables control chart that uses the subgroup average to chart central location, and the subgroup standard deviation to chart system variability. The subgroup size for this chart is usually 10 or more.

zoom To draw a drop shadow behind a symbol in the flowchart. It indicates that a detailed flowchart is drawn for that step.

References

Glossary descriptions are adapted from the following sources and used with permission.

Langford, David P., and Barbara A. Cleary. 1995. *Orchestrating learning with quality*. Milwaukee: ASQC Quality Press.

PQ Systems. 1991. *Total quality tools for education (K–12)*. Dayton, Ohio: PQ Systems.

Index

D

E

F